Unbowed

Unbowed

A MEMOIR

Wangari Muta Maathai

WILLIAM HEINEMANN: LONDON

Published by William Heinemann, 2007

2 4 6 8 10 9 7 5 3 1

First published in the United States by Alfred A. Knopf a division of Random
House, Inc., New York, and in Canada by Random House
of Canada Limited, Toronto, 2006

William Heinemann
Random House, 20 Vauxhall Bridge Road,
London SW1V 2SA

www.randomhouse.co.uk

Addresses for companies within The Random House Group Limited can be
found at: www.randomhouse.co.uk

The Random House Group Limited Reg. No. 954009

A CIP catalogue record for this book
is available from the British Library

ISBN 13: 9780434015429

This book is printed on Cyclus offset, 100 per cent recycled paper

Printed and bound in Great Britain by
Clays Ltd, St Ives Plc

TO THE MEMORY OF MY PARENTS

AND TO MY CHILDREN,

WAWERU, WANJIRA, AND MUTA

The trees of the field will yield their fruit and the ground will yield its crops; the people will be secure in the land. They will know that I am the LORD, when I break the bars of their yoke and rescue them from the hands of those who enslaved them.

—EZEKIEL 34:27 (NIV)

CONTENTS

ACKNOWLEDGMENTS

Writing a memoir was like walking down my journey through life of some sixty years. It brought up many memories and reflections of past and current events, relationships, friendships, and collaborations, as well as times of great difficulty and great joy.

Along the journey, I never walked alone. I have been supported and assisted by many people, who shaped my life through the experiences I shared with them. At the beginning were my parents, who held me by the fingers and led me when I did not know where to go, I did not know right from wrong. Then there were my teachers, as I moved from one school to another and embraced their ideas and values. Of particular importance were the nuns, both in Kenya and the United States of America. There were some like Prof. Reino Hofmann, who gave me the chance to prove myself as a teacher and a scientist.

Then there are those people I met only once or infrequently in my life; yet even they left their footprints on my path. I may remember their names but not their faces or vice versa, but they nevertheless shaped my life and destiny. It is not possible to mention them all by name, but I would like to thank all of them collectively, so that if they come across themselves reflected in these pages they will know that their part in this journey is deeply appreciated.

I am especially indebted to those directly involved in making the production of this book possible. For their unwavering patience and persistence, I wish to acknowledge Mia MacDonald and Martin Rowe. Some years back, they came to Nairobi, introduced themselves, and let me know that they would like to help me write my story. I told them I had my hands full and that I was working on a new edition of my book, *The Green Belt Movement: Sharing the Approach and Experience*, and had already developed a rough manuscript. They offered to assist me with it, and through Martin's company, Lantern Books, it was published in the United States in 2003.

During the production of this memoir they have worked with me skillfully and professionally. Mia was with me when the news of the Nobel Peace Prize was announced. In the hours and weeks that followed she joined the staff of the Green Belt Movement, friends, and volunteers who answered the countless press calls and questions, and assisted with writing and other communication needs. Besides publishing *The Green Belt Movement*, Martin aided in the development of our presence on the Internet, especially for the North America office. Their support for me and the Green Belt Movement is greatly appreciated.

Thanks are also due to my agents, Robert Kirby and Zoe Pagnamenta at PFD. I especially wish to thank my editor at Knopf, Erroll McDonald, for his warm encouragement and support. Others who have been closely connected with bringing together information and details include Alan Dater, Sr. Thomasita Homan, and Lisa Merton, as well as others. Staff and members of the Green Belt Movement both in the office and in the field assisted with aspects of research and field visits. For all of their dedication and support I am deeply indebted.

In writing this memoir and reading other works, I sometimes came across information that either reinforced what I already knew to be the case or informed me anew in a way that warrants special recognition and acknowledgment. Among these I wish to recognize, for their important scholarly contributions, Stephen Ndegwa for his thesis on the Green Belt Movement in *The Two Faces of Civil Society: NGOs and Politics in Africa*; R. Mugo Gatheru for *Kenya: From Colonialism to Independence, 1888-1970*; Caroline Elkins for *Imperial Reckoning: The Untold Story of Britain's Gulag in Kenya*; and

David Anderson for *Histories of the Hanged: The Dirty War in Kenya and the End of Empire*. I also wish to thank all participants of the Jubilee 2000 campaign for their strength, commitment, and support in this campaign, especially in Africa, and DATA (Debt, Aid, Trade, Africa) for their reports and work on how to make poverty history.

In addition, I want to extend my deepest appreciation to those who have been there for me and for the Green Belt Movement, over many years, in good times and bad. For all their steadfast friendship, insight, and financial and moral support, I wish to acknowledge wonderful friends with whom I have walked this journey so far. I cannot mention all of them by name, but there are those friends such as Huey Johnson, Richard Sandbrook, Oscar Mann, Gary Gallon, the late Anil Aggarwol, and others who literally drafted me into the Environment Movement in 1973 in Nairobi during a time when they created the Environment Liaison Center (ELC), later the Environment Liaison Center International (ELCI). And those such as Maurice Strong, the first Executive Director of the United Nations Environment Programme, who not only supported our first efforts at ELC but passed the legacy to his successor, Dr. Mustafa Tolba of Egypt, whose support and encouragement were largely responsible for our survival and growth during those early years.

Indeed the work of the Green Belt Movement over the past thirty years would not have been possible without the encouragement and support of our many friends around the world. It is virtually impossible to mention all of them by name. I want to thank in a very special way my friends and great supporters of the Green Belt Movement: There are friends who worked closely with me, such as Margaret "Peggy" Snyder of UNIFEM, and the late Bella Abzug and Mim Kelber of the Women's Environment and Development Organization (WEDO). Others include friends such as Joshua Mailman and Helvi Sipilä. I wish to acknowledge my friends of many years, Elin Enge, Halle Jørn Hanssen, Tone Bratteli, Ed Posey and Liz Hosken of the Gaia Foundation, Roger Northcott and my friends at Tudor

Trust, Tracy, Marchioness of Worcester, and Margaret Baxter of Comic Relief.

When I met Steven and Barbara Rockefeller I would not have suspected the road we would walk, starting at Kykuit with friends such as Mary Evelyn Tucker, Oscar Arias, and all the others involved in the leadership of the Earth Charter initiative.

I also wish to thank the people of Germany for making me so welcome forty years ago, both at the University of Giessen and University of Munich. The fond memories of Giessen, Berlin, Munich, and the beautiful and green countryside have stayed with me and been a source of inspiration. Many years later, the Heinrich Böll Foundation established a working partnership with us on green issues, good governance, and development in Kenya.

I also want to thank certain individuals who during the more difficult days provided me and the Green Belt Movement with sanctuary, or used their influence to get us out of harm's way. One of them is Dr. Klaus Toepfer, the just-retired Executive Director of UNEP, and the many wonderful people of the United Nations Environment Programme. They offered a literal and metaphorical haven during some of the difficult days. During the times of the efforts to reintroduce multiparty politics back into Kenya, the words and actions of then Ambassador of the United States of America Smith Hempstone; Ambassador Bernd D. Mutzelburg of Germany; Arman Aardal, Norway's representative to UNEP; and many of their colleagues in the diplomatic circle gave much needed support to me and the Green Belt Movement. When I needed to hide and remain underground, it was the voice and the intervention of friends like former Vice President Al Gore, former President of the Soviet Union Mikhail Gorbachev, Senator Nancy Kassebaum, Human Rights Watch, Amnesty International, and Kerry Kennedy of the Robert Kennedy Memorial Center for Human Rights who made it possible for me to come out of hiding, walk the streets, and travel out of the country without harassment and intimidation. One never forgets such moments, events, and friends.

I also wish to thank the members of the National Council of Women of Kenya, who entrusted me with their leadership for many years; the press, both in Kenya and around the world, which allowed my voice and that of others crying in the wilderness to be heard and respected; and my constituents in Tetu, who honored me with their votes so that I could represent them in Parliament. Subsequently, I was honored by President Mwai Kibaki, who appointed me as an Assistant Minister of Environment in the Kenyan government.

I have been the fortunate recipient of many awards and honorary degrees, some of which are mentioned in the book. Let me say here that I am profoundly grateful for the recognition extended to my work, and I will strive to live up to the trust that has been placed in me by the many distinguished universities and colleges throughout the world, which have so generously honored me. Quite obviously, the awarding of the Nobel Peace Prize in 2004 placed an invaluable jewel in the crown. It has been an extremely humbling experience.

Since 2004 I have been touched and energized by the enthusiasm of many friends, old and new. Many of them came quickly to provide the support so badly needed by the staff of the Green Belt Movement and me as we struggled to deal with the immense attention and the demand for information and answers. In New York one of the circles of friends formed around Mary Davidson of The Marion Institute, Carter Via of Bridges to Community and White Plains Presbyterian Church (which also provided free office space to the Green Belt Movement International). Other friends, such as Daniel Martin, Scott Lethbridge, Frances Moore Lappé, and Anna Lappé of the Small Planet Institute have all been involved in supporting the Green Belt Movement and the development of the Green Belt Safaris. Others such as Morten Eriksen have been instrumental in the development of new initiatives on how to institutionalize the learning experiences at the Green Belt Movement.

In Japan we initiated a campaign known as *mottainai*, which borrows on the rich Japanese culture and emphasizes the need to reuse, reduce, and recycle: to not waste, and to be grateful for and appreciate what we have. This goes well with the Japanese tradition of gift-wrapping with a cloth known as *furoshiki*. If those who are affluent and technologically advanced can lead the way toward sustainable management, good governance, justice, and equity, we might pre-empt many conflicts over the access and control of resources.

None of this journey would have taken place without the spirit, courage, and dedication of the people, especially the thousands of women who believed in me and started to plant trees alongside me in Kenya, and stood up for the environment when it became necessary to do so. Foremost among them were the women of the National Council of Women of Kenya, under whose auspices the idea that evolved into the Green Belt Movement was born, nurtured, and developed. Among the members of the Executive Committee who stayed through thick and thin were Miriam Wanjiru Chege, Lilian Wanjiru Njehu, Rahab Wanjiru Mwatha, Jane Ngugi, and the late Pricilla Mereka and Lucy Ng'ang'a. Others include my special friend and colleague of many years Professor Vertistine Mbaya of the University of Nairobi, whose friendship, commitment, and counsel have been invaluable. The greater success of the Green Belt Movement lies in the work of tens of thousands of women and men, who toil over the millions of tree seedlings they plant, water, and nurture to maturity. I know that I cannot thank them all by name. Therefore, I hope that whenever they or their relatives pick up this book and identify with the story they will accept my statement of gratitude for the faith in our vision of a green, just, and democratic society.

I have a large extended family and it is impossible to recognize all those who have touched my life in a special way. But I do thank all of them for whatever role they played in my life. I do have some special people who have been at the center of my life, and who have filled it with hope and joy. First are my parents, especially my mother, who embodied strength, wisdom, endurance, and faith. Another is my eldest brother, Nderitu Muta. Finally, and in a very special way, are my children, Waweru, Wanjira, and Muta. The path of my life did not make it easy, especially for them. However, they have grown up with grace and compassion, and I am proud of each one of them. All of the work I have done and continue to do—for Kenya, the environment, and peace—I have done and continue to do for them, and for the generations that will follow. When the road bends and I have no idea what will emerge, I think of them and gain the courage to follow the curve and walk forward, though the path ahead be yet untrodden. They are my hope and they give me a sense of immortality.

Unbowed

1

Beginnings

I was born the third of six children, and the first girl after two sons, on April 1, 1940, in the small village of Ihithe in the central highlands of what was then British Kenya. My grandparents and parents were also born in this region near the provincial capital of Nyeri, in the foothills of the Aberdare Mountain Range. To the north, jutting into the sky, is Mount Kenya.

Two weeks into *mbura ya njahī*, the season of the long rains, my mother delivered me at home in a traditional mud-walled house with no electricity or running water. She was assisted by a local midwife as well as women family members and friends. My parents were peasant farmers, members of the Kikuyu community, one of forty-two ethnic groups in Kenya and then, as now, the most populous. They lived from the soil and also kept cattle, goats, and sheep.

At the time of my birth, the land around Ihithe was still lush, green, and fertile. The seasons were so regular that you could almost predict that the long, monsoon rains would start falling in mid-March. In July you knew it would be so foggy you would not be able to see ten feet in front of you, and so cold in the morning that the grass would be silvery-white with frost. In Kikuyu, July is known as *mworia nyoni*, the month when birds rot, because birds would freeze to death and fall from the trees.

We lived in a land abundant with shrubs, creepers, ferns, and trees, like the *mītūndū, mīkeu,* and *mīgumo,* some of which produced berries and nuts. Because rain fell regularly and reliably, clean drinking water was everywhere. There were large well-watered

3

fields of maize, beans, wheat, and vegetables. Hunger was virtually unknown. The soil was rich, dark red-brown, and moist.

When a baby joined the community, a beautiful and practical ritual followed that introduced the infant to the land of the ancestors and conserved a world of plenty and good that came from that soil. Shortly after the child was born, a few of the women attending the birth would go to their farms and harvest a bunch of bananas, full, green, and whole. If any of the bananas had ripened and birds had eaten them, the women would have to find another full bunch. The fullness expressed wholeness and wellness, qualities the community valued. Along with the bananas, the women would bring to the new mother's house sweet potatoes from her and their gardens and blue-purple sugarcane (*kīgwa kīa nyamūirū*). No ordinary sugarcane would do.

In anticipation of the birth, the expectant mother would fatten a lamb that slept and ate inside her home. While the women gathered the ritual foods, the child's father would sacrifice the lamb and roast a piece of the flesh. The bananas and the potatoes would also be roasted and along with the meat and the raw sugarcane given to the new mother. She would chew small pieces of each in turn and then put some of the juice into the baby's tiny mouth. This would have been my first meal. Even before breast milk, I would have swallowed the juice of green bananas, blue-purple sugarcane, sweet potatoes, and a fattened lamb, all fruits of the local land. I am as much a child of my native soil as I am of my father, Muta Njugi, and my mother, Wanjiru Kibicho, who was more familiarly known by her Christian name, Lydia. Following the Kikuyu tradition, my parents named me for my father's mother, Wangari, an old Kikuyu name.

According to the Kikuyu myth of origin, God created the primordial parents, Gikuyu and Mumbi, and from Mount Kenya showed them the land on which they were to settle: west from Mount Kenya to the Aberdares, on to Ngong Hills and Kilimambogo, then north to Garbatula. Together, Gikuyu and Mumbi had ten daughters— Wanjiru, Wambui, Wangari, Wanjiku, Wangui, Wangeci, Wanjeri, Nyambura, Wairimu, and Wamuyu—but they had no sons. The legend goes that, when the time came for the daughters to marry, Gikuyu prayed to God under a holy fig tree, *mūgumo,* as was his tradition, to send him sons-in-law. God told him to instruct nine of his daughters—the tenth was too young to be married—to go into the forest and to each cut a stick as long as she was tall. When the daughters returned, Gikuyu took the sticks and with them built an altar under the *mūgumo* tree, on which he sacrificed a lamb. As the fire was consuming the lamb's body, nine men appeared and walked out of the flames.

Gikuyu took them home and each daughter married the man who was the same height as she was, and together they gave rise to the ten clans to which all Kikuyus belong. (Even though the youngest daughter, Wamuyu, did not get married, she did have children.) Each clan is known for a particular trade or quality, such as prophecy, craftsmanship, and medicine. My clan, Anjirū, is associated with leadership. The daughters made the clans matrilineal, but many privileges, such as inheritance and ownership of land, livestock, and perennial crops, were gradually transferred to men. It is not explained how women lost their rights and privileges.

For the Kikuyus, Mount Kenya, known as Kirinyaga, or Place of Brightness, and the second-highest peak in Africa, was a sacred place. Everything good came from it: abundant rains, rivers, streams, clean drinking water. Whether they were praying, burying their dead, or performing sacrifices, Kikuyus faced Mount Kenya, and when they built their houses, they made sure the doors looked toward it. As long as the mountain stood, people believed that God was with them and that they would want for nothing. Clouds that regularly shrouded Mount Kenya were often followed by rain. As long as the rains fell, people had more than enough food for themselves, plentiful livestock, and peace.

Sadly, these beliefs and traditions have now virtually died away. They were dying even as I was born. When European missionaries came to the central highlands at the end of the nineteenth century, they taught the local people that God did not dwell on Mount Kenya, but rather in heaven, a place above the clouds. The proper place to worship him was in church on Sundays, a concept that was unknown to Kikuyus. Nevertheless, many people accepted the missionaries' worldview, and within two generations they lost respect for their own beliefs and traditions. The missionaries were followed by traders and administrators who introduced new methods of exploiting our rich natural resources: logging, clear-cutting native forests, establishing plantations of imported trees, hunting wildlife, and undertaking expansive commercial agriculture. Hallowed landscapes lost their sacredness and were exploited as the local people became insensitive to the destruction, accepting it as a sign of progress.

At just over 17,000 feet above sea level Mount Kenya towers over the central highlands. Although it straddles the Equator, it is topped by glaciers year round. Beholding Mount Kenya for Kikuyus and other communities that live around the mountain—Kambas, Merus, and Embus—must have been awe-inspiring. The story goes that the explorers Johan Ludwig Krapf and Johannes Rebmann, upon encountering the mountain in 1849, asked their guide, a member of the Kamba community, who was carrying a gourd, "What do you call that?" Thinking the two Germans were referring to the gourd, he replied, "It's called *kĩĩ-nyaa,*" pronounced Kenya by the British. This became the name of the mountain and later the country.

Throughout Africa, the Europeans renamed whatever they came across. This created a schism in many Africans' minds and we are still wrestling with the realities of living in this dual world. At home, we learned the names of mountains, streams, or regions from our parents, but in school we were taught the colonial names, deemed the "proper" names, which we had to use on our exams. The Aberdares, for example, known locally as Nyandarua, or "drying hide," because of their shape, were named by the British in 1884 after Lord Aberdare, then the head of the Royal Geographical Society.

. . .

6

Naturally, it was many years before I was to understand the complexities of the period. I was born as an old world was passing away. The first Europeans had come to Kenya during the time of my grandparents, in the late 1800s. In 1885, Britain and the other "great powers" of Europe met at the Berlin Conference to formalize what was known as "The Scramble for Africa"—a thirty-year dash to lay claim to the entire continent. With the stroke of a pen on a map they assigned whole regions to the different powers and created completely new nations. In East Africa, Germany received Tanganyika, which later united with Zanzibar to become Tanzania. Britain acquired what became the Kenya colony and the Uganda protectorate. Prior to this superficial partitioning, many communities in Africa had identified themselves as nations, albeit micronations. The resulting countries brought these communities together in arbitrary ways so that sometimes the new citizens of the post-Berlin nations perceived each other as foreigners. Some micronations found themselves stranded between two neighboring countries. The consequences of these divisions continue to haunt Africa.

My great-grandparents, whom I did not know, lived in a pre-European world. They would probably not have interacted with any other communities outside the central highlands, apart from the Maasais, who are pastoralists, herders of cows and goats. The Maasai traditional way of life required them to transverse the large plains to the west of the highlands, the vast grassland surrounded by ridges resulting from seismic activity that ripped apart the earth's crust many millions of years ago. The "scar" stretches from Jordan to Mozambique, forming the Great Rift Valley.

At times, Maasais would raid Kikuyu villages, take away their cattle, and kill their young men, and the Kikuyus would do the same to the Maasais. But there were also times of truce, trade in the form of exchange of food, livestock, and land, and even intermarriage. These interethnic links helped cement ties between communities and foster peace. In Nyeri, mixed Maasai and Kikuyu blood was common and never viewed as a stigma. My mother had Maasai blood in her. Like her father, she was lithe, with high cheekbones and straight hair, characteristics more typical of Maasais than Kikuyus. We were told that my great-great-grandmother on my father's side was a Maasai who was abducted during a raid. When she came to the highlands, she adopted Kikuyu customs and named her second son Muta, after her father. That name was eventually handed down to my father and, later, to my second son.

Throughout the nineteenth century, European missionaries crisscrossed Africa, clearing the way for Christianity. Almost immediately behind them came numerous explorers, adventurers, fortune seekers, and those in the service of the European powers prospecting for riches in Africa (both natural and human) to exploit. In Kenya, the British, perhaps because they did not want local people to receive competing Christian messages from denominations that were already contesting fiercely in Europe, subdivided the country and apportioned different areas to different denominations. Among the Catholics, many different orders were active in Kenya: the Consolata Missionary Sisters from Italy and the Holy Ghost Order and Loreto Sisters from Ireland. Most of the first missionaries in my area were Scottish Presbyterians and Italian Catholics.

The missionaries would generally do their work by visiting villages and attending to peoples' health needs. They treated particularly stubborn conditions, such as gangrene or difficulties with childbirth, that could not be healed with local remedies like herbs and tree bark, and then established health centers. Initially, the missionaries would instruct small groups of adults in reading—only after they had converted to Christianity—but quite rapidly they established schools. I admire the missionaries' patience and ingenuity in facilitating communication among people who did not understand one another's languages. They did their work well.

The art of reading and writing must have hit people like lightning. It must have been extraordinary to them that lines and dots on a page or a slate when taken together could transmit a message that a person many miles away could receive. It must have seemed like a new form of magic that overshadowed what Kikuyus had known until then. Reading and writing fascinated them and they embraced it with a passion.

Before the arrival of the missionaries, Kikuyus and all the Kenyan communities had largely oral cultures. The ways they delivered a message or passed information included the use of drums, horns, shouting, or sending somebody. Among Kikuyus, one interesting form of message transmission and education was *gĩchandĩ*, which was made from a gourd. When you shook it, the beads on strings on the outside and the seeds and stones inside made music. As players or actors shook the gourd, they relayed riddles, proverbs, and other folk wisdom and information. These gourds were also inscribed with symbols and marks that represented a form of writing that these artisans would use for recitations and conveying information.

Ironically, the missionaries described such instruments in detail, but then encouraged the local people who had converted to Christianity to destroy them. Even as they trivialized many aspects of the local culture, including various art forms, they also recorded them and saved some of the artifacts, which now reside in European museums. I have heard that one of these *gĩchandĩ* is in a museum in Turin, Italy.

To consolidate their hold on their new territories in Africa, during the first decade and a half of the twentieth century the European governments encouraged people of European descent—among them South Africans, Australians, Canadians, Britons, Germans—to settle in their colonies. In Kenya, these settlers began arriving in increasing numbers and the British authorities gave them land in the highlands. The settlers found the highlands very attractive for the same reasons the local people do: the soil was fertile, debilitating diseases like malaria were absent, and it was neither too hot nor too cold—perfect weather.

The settlers received title deeds to most of the land in areas where they preferred to settle, near emerging city centers or regions that seemed promising for successful wheat, maize, coffee, and tea farming, and for grazing livestock. To make way for them, many people were displaced, including a large number who were forcibly relocated to the Rift Valley. Those who refused to vacate their land were transported by the British elsewhere.

By the 1930s the British had ensured that native communities, including Kikuyus, had been restricted to designated regions known as native reserves while their land was subdivided among the new arrivals. People within the native reserves were able to keep their land. Ihithe was in the Kikuyu reserve and my father owned land there. Some he had bought and some he inherited from his father, who purchased it when he migrated to Ihithe from Kahiga-inī, a village nearby. After both the First and Second World Wars, war veterans came to Kenya and received land—one of the ways the British government thanked them for defending the crown. By the early 1950s, about 40,000 settlers, most of them British, had moved onto about 2,500 farms in what became known as the "white highlands," which included the hills outside Nairobi, the highlands of the central and western regions, and large tracts of grassland in the Rift Valley.

However, even after the arrival of missionaries and then the British administration, pockets of the old way of life persisted. Three of my grandparents never converted to Christianity, but I am informed that my mother's mother was baptized on her deathbed. Their children, however, converted as adults, the first generation of Kikuyus to become almost wholly Christian. They must have been among the early converts of their generation, because when I was growing up, my uncle Kamunya, charismatic and progressive, was already a leader in the African Independent Church. This church embraced both Protestant and Catholic teachings as well as aspects of Kikuyu culture discouraged in the other two denominations.

At the time of my birth, in 1940, there were still people who had not become Christians and competition for converts among the many churches that had been established was intense. In and around Nyeri, the Catholics, the Presbyterians, and the Independent Church were very active. Those who had not embraced Christianity, who still held on to and advocated for local customs, were called Kikuyus, while those who had converted were called *athomi*. Literally translated, this means "people who read." The book they read was the Bible. One of the first local language translations of the Bible was into Kikuyu, which made the Christian teachings much more accessible.

In general, local Kenyans who converted to Christianity were given preference within the British colonial administration and were often appointed chiefs and subchiefs in villages and towns. In addition, the *athomi* culture was presented by those who embraced it as progressive, its members moving forward into a modern world while the others were presented as primitive and backward, living in the past. The *athomi* culture brought with it European ways and led to profound changes in the way Kikuyus dressed and adorned themselves, the kinds of food they ate, the songs they sang, and the dances they performed. Everything that represented the local culture was enthusiastically replaced: Millet gave way to maize, and millet porridge, then the most common Kikuyu drink, was displaced in favor of tea. As the crops changed, so did the tools used for agriculture and cooking: Corrugated iron pots replaced earthen ones, plates and cups replaced calabashes, spoons replaced fingers and sticks. Clothes of animal skin were put aside in favor of cotton dresses for women and shirts, shorts, and trousers for men.

In traditional Kikuyu society, young men and women braided their hair; once married, they shaved their heads completely. When you became a *mūthomi* ("a person who reads"), you no longer braided your hair or shaved your head. Men cut their hair short while women let theirs grow long to resemble that of Europeans. Women also tied scarves around their heads to approximate veils. Dancing and non-Christian festivities and initiation rites were discouraged or even demonized and banned by missionaries and converts. A nearly complete transformation of the local culture into one akin to that of Europe had taken place in the generation before I was born.

Among the critical mass of Kikuyus in the central highlands who had converted to Christianity by the time of my birth were my parents. Because my parents were *athomi*, they dressed like Europeans, as did I, because I was a child of "those who read." I remember seeing some "Kikuyus" in and around Ihithe, including my paternal grandfather, Njugi Muchiri, wearing either a goat skin or a blanket that hung over his shoulders and fell long to the ground. I have almost no memory of his face, just his blanket dragging behind him as he walked.

My father was tall, well over six feet, and muscular. He had an authoritative voice and was a dominating figure in our household. He was born around 1903—there were no written records then—and attended primary school. He could read and write in Kikuyu, which is how he read the Bible, and he also spoke some Kiswahili, a language that had traveled throughout Kenya from the coast. Although his father, my grandfather, would not have gone to school, he saw to it that his sons did, if only for a few years.

My father's physical strength was legendary. Some of the older people still remark on it: "Your father was so strong, he didn't need the jack to change the wheel of his car." I have also heard that when he went to a storehouse to load his truck with bags of wheat or maize, he would take the bags in his hands and simply throw them in. Most other men would put the heavy bags on their shoulders before they moved them. Men knew not to pick a fight with my father, because he never lost. My eldest brother, Nderitu, inherited a bit of that physical strength, so my mother told us. In later years, when my brother's car would get stuck in the mud, he would get out, tie a rope around the fender, and pull the car free, *almost* single-handedly.

Physically and in her demeanor, my mother provided a striking contrast to my father. Throughout her life she was thin and tall, at least five feet eight inches. She walked very straight and it was only in her late eighties that she began to bend. Next to the imposing physique of my father, my mother looked almost fragile. However, in character and body she was sturdy, and very hardworking. She was also very kind. I always think of her as gentle and quiet, never shouting or scolding.

My mother was born around 1906 and married my father in her mid-twenties, the usual age for marriage then. Although my mother attended classes for adults that taught her sewing, ironing, and some agricultural practices, she never learned to read or write. Her life remained mostly rural: She cultivated crops and produced food well into her eighties. When she got sick, we children always had enough, mostly because of her hard work and the deep sense of duty and responsibility she had toward us.

I was her eldest daughter, and that naturally made us very close, because almost as soon as I could walk she would ask me to help her. When you are the first girl in a Kikuyu family, you become almost like the second woman of the house. You do what your mother does and you are always with her. The two of you become almost like one. As far back as I can remember, my mother and I were always together and always talking. She was my anchor in life.

My father was also part of the first generation in Kenya to leave their homes and families behind to find jobs and accumulate money, which could be found only in the cash economy the British established. He, like approximately 150,000 other young Kikuyu men, migrated from the Kikuyu native reserves to white-owned farms. Before the British arrived, animals, especially goats, were the main form of exchange. "How many goats (mburi)?" you would be asked if you were selling land, or paying a marriage dowry or compensation. The life of a man was worth about thirty goats, that of a woman or a child less.

When the British decided to collect revenue and finance local development, they did not want to be paid in goats. They wanted cash. They also wanted to create a labor force, but they did not want to force people to work. So they introduced an income tax for men

in most parts of the country that could be paid only in the form
of money. This created a cash-based rather than a livestock-based
economy. Of course, the colonial government and the British settlers were the only ones with money in their hands. So the local people, especially men, were indirectly forced to work on settlers' farms
or in offices so they could earn money to pay taxes. By the 1940s,
settlers' farms constituted a major source of employment.

This kind of economy accepted, indeed often required, that when
men went to work in towns or cities, their wives and children would
be left behind in the rural areas. Generally, men could visit only
every three months, or sometimes as rarely as once a year, when
they received time off or could afford the cost of travel. This separation of men from their families was completely new and resulted
in large numbers of women-headed households, which had not been
the case before. It also introduced negative phenomena such as
prostitution, absent fathers, and sexually transmitted infections that
were unknown until then and persist as significant challenges in
society today.

On the settlers' farms, however, men were not only allowed but
encouraged to bring their families with them, because the wives and
children contributed to the farm's labor force. At that time, farmers
in the Rift Valley badly needed workers, because much of the agriculture was manual. There were very few tractors and plows, and
even after mechanization was introduced in the 1930s, much digging, planting, harvesting, transporting, and milking of livestock
continued to be done by hand.

Around 1943, before I developed the capacity for memory, my
mother and I left Ihithe to join my father in Nakuru in the Rift Valley, about one hundred miles away, where he worked as a driver and
mechanic on the farm of a British settler, D. N. Neylan. My father
had no title to the land where he had established his household—he
was effectively a squatter on the farm—but he could build housing
for his family and cultivate crops on land Mr. Neylan apportioned to
him. Often the settlers' farms were so large that this land would be
substantial, but the settlers could move squatters at any time.

Going to the Rift Valley to work was an attractive option for men, especially for Kikuyus, many of whom had been forcibly displaced from their land in the central highlands to make way for the settlers and new towns. The soil was fertile, which made it possible to grow a lot of food. We and other squatters' children never went hungry. But there were no schools on or near the settlers' farms. Even as I was growing up, it was not easy for the workers to send their children to school. This was a reality that was to shape my life.

Although my family could grow food for our household on the farm, if my father wanted to sell maize, for example, Mr. Neylan had a monopoly. To sell your harvest to a cooperative you had to be a member, a privilege afforded only to the settlers. While my father could sell as much as he wanted to Mr. Neylan, his remuneration was rather minimal compared to what Mr. Neylan himself was making selling to the markets. Squatters like my father would also receive maize flour and about a quart (or liter) of milk from Mr. Neylan as a daily portion for the work done on the farms. Even then, the man, his wife, and children were all required to provide labor. They were really glorified slaves, although of course they had the freedom to leave if they wanted.

Unlike many Kenyans on Mr. Neylan's farm who could provide only manual labor such as digging and harvesting my father was skilled: He could drive and he knew how to repair machines, trades he had learned as a young man. This gave him an advantage, and in time he became one of Mr. Neylan's most trusted employees.

My first memories are of being on that farm in Nakuru, helping my mother. When we arrived in Nakuru, my parents already had my two older brothers, Nderitu and Kibicho, and me. While we were there, my mother gave birth to my two younger sisters, Muringi (also known as Monica, her Christian name) and Wachatha (also known as Beatrice). As a young child, I went with my mother into the fields to help her take care of my sisters. She would put us down on the ground near her, and we spent the day playing in the soil and chattering among ourselves.

I also watched my mother work. She planted seeds, tilled the soil, plucked weeds, and harvested crops. Most were food crops, such as wheat and maize, as well as pyrethrum, a plant brought to Kenya by the British that was popular and highly valued as an insecticide. Pyrethrum was about the height of small children, so the settlers used children older than me to harvest it. In my mind's eye I can still see the little children in the fields picking the pyrethrum's white flowers. To me, then, it looked like a pleasant job.

On Mr. Neylan's farm, fields of maize and wheat stretched as far as my little eyes could see. When the wind blew over that wheat, the movement was beautiful, like waves. Before the harvest, the wheat turned golden brown, springing from a soil that was whitish gray and flecked with flickering grains of minerals. *Managu*, a green vegetable, flourished in maize fields after the harvest. Although it was considered a weed, it was a popular food, especially when used as an accompaniment to *ugali*, a maize cake something like corn-bread that we ate. I recall the older women making a big fuss of collecting the *managu* leaves for sale in markets in neighboring Nakuru town.

For me, the pleasures of *managu* were closer by. Small, yellow, juicy berries sprouted amid the *managu* leaves. Whenever I was sent with my siblings to look after our sheep and goats as they grazed in the freshly cut fields, I would feast myself silly on those berries! I ate so many that I would not be hungry for dinner when I got home. At that time, nothing in life was more pleasant than to be asked to take the animals into the fields. Unfortunately, one does not see the *managu* plants a lot these days—one of the negative consequences of overcultivation and the use of agrochemicals.

Like many men of his generation, even among the "people who read," my father was a polygamist. Some churches were very strict and required men to have only one official wife at a time. Others were less so, including the church my father belonged to, the African Independent Church. My father had four wives, including one he married after I was born. My mother was the second wife. At the time I was living in Nakuru there were about ten children in my father's household.

All of us, the wives and the children and my father, lived in a single compound, a typical Kikuyu homestead. Our homestead covered a large open space and included several houses and a big courtyard with a fence and gate surrounding it. My father had his own hut, called a *thingira*, which was one large, round room constructed of mud and wood and covered by a sloped, grass-thatched roof. Here he ate, slept, and received guests, including strangers, who were not supposed to go beyond the *thingira* without permission from the man of the house. I would sometimes take food from my mother to my father in his hut, but as a girl I would not be expected to stay. This was the realm of men, boys, and male visitors.

Each of my father's wives had her own house, called a *nyũmba*, similarly constructed but with several compartments. This was the realm of the woman, her children, and female visitors and relatives. Each house was between twenty and thirty feet across and divided into several separate areas by walls or sticks. My mother had her own place to sleep, while my sisters and I slept together in our own compartment, as my brothers did in theirs. Our beds were wood planks topped by mattress covers that we stuffed with leaves, ferns, and grass.

The houses had no electricity or running water and were dark inside. There were small windows, but with no glass in them. In the middle of the *nyũmba* was the fire where my mother prepared meals. This cooking area was the family's space, around which members talked, told stories, and shared their experiences of the day. Firewood was abundant and people mostly used dry wood, which produced very little smoke along with beautiful flames that illuminated the house. The mud walls and the thatched roofs retained the heat from the fire, so I do not recall being chilly, even during the cold season in July.

Sheep and goats also lived in the compound and some were kept inside the huts at night. I recall having a goat in the house with us that was fattened, slaughtered, and eaten when my mother gave birth to one of my younger sisters. By the time I was born, latrines had become a permanent feature of homesteads. Commonly, there would be two or three for a compound like ours and the women would keep them clean. As children got older, they were asked to help clean them, too.

Even though the living area inside the house was comparatively small, it did not feel crowded. We usually stayed in the house only at night. If you were inside during the day, it was because you were sick. Otherwise, someone would ask you, "What are you doing in the house? You're supposed to be outside working"—or, if you were a young child, basking in the sun. Today, many Kenyans, even in the rural areas, build houses made of bricks and metal and in the shape of squares or rectangles. Square corners are now perceived to be very progressive. To see a "traditional" Kenyan homestead, you have to go to the National Museum in Nairobi. But when I was growing up this was the only reality I knew.

As a child, I did not realize that some of the children were not my full siblings. In a polygamous homestead, we learned to live with our half siblings as part of a small community. I felt like everyone in the homestead was a member of the family. I could go to any of the other houses and be welcomed and feel at home, as could any other member of the family in my mother's house. We would call the other wives "mother" (*maitū*), but with an adjective: younger mother, *maitū mūnyinyi*, or older mother, *maitū mūkūrū*. My mother we called plain *maitū*. I did not sense any of the jealousy or hatred that is sometimes portrayed as being rampant in such a homestead.

In traditional Kikuyu society, a man had the freedom to marry as many women as he wanted. But, unlike today, he was required by cultural norms to take care of all his children. The society would not allow men to escape these duties. For one, a man was under strong peer pressure to embrace his responsibilities. If he did not behave properly, his peers could ostracize him from the community. Few people could withstand such public rejection. Today, that peer pressure, which was part of the culture, is gone. People can go to court, but they can still escape justice and abandon their responsibilities by disappearing to distant places or into the urban jungle. Some men do not seem to have the slightest feelings of guilt when they abandon their children. That was not the case when I was a child. Then, children were protected and attended to.

In many ways, the polygamous system worked well for children. Even though my mother went to work each day in the fields, my brothers and sisters and I never felt we were alone. If we were at home, we would be taken care of by whichever adult was also home. I am sure that there were conflicts in the household, especially between the wives, and that my father beat them, including my mother, because when I was much older they complained. But I never saw or heard about any of this as a child.

When there was a calamity, like a death in the family, we children were protected from that phenomenon, which of course is overwhelming even for adults. For instance, the first time I saw my mother crying, I learned from her that my uncle Kamunya had died young, his dreams unfulfilled. But I was shielded from all aspects of the death, so the memories I have of my uncle are of him herding his cows, working around his compound, or sitting in his home with a cup of tea. The adults seemed to appreciate that their children might not be able to process such profound experiences and so they would not give them information their young psyches could not comprehend. Today, young children are exposed to cadavers, coffins, and burials, experiences that might be too much for their young minds.

What I know now is that my parents raised me in an environment that did not give reasons for fear or uncertainty. Instead, there were many reasons to dream, to be creative, and to use my imagination. As I grew older, I learned that we can convince ourselves and our children, and if we are leaders we can convince our citizens, that we are in danger, either from what people might do to us or what we might do to ourselves. I know my parents occasionally told me things to keep me unaware and therefore unafraid. But parents have to do that sometimes to allow their children to grow up confident and resilient and able to confront challenges later in life.

My father and mother were very reserved with each other, which was typical of relationships between women and men at that time. Similarly, my siblings and I had formal relationships with my father. My early memories of him are as a serious person who kept his distance. When I met him on the farm, he would not say, "Oh, Wangari, there you are." I would just know "That's my father." That was all I needed. If you are trained to be satisfied seeing your father at a distance, you accept it. You are just happy he is there.

Most often, we children would see my father late in the day. Each evening, a fire would be made at the gate of our homestead and he, friends, visitors, and his sons would sit there. Everyone would pass by: the wives, the younger girls, and the livestock. I later learned that this ensured that my father knew that everyone had come home. When they had, he would close the gate and go into his hut, usually when dusk fell. This evening ritual made me feel secure and protected.

There is one memory of my father that has remained with me. He was in Nakuru town driving a large truck that was high off the ground. He had parked next to a café, now called the Ihithe Hotel, where we used to have tea if we were in town. The hotel belonged to one of my father's step-uncles, which is why we stopped there. I was standing on the hotel veranda and I had to look way up in the sky to see my father. Because the truck was so high, when my father got out of the cab he had to leap down. I saw this huge figure in heavy black boots jumping to the ground.

When he landed, he leaned down and said, "Hello! How are you?" and touched my forehead, the way adults customarily greeted children. For much of my early life my father was an overpowering figure. Yet here he was, singling me out, down at my level on the earth. In his prime, my father seemed like a mountain to me: strong, powerful, invulnerable, immovable. Many years later, when he got old and sick with cancer of the esophagus and could hardly move, that fantastic picture of him would come back. It helped me understand how wonderful it is to be healthy and able to move, how quickly those youthful years pass, and how vulnerable we are.

As he grew older, my father changed a lot. He became less formal and more interactive with his children. Consequently, my youngest brother and my younger half brothers and half sisters were able to have a much closer relationship with him as children than those of us who were older. As it turned out, for most of my childhood I lived with my mother and my sisters and brothers in Nyeri while my father stayed in Nakuru. Perhaps if he had been in the household during those years, I might have had a stronger relationship with him than I did. For many years, though, I saw him only occasionally when I would visit him in Nakuru.

In all the years we were together, my mother and I never disagreed. Sometimes you get to a point when you feel that your mother is pushing you a certain way, and you get fed up and even rebel. I never had that with her. I know now as a mother myself that it was a great gift and privilege that she lived long and that I was able to take care of her and be with her when in her eighties she became weak. The fact that we never had an upsetting word between us is a source of great personal peace.

One memory of her has remained with me all these years, partly because it caused me to question my behavior. It was Sunday and I had been to church. After the service, I followed a group of Pentecostals, a denomination that was becoming strong in Ihithe and nearby villages, to the Gĩtherere shopping center. The spirit was with me! When I arrived home I leaned against the wall of our house, singing my heart out, as I had just heard a young boy preacher do. My mother was sweeping the compound, and without saying a word, she took her broom and swept all around me as I sang my hymns.

"Now, why didn't she ask me to move, or why didn't I move instead of standing there in my bare feet singing while my mother worked?" I asked myself when my mother was finished sweeping and had gone to do errands. Was it my responsibility to move, or my mother's to tell me to? Is it that she was listening to my Pentecostal songs or did she think, "She ought to know better and move"? I never talked to my mother about the incident, but it taught me profound lessons—to question myself and assess my actions and then do what is right. My mother did not force her sense of justice and fairness on me—after all, she could have hit my dirty feet with the broom and said, "Get the hell out of here." But she didn't. She just let me carry on singing. Her contentment and composure inspired me when I was old enough to appreciate it. Whatever disappointments my mother had, and I am sure she had some, she kept them to herself, a trait I learned to admire as I grew older and, inevitably, accumulated my own.

On Mr. Neylan's farm, people from many communities worked, including Luos, Kipsigis, and Kikuyus, who without the economic and labor system the British instituted would not have lived in proximity to each other. Each community kept to the category of jobs assigned to it. Kikuyus worked in the fields, Luos labored around the homestead as domestic servants, and Kipsigis took care of the livestock and milking. The communities also lived separately, which of course was deliberate. It was probably the master's way of making sure that everybody kept to their roles and remained apart. You would see a Kikuyu village here, a Luo village there, and a Kipsigi town down there.

My father was very good with languages and could communicate quite fluently in Kipsigis, Luhyia, Luo, and Kiswahili, which he picked up around the area. But most of us on the farm rarely met people from other communities, spoke their languages, or participated in their cultural practices. Except for the skin color we shared we were as "foreign" to one another as the British setters were to us.

I grew up knowing that I was a Kikuyu and that the other communities were different from us. I would, though, overhear the adults around me expressing their views about some of our differences. If, for example, one of the women was very well dressed, they would ask her with a smile, "Where are you going, smartly dressed like a Luo?" Other people were known to expect things for free. These ethnic biases, many of which were planted early in one's childhood, became amplified and were embraced by national political rhetoric. They are still used today to divide Kenyans from one another.

During my years on the farm, I never thought about the fact that Mr. Neylan and his family were white while everyone else was black, and I never heard my parents or other adults talking about it; for them, skin color was not an issue. But we did recognize the differences in our lifestyles and privileges, which were taken as given. In my child's world, though, there was a time when I thought life was at a standstill: Those of us who were children would always be children, and those of us who were old would stay that way. "That's the way they are," I said to myself. It took me a long time to realize that people grow old and die and that even I was getting bigger and taller.

I never spoke to Mr. Neylan, his wife, or his children, but I did observe them. Mrs. Neylan always wore a large hat, probably to protect herself from the strong, hot sun. She also wore light, flowery cotton dresses that came to just below her knees. People called her *nyakīneke,* which means "a large person," perhaps because she was pleasantly round and walked briskly. We had nicknames for all the settlers and, in fact, I never learned her real name. When I saw Mrs. Neylan it was usually in the evenings when I would come to collect our family's allotment of wheat flour and skimmed milk (the settlers kept the butter). There she was, basket in hand, moving purposefully from one coop to the other collecting eggs from her chickens. I loved watching her. If she were alive today and we met, she would probably say with a chuckle, "Well, look at you! Who is *nyakīneke* now?"

Mr. Neylan and *nyakīneke* had children, including a daughter about fifteen years older than I. The people on the farm fondly referred to her as *kairītu*, or "the sweet young girl." Occasionally, my father would work around the Neylans' homestead. One time I went to see him there and found myself very close to *kairītu*'s room. Through an open door I saw a compartment full of clothes. More than twenty dresses must have been inside—the closet was completely stuffed. I can still see the colors: blue, white, and red. "How can anybody have so many dresses?" I asked myself. It was as many dresses as I had seen in my whole life. At that time, I think I had two dresses, maybe three.

Over the years, my father and Mr. Neylan grew to be close friends—as good friends as a master and his employee can be. My father valued that friendship, perhaps even more than Mr. Neylan did. One time, when he got older, my father took Mr. Neylan a he-goat. Traditionally, when an old man takes a he-goat to another old man it is a sign of great friendship and respect. The man receiving the goat is supposed to slaughter and eat the goat, and return the front leg to the man who gave it to him. I don't know whether Mr. Neylan knew what to do with the goat or whether he returned the leg, but giving the animal to him meant a lot to my father.

Among the British were some wonderful people, like the Neylans. The power between my father and Mr. Neylan was never equal, of course. We remained squatters on Mr. Neylan's land until Kenya's independence. But when independence came and a wave of British settlers sold their land to local people, Mr. Neylan decided to give my father twenty-five acres of the farm as a gift. My father then joined a cooperative and with the other members bought what remained of Mr. Neylan's farm. When my father died in 1978, his remains were buried on that farm, not far from where our homestead had stood and where I had eaten *managu* berries as I tended our sheep and goats. My eldest brother and some members of my extended family now live on that land.

. . .

Occasionally I would accompany my mother or other members of my family to Nakuru town, about ten miles away, where the women would sell vegetables in the markets. In those days, there was no public transport, so we walked. We would leave early in the morning, long before the sun rose over the ridges of the valley, and arrive in Nakuru at dawn. The area around Nakuru is largely grassland, with occasional trees, especially acacia. Up on the ridges, there were natural forests but also plantations of exotic species, such as pine and eucalyptus. I remember thorn trees along the riverbanks and I used to collect firewood from the fallen branches. I always wondered how those trees got to be set along the river—why they were only there and nowhere else. I did not realize then that most of the other trees had been cut to make way for farms.

For me, a rural child, going to town was very adventurous. In Nakuru, I would see cars, lots of people, and clothing and other goods for sale. We would have a cup of tea at my father's relative's hotel and eat *mandazi*, fried dough sweetened with sugar. All this was fascinating to me then so I did not mind the walk. In fact, I practically ran.

In those days, the upper part of Nakuru town was still enclosed by forests and was extremely clean. It was an affluent town, surrounded by wealthy settlers. Approaching Nakuru from the east, you always knew you were close because you would see jacaranda trees, which, when they bloom, have beautiful, bright blue-purple flowers. Jacarandas are among the many foreign species of trees and plants the British must have brought to Kenya. As you walked toward the town, on the right was a ridge and, beyond it, the lake. Because Mr. Neylan's farm was out of town, I saw the lake only from a distance. To me it looked shiny white, from the saltwater, with a flush of pink, which I learned much later was due to the millions of flamingoes that make it their home. The lake is now a national park, where you can see rhinos, lions, hippos, and, of course, the flamingoes.

Like many towns in colonial Kenya, Nakuru at that time was segregated, with separate areas for Europeans, Indians, and Africans. The European section was on the slopes of a ridge overlooking the lowlands. The houses had a very particular style: red brick with red, blue, or white walls and sloping roofs, surrounded by jacarandas and bougainvillea, which the British seemed to love, since you always saw them in their homesteads.

The Indians occupied the middle ground on the hill and their houses had a distinctive architecture of mostly flat roofs, elaborately decorated walls, and small gardens. About thirty-five thousand Indians were brought by the British to Kenya in the 1890s as low-wage laborers to build the Kenya-Uganda railroad. Many Indians died completing the railroad, but those who survived were encouraged by the British to stay in Kenya and Uganda. Many did and set up shops along the railroad line and sold goods, such as blankets and cotton products, along with salt and other foodstuffs. These goods were being imported for the first time.

The Indian immigrants also brought with them their traditional foods and cuisine and successfully introduced them to the local populations. Salt, fat, sugar, and oil, virtually unknown in local food preparation, tasted good and were heavily promoted. Today, many new diseases associated with nutrition find their roots in this sudden change in people's diets, which for many communities, including Kikuyus, had been largely maize, millet, roots, beans, sugarcane, and green vegetables.

In Nakuru, as in other cities at that time, Africans lived in the most crowded part. There were many people and the homes, built from stone, mud, or brick, were small and crowded together. Even as a child, I could see the difference. Of course, I did not think any of this was deliberate: It was just the way it was and we belonged in that part of town. Today, Nakuru is Kenya's fourth-largest city—busy, bustling, noisy, and full of houses and people. If you go to Nakuru now, it is very different. The jacarandas are still there, but the city is not nearly as beautiful. While there are still a large number of Indians and Europeans, there is not much separation between them and Africans. Today, money talks. If you have it, you can live anywhere.

Every family has a secret, and ours is no exception. In my family, there was a missing member, someone I did not find out about until I was well into adulthood. During the First World War, Africans in the colonies were conscripted to fight or serve as porters. In Kenya, if parents had an able-bodied son old enough to go to war, they were supposed to encourage him to join military training and then fight with the British army in East Africa (most of the battles were against the Germans and Italians and fought in Somalia and Tanganyika). If he would not go on his own, the parents were expected to surrender him to the authorities.

My grandparents had such a son, Thumbi. My grandmother did not want her son, who was no more than twenty at the time, to join the war. She was in despair. So she advised him to hide in the dense vegetation near a high waterfall in the Tucha River near Ihithe, and brought him food from her farm every day. However, the British had developed a system to deal with parents who were reluctant to give up their sons to the war effort. They would confiscate all of their livestock. For people at that time, especially men, livestock was everything, as important as land. The authorities confronted my grandfather and threatened to take all his cattle and goats. The pressure worked. He told them where his son was hiding and they went and seized him.

"Ah, he'll come back," my grandfather said to his wife and anyone else who would listen once his son had gone to war. "He'll never come back," my grandmother replied, crying. And he never did. He became one of the more than one hundred thousand Kikuyus who died on the battlefield or from starvation or influenza during the First World War. When the war ended in 1918, my grandparents waited for their son to return from Tanganyika. But he didn't and they received no news about him. Then one day a man who lived nearby and who had also gone to the war said to my grandparents, "Make beer and I will come and tell you what happened to your son."

So my grandfather made beer. That was typical: to make beer and have guests come and drink and talk. That afternoon, the man came. Perhaps the beer gave him the courage to tell my grandfather what he knew about his son's fate. "I saw him get shot. He fell, and he didn't get up," he said sadly. My grandmother cried for her son for the rest of her life, and she always blamed my grandfather for the loss. "I told you he wouldn't come back," she would say.

My mother told me this story because I asked her why my uncles and aunt were naming their children after my father. In Kikuyu culture, traditionally the first son is named for his paternal grandfather, so I always thought my father was my grandparents' eldest son. Later, I learned that my father was named after my grandmother's father, so there must have been another son. In explaining this, my mother told me that my grandmother had been so distraught by what happened to her son that she decided that none of her grandchildren would be named for him, lest she be reminded of that loss. The name of that young man—my eldest uncle—was lost with him, wiped from the face of the earth.

My grandparents and other families like them who lost sons in the First World War never received any official word about what had happened to their children, or any compensation. This is still an open wound. I want to say to the British government, "My uncle went to war and never came back, and nobody ever bothered to come and tell my grandparents what had happened to their son."

2

Cultivation

Late in 1947, my father sat me down, which, given our relationship, was unusual. "You are going to Nyeri so you can help your mother take care of your younger sister," he said. I imagine I just nodded. As long as I was going with my mother, it was all right by me. If I had been told I was to be separated from her, I would probably have thrown a tantrum.

My two older brothers were already in Nyeri attending school, living with my uncle Kamunya, whose children were also in school. It was decided, presumably by my father in discussion with my mother, that we would return to Nyeri so my mother could relieve my uncle and his family of the care-taking duties for my brothers. My mother, my youngest sister, Wachatha (then about two), and I made the journey together. My other sister, Muringi, had injured her leg chopping wood, so she stayed behind and joined us later.

My father had sent my brothers to school in Nyeri because, even in the late 1940s, it was rare to have schools on settlers' farms. Not even the missionaries tried to establish schools on private land. Also, educating African children was not a priority for the settlers. Indeed, when Mr. Neylan heard of what my father was doing, he is said to have asked him who would pick his pyrethrum. "Don't worry," my father replied, "there are still many children in my homestead." As it turned out, because of the conflict following the outbreak of the Mau Mau resistance movement and the state of emergency that followed, none of my other siblings managed to follow us to Nyeri to attend school.

To get from Nakuru to Nyeri in those days, you first had to travel north and then east in a sixty-mile journey that today lasts only three hours but at that time took all day. This would be the longest conscious journey of my young life. Our adventure began the previous day, when we spent the night at our relative's hotel in Nakuru town—more a place to have tea than to sleep. This was an extraordinary experience in itself, *to sleep in town*. It was very warm, so much so that we did not even want to cover ourselves. I hardly slept because the surroundings were so unfamiliar: There were lights, cars passing, people talking and working in the kitchen throughout the night.

Early in the morning, we boarded the bus and started our long journey to Nyeri. Until then, I had thought that the whole world was contained between the ridges that ran along the edge of the Rift Valley and Lake Nakuru. So you can imagine my shock when we climbed the ridge through Ndunduri and I discovered that on the other side of the ridge lay another world. I was completely overwhelmed by this discovery and hardly remember what happened between Ndunduri and Nyahururu (in English, Thomson's Falls). When we passed Nyahururu my mother told me that its name meant "place of falling water" and that it was called after a waterfall nearby.

The packed bus rattled along past the waterfall and, as it did, I glimpsed the fast-flowing waters that disappeared into the steep fall and heard them rolling down the cliff. We were soon traveling across the open grasslands and interminable scrub on the eastern edge of the Rift Valley. Looking out through the bus's open window and enjoying the cool breeze on my face, I watched the great herds of cattle grazing on ranchland owned by the white settlers. Zebras, giraffes, antelopes, and the occasional buffalo were dotted throughout the plain. Together our little family and our fellow travelers— farmers, businessmen, and visitors returning home—jostled and bumped and hoped that our luggage would not fall off the roof and be lost in the huge cloud of dust that spread out in a plume behind us.

At one point in the trip we drove past acre upon acre of blackened tree stumps. These were *mītarakwa* (tropical cedars), which had been destroyed by what my mother said had been a forest fire. When we reached Ngobit, there was a police checkpoint where we were stopped and asked to exit the vehicle. The uniformed officers looked very serious, well-dressed, and disciplined. Much later, I understood that they were ensuring the bus had a valid road license and that vendors weren't transporting diseased livestock.

It was around dusk as we approached Nyeri, dipping into the valleys and climbing up the rough roads around the hills. Everywhere I looked I could see woodlots, and between them farms and rows of crops. Far in the distance, seeming to hover above the horizon, were the imposing outlines of the snow-capped peak of Mount Kenya to the north and the Aberdare Range to the west. Both were covered by thick forests that to my eyes seemed like blue-black blankets.

We arrived in the bus depot in the center of Nyeri. Most of the passengers disembarked here, but we stayed on until the last stop, Huho-inī, where the bus owner had his homestead. Since it was too late for us to continue the journey, we slept there as the bus owner's guests. Everything was new and unusual and it took me a long time to fall asleep as I stared into the darkness, thinking about what I had seen that day and the final leg of the journey that lay ahead. It was so quiet I could almost hear my own breathing.

The following morning we woke up early and ate porridge. Typical of the hospitality in those days, we didn't have to pay for the bed or the breakfast. Our feet took us the final three miles to Ihithe, my mother carrying much of our luggage, Wachatha wrapped around her chest, and me walking in front. Near the top of Gatumbīro, which is seven thousand feet above sea level, I saw my home—a series of valleys, bright green and luxuriant, punctuated with yams, bananas, sugarcane, and arrowroots. Even though I had eaten these foods, I had never seen them growing in the soil.

On the horizon was the thick, deep green of the Aberdare forest, stretching as far as the eye could see in the early morning sun. I drank in the beauty, overwhelmed. The contrast between Nakuru and Ihithe could not have been greater. Nakuru means "dusty place" in Maasai, while Ihithe was a landscape full of different shades of green, all springing from soil the color of deep terra-cotta—smooth and dark and richly fertile, but mostly hidden behind the mass of wet, fresh vegetation.

Finally, my mother led us down a narrow path overhung with plants into the homestead of her father, my grandfather, Kibicho Ngetha. He received us warmly—giving her his hand and saying, *"Wakĩa maitũ"* ("How are you, my mother?"). She replied, *"Wakĩa awa"* ("I'm fine, my father") and he laid his hand on my sister's and my foreheads and blessed us. To me, he seemed very old. He wore a blanket around his shoulders and was richly adorned in a necklace, with long pierced ears and colorful earrings. This was the first time he had seen my mother since her own mother had died. We sat down and were treated to a welcome drink—delicious millet porridge in a calabash, a large one for my mother and my little sister and a small one for me.

Shortly after we arrived, people in the neighborhood came to welcome my mother home. As they engaged in conversation, I saw a group of excited children running to the homestead. They were my uncle Kamunya's children, and they immediately invited me to go with them. My mother encouraged me and off I went with my cousins. To get to my uncle's homestead, we had to cross a valley at the bottom of which was a small stream. Valleys were new to me. I was afraid I would fall as I walked down the hill. My cousins assured me I would not, but, unconvinced, I came up with a solution: I walked down the hill backward, on all fours. My cousins laughed. They were used to racing up and down the hills, even competing during the rainy season as if skiing downhill on the mud. It didn't take me much time to get used to the hills. Before long I, too, was an expert downhill mud-skier.

Ihithe was one of a cluster of villages of about three hundred households, about nine miles from Nyeri town. Nearly everyone, men and women, were farmers, growing food for their families. There were no settler farms nearby, so everyone lived and worked in one place. It rained frequently, but the rivers were always clear and clean because the land and the riverbanks were covered by vegetation. We were encouraged to play in light rain and made to believe that, like the crops, we would get tall as a result. I loved it. Hailstorms, too, were frequent and as children we enjoyed collecting, playing with, and eating hailstones much as children play with snow. One hailstorm was so intense it turned the landscape in Ihithe white for a week.

Although some of the roads in Ihithe are now paved and there are many more motorized vehicles, the village today looks not that different from what it was like when I was young. Infrastructure was minimal then, and it still is: Running water was not available until the 1960s and electricity has only recently begun to arrive. But the population has greatly increased and many of the woodlots have been replaced by tea plantations and houses, now made mostly from stone with corrugated iron roofs.

Even though there is a hair salon, the M.K.M. General Shop, a medical clinic, the Karuma-Indo butchery, and the By Grace Café, sheep are still grazing on the side of the road. The men have still not finished the conversation they began centuries ago while the women are still selling vegetables by the roadside or carrying firewood on their backs or are bent over in the fields cultivating crops—although today it is coffee or tea more often than their own food. Children are still tending goats or running errands or walking to and from school, although now the schools are built of stone, not mud.

Created by the British as an army camp, Nyeri during the 1920s and 1930s grew into a market town for the surrounding settlers, mainly ranchers and wheat farmers. Though a bustling place of commerce today, in the mid-1940s Nyeri had relatively few inhabitants. People came to town because they were bringing something

33

to sell or buying something to take home. For rural people, traveling to town was a novelty and you didn't go unless you had something to do, since it was not a place to hang around. In fact, the British established rules and regulations that meant you could be arrested if you were caught loitering. Ironically, because you weren't allowed to loiter, the town looked organized, clean, and orderly.

As in many other towns throughout Kenya at that time, Nyeri's shops were owned by Indians while the administrative offices were managed by British civil servants, who held various ranks such as provincial commissioner, district commissioner, and district officer. British civil servants, especially provincial administrators, always wore very impressive uniforms, and people in uniform tend to look orderly and disciplined, and to have a mystique about them. Their uniforms were a deliberate means of enforcing respect and fear of authority as a means of making the local people subservient and therefore easier to govern. This fear is entrenched even today.

Beneath the rank of district officer, which was always held by a white man, there were local people whom the British appointed to positions that were closer to the people. The British authorities found it more convenient and effective to have local administrators acting as the ears and the eyes of the colonial administration. Initially, other local people saw these administrators, who included criminals and tricksters, as seekers of advancement at others' expense without any relevant qualifications. They were thought of as collaborators, whose allegiance was to the British and not their own people. While eventually the jobs' aura and power attracted better candidates, the legacy of corruption, lack of accountability, patronage, and incompetence surrounding government positions has been hard to shake off.

Occasionally you would see white women around Nyeri, the wives of the British administrators. They did social work, and turned these voluntary positions into their occupations. They established many charities that cared for disabled, abandoned, or orphaned children, especially during the Mau Mau resistance in the 1950s. Some of the colonial wives in Nairobi also set up the Kenyan branches of well-known organizations such as the Red Cross, the Business and Professional Women's Association, the Association of University Women, and the Young Women's Christian Association.

These days, Nyeri, like most other towns in Kenya, has seen an explosion of immigration from the rural areas. With the focus on a cash economy and cash crops (which have not delivered the expected returns), life in villages is poorer in relative terms than it was during my childhood, so people have moved to towns to look for better lives. Nyeri is crowded with people trying to make a living in every way they can—beating metal, selling fruits and vegetables, growing plants, and buying and selling merchandise, both new and second-hand.

When I look at Nyeri today, I am reminded that when I was a child, people carried beautiful, colorful baskets of different sizes and types made from sisal and other natural fibers to and from the markets to transport goods. These baskets were part of the local handicrafts industry. Today, these baskets are hardly used and instead are made for tourists. The people meanwhile use flimsy plastic bags to carry their goods. These plastics litter the parks and streets, blow into the trees and bushes, kill domestic animals (when they swallow them inadvertently), and provide breeding grounds for mosquitoes. They leave the town so dirty it is almost impossible to find a place to sit and rest away from their plastic bags.

When we first arrived in Ihithe in the early 1940s, we stayed with my uncle while a house was built for us adjacent to his homestead. This did not take long. Over the period of a month or two, my uncle would have purchased and assembled the necessary materials and sought the assistance of other men to construct the house's frame. Young men and women would have filled the walls with mud and my mother would then have asked her older female relatives and friends to help her thatch the roof. At the end of each day my mother and her women friends and relatives would provide millet porridge, arrowroots, and ripe green bananas (*mīraru*) to nourish those working on her new home.

When it was finished, our first house in Ihithe was a rectangular mud hut with two rooms: One for my mother, my sisters, and me, and the other a common area for cooking and sitting. Later, my mother and older brothers built a small hut where the older boys lived. Behind this was a small woodlot where I would disappear, emerging only when I had a small pile of firewood on my back. I loved imitating my mother and the other women I would see in the village, with firewood on their backs, singing as they walked home. When I got home I would throw off the wood, sit on it, and act very tired, much like I had seen my mother and other women do.

Some months after our arrival in Ihithe, my mother gave birth to her last child, my brother Kamunya, who was named for my uncle. I did not know that my mother was having a baby, but I remember her calling me and telling me to call my maternal great-grandmother Wangui, who lived nearby. I ran and urged her to hurry to our home because my mother was unwell. The next thing I knew, my mother had a new baby.

My great-grandmother was a link to my community's past. My mother would often send me to her house to take her food and firewood to keep warm, especially during the cold season. My great-grandmother made a delicious sorghum meal, which she would fondly share with me when I arrived. She was grateful: "Bless you, the child of my child," she would say. "May your children remember you and bring you firewood and food." She was in her mid-nineties, an age that was not unusual in those days. Because of the fertile soil, good climate, and abundant food, the people of the central highlands were very healthy. They worked very hard and then did not suffer from many debilitating diseases.

It was common for older men and women, anticipating their passing on, to gather their families around them, bless them, declare their will, and appoint the administrator of their estate, who was often their first son. In those days, the prevailing belief was that after death, rather than go either to heaven or hell as Christians believe, the newly departed joined the spirit world of the ancestors. "May you sleep where there is rain and dew" was the final blessing given when someone was laid to rest.

The arrival of my youngest brother, to whom I grew very close, did not change the shape of my life. I continued to wash my older brothers' clothes, clean up after them, and bring them food, as was expected. Luckily, both of them were very nice to me. I often accompanied my mother as she worked in the fields. Like many African girls with their mothers, I saw her cultivating the soil and so I did the same. We did not have refrigerators or coolers, so each day we had to harvest food for that evening, especially roots and green vegetables. Although the work was hard, it was rewarding. Because of the frequent rainfall, the soil of the central highlands was often wet enough that you could make a ball with it, but still porous and smelling fresh. When you rubbed it between your fingers you could almost feel the life it held.

In addition to food crops like peas, beans, arrowroots, millet, and maize, my mother continued to grow pyrethrum, as she had in Nakuru. At the time, it was the only cash crop black farmers were allowed to grow. Tea and coffee cultivation was restricted to the white settlers. My mother also had two cows, a few goats, and chickens—just enough to provide for our household needs.

Although occasionally Kikuyus would eat meat, they did not eat wildlife and were mostly vegetarian. For that reason my mother did not eat chicken or eggs, which she considered wildlife. However, we, her children, loved to eat them. We had a dilemma, though. My mother would not allow us to use her pots and utensils to cook this "wildlife." But we did it anyway, when she was out of the house, and scrubbed the pots and spoons clean before she returned. Sometimes, we obviously did not do a very good cleaning job. If my mother smelled the aroma of the chicken in the pots, she would discard them. There were times, however, when she inadvertently used the same utensils we had used and only after the meal did she learn that chicken had been cooked with them! I believe this eventually persuaded her to accept, and even enjoy, eating chicken and eggs and stop discarding her utensils.

My mother gave me my own small garden of about fifteen square feet in the middle of her farm and provided me with instructions on how to plant and care for crops. When the rains came, she would say: "Don't idle around during the rains, plant something." So I did. Whenever the rains came, I planted sweet potatoes, beans, maize, and millet. Because my plot was so small and I planted so early in the growing cycle, I spent a lot of time literally watching the seeds germinate. Occasionally, I would lift the seeds out of the ground to see how quickly they were growing. "No, no, no," my mother would say. "You don't remove them. You have to cover them. You have to let them do all this by themselves. Soon they will all come above the ground." To my utter amazement, they did.

Maize produces a tassel when it grows. This seemed miraculous: "Where did that come from?" I would ask myself. Then the maize would produce a cob, and the minute the cob appeared, so did the birds. I enjoyed watching the birds trying to eat my maize, although sometimes I covered the cobs so the birds didn't finish them all off! When my beans produced flowers, I loved seeing the bees and the butterflies. They would come to my field first because I had planted early, and I would excitedly tell my mother what was happening in my little garden. She didn't know anything about pollination, but she explained that the presence of bees and butterflies meant that my plants were doing fine and soon we would have beans.

At about this time, something profound started happening in the hitherto pristine Aberdare forest. The colonial government had decided to encroach into the forest and establish commercial plantations of nonnative trees. I remember seeing huge bonfires as the natural forests went up in smoke. By the mid-1940s, the British had introduced many exotic tree species into Kenya. Pines were transplanted from the northern hemisphere, and eucalyptus and black wattle from the southern hemisphere. These trees grew fast and strong and contributed to the development of the newly emerging timber and building industry.

To popularize them, foresters gave many such seedlings to farmers free of charge. Farmers appreciated their commercial value and planted them enthusiastically at the expense of local species. However, these trees did damage, too. They eliminated local plants and animals, destroying the natural ecosystem that helped gather and retain rainwater. When rains fell, much of the water ran downstream. Over the subsequent decades, underground water levels decreased markedly and, eventually, rivers and streams either dried up or were greatly reduced.

Soon after we arrived in Nyeri, my brother Nderitu posed a question to my mother: "How come Wangari doesn't go to school like the rest of us?" Nderitu was about thirteen at the time and had just started high school. It was not a wholly shocking question. There was a precedent in my family for educating girls. My uncle Kamunya was sending all his children, including a daughter, to school, but it was still not a common practice.

My mother thought for a moment and then replied, "There's no reason why not."

Although I do not know what happened next, I suspect my mother consulted my uncle, who would have acted as my father's representative as the head of the homestead. He must have agreed, because it was decided that indeed I should join my cousins at Ihithe Primary School. Nonetheless, this was a big decision for my mother. My sister Monica had joined us, so mother had three children younger than me to look after. There were also school fees to consider. Even though they were only one shilling and fifty cents per term, that was a lot of money for a rural family then.

My mother could easily have said, "We don't have enough money, I need her at home. What is the point of a girl going to school?"

Yet, although she had almost no formal education, she agreed with my brother. How grateful I am that she made the decision she did, because I could not have made it for myself, and it changed my life! I have often wondered what would have happened if Nderitu had not asked my mother his question, and if she had not answered as she did. To this day I do not know where the money for my education came from, but my mother probably raised it by working for people in the village, cultivating their land. At that time you could earn up to sixty cents a day doing such work.

My first day at Ihithe Primary School sticks with me. Actually, it is what happened *before* I got to school that is most vivid. I had a slate, an exercise book, and a pencil to write with and a simple bag made from animal skin. Later on, my uncle gave me a cotton bag from the shop he owned. Although it would not have been unusual for a girl of eight to walk the three miles to school alone, my cousin, whose name was Jonothan, nicknamed Jono, came to pick me up and take me to school. He was a little older and could already read and write.

As we walked barefoot along the dirt path up the hill to the clearing where the primary school stood, my cousin suddenly stopped and sat down at the side of the road. He beckoned me to do the same. "Do you know how to read and write?" he asked. "No, I don't," I replied. "Can you write at least?" he said, trying his best to intimidate his little cousin. I told him that I could not. I am not even sure I knew what writing was, really, but I did not want to let on that much. "Well, let me show you something," he said mysteriously. "What's that?" I asked, intrigued. "Let me show you how to write." He took out his exercise book and wrote something on it with a crayon-like pencil, which you had to lick in order to get it to write. Believe me, cousin Jono made the most of that lick! He then presented me with what he had written. Now, of course I couldn't understand what he had scrawled on the page, but I was mightily impressed. "Wow, so you can write," I said, my eyes widening.

My cousin nodded and then did something I thought was truly

miraculous. He took an eraser out of his bag and rubbed out what he had written. The writing simply disappeared. I had never seen an eraser before and it seemed like magic. "Can you do that?" he asked me, with more than a touch of pride. "No, I can't," I replied sadly, thinking my cousin was some kind of genius. "This is what you will learn in school," he intoned. With that, we continued our journey. I never forgot that day. It was a great motivation for me. How I longed to be able to write something and rub it out. When I finally learned to read and write, I never stopped, because I could read, I could write, and I could rub!

My school was typical for its time. It had walls of mud, a floor of earth, and a tin roof. Every Friday we had to bring ash from home, put it on the floor, go to a nearby stream to bring water, and pour it on the ash. Then we swept the floor, a common way of cleaning in those days that kept the dust from building up in the classroom and got rid of pests, like fleas. From June to August, the coldest and foggiest months of the year in the central highlands, our school would be freezing cold. During this time, the teachers would have a fire burning so we could warm our hands and be able to write. Today, the central highlands are no longer as cold as they used to be, probably the impact of climate change.

Ihithe Primary School was established by the Presbyterians. While some teachers were from the surrounding area, others had come from far away, and they all lived in a large house on the school compound. The teachers were very responsible, especially toward children, but they were also very strict. You could be beaten if you didn't do what the teacher said and if you were mischievous you could be thrown out for the whole period.

Because I was only the second generation in Kenya to go to school, adults joined the education system and some were in my class. As I was so young, I didn't think there was any difference between men and women and girls and boys. But my older classmates did. They would often complain when they were told to do things they thought children should do, such as sweeping the compound or fetching water. Sometimes they would protest when they were asked to move from the back of the room to sit next to a child in a little chair. But the teacher was adamant. "No, you sit here with this child." Some of the men were very disruptive and one day they were forced to dig a latrine as a punishment. I thought it odd to punish grown-ups.

During my early schooling, we started in Standard A and then Standard B (both half a day) during which we learned the ABCs and how to count. The language of instruction was Kikuyu. After my cousin Jono's roadside performance, the ABCs and counting didn't impress me much. A lot of what we did was simply rote memorization. Things got more interesting once I started Standard 1, the next year, and went to school all day. Over the next three years, through Standard 4, I learned mathematics, Kiswahili, English, and geography. Our Kiswahili teacher was named Muchai. He was a very dedicated and generous teacher who died only a few years ago. In later years when I would visit Ihithe he would follow me around, sharing with pride the fact that he had been my teacher.

In Standard 4, when I was eleven years old, we began to learn English. My first English teacher was a short, muscular man who usually wore white shorts, a decision that did little to flatter him and only highlighted his very thick calves. His teaching style was very colorful. He would stand in front of us and dramatize the language. "I am going to the door," he would shout, emphasizing each syllable with great seriousness and purpose as he made his way to the door. He would urge us to repeat after him: "I am going to the door," even though we were all sitting in our chairs.

"This is the door," he would say, helpfully pointing in the direction of the door. We confirmed that, yes indeed, that was the door. "That is the wall," and he indicated the wall on the other side of the room. "I am going to the wall," he announced, and you don't need me to tell you where he went. That's how we learned English: We may not have been able to write a sentence, but we soon became experts at identifying basic architecture.

Every time I think of my English teacher with his shorts and thick calves, I have a smile on my face. But it wasn't funny then; we took it very seriously. When I went home and repeated all this to my mother, she wasn't impressed. "What are you saying?" she asked, mystified. Even though we liked to laugh as children, I recognized that the teachers were serious, responsible, and kind. They also provided me with a good enough grounding that I could excel in the national exam we had to pass to proceed to Standard 5.

I was always attentive to nature. Ihithe borders the Aberdare forest and our area had many wooded plots. As a result wildlife was abundant. I knew there were elephants, antelopes, monkeys, and leopards in the forest. Even though I never saw these animals, my mother encouraged me not to be afraid of them. Leopards were seen often and were among the most feared wild animals around. My mother told me that leopards would lurk in vegetation, their long tails draped across a narrow path in the forest. The Kikuyu word for leopard is *ngarī* and the possessive form, "of the leopard," is *wa-ngarī*. "If you are walking on the path and you see the leopard's tail," my mother said, "be careful not to step on it. Instead, as you keep on walking, tell the leopard, 'You and I are both leopards so why would we disagree?' " I believed that the leopard would recognize me as *wa-ngarī* and not hurt me and that I had no reason to fear it.

Many people in Kenya these days get so scared when they see a large wild animal that they overreact and frighten it, which in turn may lead to an attack. Recently, I received a call at six o'clock in the morning: "Three elephants are roaming about in your constituency and people are going wild." The elephants had strayed into a populated area out of the corridors they use to travel between Mount Kenya and the Aberdare mountains. "The elephants are by your mother's place," said the caller.

The villagers were trying to scare the elephants away by yelling and bashing their cooking pots together. However, the more noise the villagers made the more frightened the elephants became.

In their confusion they got agitated and began to trample farmers' crops and threaten human lives. So, to calm the public, the staff of the Kenya Wildlife Service came and shot and killed the elephants. When asked why they could not have tranquilized the animals and moved them to another area, they claimed they didn't have the necessary equipment to move them fast enough away from the panic-stricken community. This sad state of affairs is caused by a lack of understanding of animal behavior, something my mother's generation seemed to grasp.

When I was a child I loved listening to the birds around our homestead and learning their names. One particular bird sang at dusk and had a very special call that sounded like *"ikia ngū, ikia ngū, ikia ngū,"* which translates as "toss the firewood." When I asked my mother what the bird was saying, she told me it was warning us: It is getting dark, so it's time to bring the firewood into the house. When I visit the countryside today, I still hear that bird, although not as often as I did when I was a child and there were more forests. However, when I do, I remember with delight what my mother told me. When children communicate with adults they learn a lot as they grow.

Collecting firewood for the household was a frequent activity and I would often help my mother do it. The country was dotted with hundreds of huge *mīgumo*, or wild fig trees, their bark the color of elephant skin and thick, gnarled branches with roots springing out and anchoring the tree to the ground. Fig trees had great green canopies beneath which grew dense undergrowth. This tree's canopy was probably sixty feet in diameter and it produced numerous fruits that birds loved. When the fruit was ready you would find hundreds of birds feeding on them. The undergrowth of the fig tree was also very fertile because people did not cut anything near those trees but allowed the undergrowth to flourish. All this added to the tree's mystery.

When my mother told me to go and fetch firewood, she would warn me, "Don't pick any dry wood out of the fig tree, or even around it." "Why?" I would ask. "Because that's a tree of God," she'd reply. "We don't use it. We don't cut it. We don't burn it." As a child, of course, I had no idea what my mother was talking about, but I obeyed her.

About two hundred yards from the fig tree there was a stream named Kanungu, with water so clean and fresh that we drank it straight from the stream. As a child, I used to visit the point where the water bubbled up from the belly of the earth to form a stream. I imagine that very few people have been lucky enough to see the source of a river. At the point where the stream came out of the ground, were planted arrowroots, and along the stream were banana plants, and sugarcane, which were typical food crops. Arrowroots, when cooked, provide a starchy tuber like potatoes, and grow only where there is a lot of water. At that time they were planted all along the banks of small, slow-flowing streams. Their large, deep green, arching leaves provided a hideaway big enough for a small child such as me to sit underneath. When it rained the silver drops of water would dance on the broad fronds above me and cascade to the ground. We also used these leaves to fetch water from the river and drink it. The water looked clean and fresh against the sparkling green leaves.

Underneath the arrowroots, there would be thousands of frogs' eggs. They were black, brown, and white beads that I thought would make a beautiful necklace. I would spend hours trying to pick them up as gently as I could, hoping that I could put them around my neck. However, each time I placed my fingers below to lift them, the jelly that held them together would break and they would slip through my fingers back into the stream. I was so disappointed!

Time and time again I would return to that stream to play with the frogs' eggs. Suddenly the eggs would disappear and subsequently I would see what seemed to be an army of black tadpoles wriggling in the water. I would try to catch them by their tails but they, too, were elusive. In time, these also would disappear and later on I would see many frogs hopping around the area near the stream. However,

I never made the connection between the eggs, the tadpoles, and the frogs until I went to school and learned about the life cycle of amphibians.

In my mind's eye I can envision that stream now: the crystal-clear water washing over the pebbles and grains of soil underneath, silky and slow moving. I can see the life in that water and the shrubs, reeds, and ferns along the banks, swaying as the current of the water sidles around them. When my mother would send me to fetch water, I would get lost in this fascinating world of nature until she would call out, "What are you doing under the arrowroots? Bring the water!"

I later learned that there was a connection between the fig tree's root system and the underground water reservoirs. The roots burrowed deep into the ground, breaking through the rocks beneath the surface soil and diving into the underground water table. The water traveled up along the roots until it hit a depression or weak place in the ground and gushed out as a spring. Indeed, wherever these trees stood, there were likely to be streams. The reverence the community had for the fig tree helped preserve the stream and the tadpoles that so captivated me. The trees also held the soil together, reducing erosion and landslides. In such ways, without conscious or deliberate effort, these cultural and spiritual practices contributed to the conservation of biodiversity.

When I wasn't in school my mother would send me on errands away from the homestead. I would go to buy maize, beans, and bananas from the market in Mūkarara or walk to the mill by the Gura River, eight miles away. At that time, all the grinding mills in our area were driven by water, so when I went to have our maize ground into flour I would often spend all day playing with other children while we waited our turn. The waters of the Gura River were fast and clean. The stones beneath the water were black and round. Therefore, the waters appeared black but had a lot of foam.

As I grew older, I took on more responsibilities on my own initiative. I particularly loved to cultivate in the fields late in the afternoon. Even when I was older and away at boarding school much of the time, I had my own plot and my mother would look after it. I would eagerly anticipate the holidays when my classmates and I would return home to work in the fields and touch the soil.

Nothing is more beautiful than cultivating the land at dusk. At that time of day in the central highlands the air and the soil are cool, the sun is going down, the sunlight is golden against the ridges and the green of trees, and there is usually a breeze. As you remove the weeds and press the earth around the crops you feel content, and wish the light would last longer so you could cultivate more. Earth and water, air and the waning fire of the sun combine to form the essential elements of life and reveal to me my kinship with the soil. When I was a child I sometimes became so absorbed working in the fields with my machete that I didn't notice the end of the day until it got so dark that I could no longer differentiate between the weeds and the crops. At that point I knew it was time to go home, on the narrow paths that crisscrossed the fields and rivers and woodlots.

The freshness of the evening air lifted the burden of labor off my shoulders. Strips of moonlight threw shadows into the trees' canopies and down the ravines. Deep in the valleys were many streams that I had to cross as I wound my way home. It was so dark I had to listen carefully to the water flowing down the hillsides and through the gullies bordered by arrowroots and dense vegetation so I could work out where I was and where I was going. The streams would *hiss* and *whoosh* as they joined the Gura River, which swept along the valley floor until it slid over a waterfall and crashed onto the rocks below.

When I climbed a particularly steep hill I knew I was nearly home. As I got to the top, if it was not during the June to August foggy season, I could see the sky exploding with stars and the Milky Way spread across the heavens. Once I arrived, quite often I didn't even want to go inside. My mother would bring the food she had cooked and we and other members of our family would eat together under the bright, starry sky. Everyone would want to know how the day had gone, how much we had cultivated, and what remained to be done. These were the experiences that made me feel very close to the land and appreciate the beauty of the environment. I have never lost that closeness to the soil. I knew that the soil should remain on the land and painfully recognized the destruction of the land when I saw the silt in rivers, especially after the rains.

Sometimes I overextended myself and my mother would remind me that I was still too young to take on some tasks. One school holiday, my mother fell ill and was taken to Mathari Hospital in Nyeri where her appendix was removed. Rather than visit her every day in her hospital bed, I decided that it was important for the planting to be done. Whatever became of my mother, food would be a priority for the family. Therefore, I visited her only rarely (I later learned that my mother would have preferred me to visit more often). Nevertheless, when she came home, she was amazed at how much work my sisters and I had done during her hospitalization.

Three months later, when I returned home for the next holiday, it was time to harvest the red kidney beans I had planted earlier. I borrowed a donkey from a neighbor and went to our farm in the Gura valley. The harvesting and thrashing took most of the day and by late afternoon I had harvested about one and a half sacks of beans. "Well," I thought to myself, "I'm strong and the donkey looks sturdy enough," so one sack went onto the donkey's back and the remaining half sack I took for my own. Off we went, two beasts of burden crawling up and down the hills on narrow paths, bent over trying to carry these heavy loads. By the time we reached the Tucha River, it was getting dark and I was very tired. I may not have guided the donkey properly and before I knew it she slipped and rolled down the slope.

I didn't have a clue what to do. Gathering my senses, I found a place to leave my load of beans and rushed to assist the donkey, who luckily had not been hurt in the fall. I helped her up, loaded the bag of beans onto her back again, and encouraged her back onto the path.

I heaved my own sack onto my back and off we trudged again. As we neared our homestead at Ihithe village, we both had had enough and collapsed in a heap. My mother ran out of the house and could not believe what she saw: a donkey and her daughter lying exhausted next to each other. "How did you make it?" she cried. "These are enormous sacks of beans! I never expected you to carry so many beans. You shouldn't do that." The donkey and I were too tired to reply.

That incident has remained with me through the years and reminds me that, while it's perhaps sometimes foolhardy to take on something that's too big for you, it is incredible what you can achieve if you are single-minded enough. To walk all that way and thrash the beans and then carry them back: Even my mother never forgot that journey!

My mother always told me that I looked and behaved like my paternal grandmother, Wangari, after whom I am named. She was known to be industrious and very organized. It was said that my mannerisms, the way I spoke, walked, and arranged my things, were like hers. When we worked in the field, I always carefully put the food or animal fodder I was harvesting in neat piles, so I was well prepared for the journey. "You remind me of your grandmother, the way you organize yourself," my mother would say. I was happy to hear the comparison and always wished I had known her. The Kikuyu system of naming children is meant to make you feel as if you are a duplicate of the relative whose name you bear. I felt I was the living Wangari, and as my mother and I walked home carrying food crops, firewood, and animal fodder, I would reflect on my grandmother and feel good that I reminded my mother of her. In my community, children gave the people a sense of immortality.

The art of storytelling around a fire was an essential dimension of life in the countryside. Many evenings, at the end of a day in the fields, children would gather and listen to stories their mothers would tell as they waited for the meal to cook over an open fire and three stones. Children also told stories around the fire. Stories were a way to keep children entertained—and awake—as they waited for dinner, and could be as short or as long as the cooking required. Green maize or sweet potatoes could take about thirty minutes to cook, while arrowroots could take two hours. The Kikuyu stories served to entertain, educate, and encourage creativity in children. It was an effective informal education.

Because Kikuyu culture was oral, refined methods had been developed of passing knowledge to, and shaping the values of, future generations through, among other activities, stories. Many of the stories had become very elaborate and subtle, like myths, because they had been told in various forms over many generations. Kikuyu stories were filled with animals with human characteristics—both bad and good. One very dominant character in stories was an *irimū,* or a dragon.

The *irimū* usually appeared in the guise of a handsome young man, but could also take other forms. He was a trickster and was ready to scare children and seduce young maidens with promises of good things, including marriage. Although the *irimū* looked like a handsome young man, he could transform himself into anything—even a tree, a giant gourd, or a plant—and disappear into rivers and ponds, usually reappearing when young maidens went to fetch water. These stories so impressed my young mind that whenever I passed by a waterfall, I always imagined that an *irimū* would leap at me through the wall of water, so I preferred only to travel near waterfalls and rivers with my mother or other adults!

When I went to school I was exposed to books, all of which told different stories from the ones I had heard around the fire. I read "Cinderella," "Little Red Riding Hood," "Sleeping Beauty"—stories that Westerners told their children for their moral development but which did not mean as much to me as the stories I was told around the fire. The Kikuyu stories reflected my environment and the values of my people; they were preparing me for a life in my community. The stories I read in the books had a completely different dimension. Half the time I did not understand what I was reading and merely memorized the words on the page for examinations.

We found it impossible to doze when a story was on: Sometimes we were scared and sometimes we laughed, but we were always entertained. We would ask to hear stories again and again because we loved them so much. When the story was over, we were encouraged to tell our own, but we preferred it when the adults told them. I loved the calm, warm atmosphere as we sat and listened to the women—mothers, aunts, grandmothers. (Men did not tell stories.) My aunt Nyakweya, who is now in her late eighties, was a great storyteller. She would sing and imitate the movements of the characters. One of my favorite stories was *Konyeki na ithe*, or "Konyeki and His Father." I asked my aunt to tell this story over and over again, which, being the jolly person she is, she did—with a loud laugh—while we were all ears. (You can read the story of Konyeki and his father in the appendix.)

I like this story because my aunt told it very entertainingly and because it reflects character traits that I easily identify with and encounter in other people. There is the women's naïveté—or is it deliberate refusal to face the obvious? Instead, they choose to close their eyes and ears to the truth, seeing and hearing nothing. This is indeed a case of "love is blind." I also have had moments when I've been blinded and could identify with the women, who pursued the *irimū*, no matter what they had come to know about him.

Nevertheless, the women were shrewd. Those who decided to leave were wise enough not to confront the dragon's power directly, because they would have been eliminated. Another lesson from the story is that sometimes you need to be careful what you say in certain places, and make decisions based on your situation. So the women were wise when they did not respond accurately to the dragon's question about his dinner. But once you make a decision, you must be prepared to live with the consequences. The woman who stayed behind married the dragon and gave birth to a son, who was a dragon as well. She had to live the life of a dragon's wife.

These stories often had evil competing with good, and good often triumphing, while the evil character eventually perished. Stories could always be extended if the food was still not ready, and so some stories were very short while others were long. It was also possible to cut a story short, but it had to end appropriately: A story was never left unfinished. It was important to have different people tell stories. If you hear a story, you are indebted to others and should tell your own story.

These experiences of childhood are what mold us and make us who we are. How you translate the life you see, feel, smell, and touch as you grow up—the water you drink, the air you breathe, and the food you eat—are what you become. When what you remember disappears, you miss it and search for it, and so it was with me. When I was a child, my surroundings were alive, dynamic, and inspiring. Even though I was entering a world where there were books to read and facts to learn—the cultivation of the mind—I was still able to enjoy a world where there were no books to read, where children were told living stories about the world around them, and where you cultivated the soil and the imagination in equal measure.

3

Education and the State of Emergency

Have you ever woken up and the day looks ordinary and then
the most extraordinary thing happens that changes your life
forever? Such was the day when I discovered that my mother, my
brother Nderitu, and one of my distant cousins, named Wangari
Wanguku, were meeting and deeply engrossed in a conversation
about me. My mother noticed me eavesdropping and, to my disappointment, quickly sent me to fetch water. I really wanted to hear
what they were saying, but I knew I had to do as I was told. So I practically flew down the hill with the cooking pot high in the air, and
raced back as fast as I could, trying not to spill too much water on
the way back.

Breathing hard from a mixture of exertion and excitement, I reen-
tered the house and learned that, despite my speed, the conversation
was over and they had already made their decision: I would join
my cousin Wangari at St. Cecilia's Intermediate Primary School, a
boarding school at the Mathari Catholic Mission on the slopes of
Nyeri hill. The school was run by the Consolata Missionary Sisters
from Italy.

"Wow!" I thought. "They've already decided? It did not take me
that long to fetch the water!" It is impossible to describe the emotions I felt at that moment: happy because I would be joining St.
Cecilia's, secure because I would be with Wangari, sad as an eleven-
year-old that I would be separated from my mother for the very first
time. I would also be leaving behind the landscapes that I woke up
to, our animals, our gardens and food crops, friends and relatives,
and the small stream I visited each day.

Despite all those emotions, I knew my family had made the right decision for me. St. Cecilia's had a reputation for good teaching and discipline. As a boarding school, it was thought to offer no distractions or disruptions to studies. I later learned that my family had one concern about St. Cecilia's: that I might convert to Catholicism and that the Catholic sisters would woo me to become one of them. A nun's way of life was completely unknown to the Kikuyu community, which expected girls to marry and have children. Becoming a nun was considered a major loss to the community.

During the next several weeks, not a day passed without my thinking of the major journey I would soon be making. My mother bought me a small wooden box in which to pack my few belongings. Once my parents had paid the school fees, I would get practically everything I needed at school—bedding, a uniform, books, utensils, soap, and food. In preparation for my journey, my mother cut my hair very short to make it easy for me to manage. She also bought me a new dress. My brother got me another. He had purchased green-gray material to have a pair of trousers made for himself, and had deliberately bought extra so a dress could be made for me from the same material. I liked the material and style of the dress, since it did not wrinkle and was easy to wear. Such a thoughtful gesture from my brother endeared him to me. It is nice for me to think that my brother and I were cut from the same cloth in more ways than one. He was always there for me and all other members of the family.

There is one thing I did not have to pack—a pair of shoes, since I had none, until a local shoemaker made my first pair four years later when I went to high school. On the day of my departure, I carried my belongings on my back, much the same way I learned to carry firewood. The load was suspended from a string around my head. My family accompanied me up the hill to where I met my cousin. There I bid them farewell and set off to a new life. The journey would take the whole day.

We walked past the Tetu Mission, crossed the Chania River, walking on a footbridge for the first time. The river roared and frothed as it tumbled headlong downstream. Dense vegetation overhung the river and the air was thick and damp. Beneath me, the river was black but foaming, and I was worried I would fall in if I looked down and saw the mesmerizing currents below me. So, as I'd been told to do, I focused my eyes on the other side and walked across. After climbing the steep slope to the Mathari Mission, we reached the top of the valley, and I could see the expanse of the school and hospital, built in an Italian style: beige stone buildings, red-tile roofs, and a clock tower, all set in a valley. As far as the eye could see, through the valley and into the hills, the Catholic Church owned the land.

Once we arrived, Wangari and I were separated. While Wangari joined the girls in her class, I was directed to a dormitory where first-year students slept. It was quite an experience to be in a dormitory with about thirty other girls I had never met before. The bed was comfortable—it had one set of sheets and a pillow and mattress stuffed with grass, which I could smell. Every time I turned over, that grass made a crunching noise. Nevertheless, by my standards, it was a bed fit for a queen. At bedtime, a nun came into the dormitory, her habit as white as snow and a long black rosary around her waist. It was my first encounter with a Catholic nun. She led us in an English prayer, turned off the lights, and wished us good night. We were all tired and went straight to sleep.

The following morning I woke up to what would become a routine for the rest of my time at St. Cecilia's. At dawn each morning, one of the sisters would ring a bell to wake us up. We would spring out of bed, get down on our knees, and say our morning prayers. Then we would all rush out to wash our faces and rush back to tidy our beds, and then get dressed. By the time we left for church everything in the dormitories would be very neat and orderly. We had an hour-long Mass every day, after which there was a breakfast of maize flour porridge. After breakfast we had what was called a cleaning session. Everybody had something to do to keep the school compound spotless: cutting the grass, keeping the path clear, scrubbing the bathrooms, or tidying the dormitories. Finally, we would go to the classrooms to study. At mid-morning we broke for play and relaxation.

We had lunch at midday and then continued studies during the afternoon, until five o'clock, when we ate the evening meal. The food never changed: corn and beans at lunch, at dinner *ugali* and vegetables, such as cabbages, spinach, pumpkins, and onions. Meat was rarely served. This was fine for us, since our traditional diet contained very little meat anyway. We had no snacks, so when we got to the dining room we were hungry and ate whatever was placed before us, even though weevils regularly attacked the maize and beans. Despite the fact that we could see the weevils, we learned to navigate around them as we ate. After dinner, we went back to the classrooms and often did our homework under the supervision of one of the nuns. At ten o'clock it was time to go to bed.

Sports were an important part of our routine. During recess and breaks we would play a variety of games, all foreign sports. I enjoyed playing netball and tenniquoits, in which two players toss a ring across a net, and at which I became a champion. During those days, even for those of us who had them, we did not wear shoes except on special occasions, so at night it was very important to wash our feet. To keep them clean once we had washed, my friends and I would take turns carrying each other to bed, chatting and laughing as we did. The last to carry would always have shoes to wear to keep her feet clean. Once we were all in bed, the last thing we did was pray.

I really enjoyed learning and had a knack for being an attentive listener and very focused in the classroom, while being extremely playful outside of it. When you focus and do well, school becomes a pleasant experience. You do not hate it and long to drop out. At St. Cecilia's I was never bored since I was kept very busy. Never was there a time when I had nothing to do but just lie in the sun and enjoy its warmth. I *should* have found some time because it is good, particularly for a young person, to enjoy the sun and gaze at the clouds as they move and change shape.

Although the school had electricity and running water, conditions were still spartan. Unlike the mud house where my family lived, which trapped heat, the stone walls at St. Cecilia's let in the cold and the dormitories had no heat or hot water. During the cool seasons this was not very pleasant, but it did mean that if you were not awake when you got up you certainly were after you washed your face in the ice-cold water!

Paying for St. Cecilia's was a burden for my family, and my brother Nderitu, then at Kagumo High School, would do odd jobs to earn some cash to contribute to my school fees and pocket money. He had a small stove in his room on which he would boil water for other students who would pay him a few coins. There was not much to buy in Mathari so I often saved the pocket money to do some shopping for my family on the way home during school holidays.

Nderitu's role in my education didn't stop there. He was always very interested in how well I was doing in my studies and would regularly visit St. Cecilia's, even in addition to the one day a month when visitors were allowed. "Your brother was here," the sisters would inform me. I accepted the rules for visitors, so did not make a big fuss about the fact that he had not asked to see me. On one occasion, I heard him and his friend speaking to the headmistress and laughing, and I knew he must have come to check up on me. I did not have the courage to ask to see him, but I always wished the sisters had allowed us a short visit and regretted that the nuns deprived us of contact with our family members, except for the occasional auhorized visit.

Initially when I arrived at St. Cecilia's I was homesick. However, there were many opportunities to nurture friendships, some of which have lasted a lifetime. One day, during a Kiswahili class, the teacher was explaining and translating English words into Kiswahili for us.

He came across the word *somo*, which means "namesake." I immediately turned to my friend Miriam Wanjiru, who was sitting behind me, and said to her fondly "my *somo.*" This is because my baptismal name is also Miriam. She replied *somo*, as well, and with that we formed a lifelong bond: Two *somos* together. Even today, this is the nickname we often use for each other.

One of the other reasons I was not homesick is that the nuns, bless them, quickly became our surrogate mothers. I found them nurturing, encouraging, and compassionate. One nun, Sister Germana, came from Milan in northern Italy. She was tall, elegant, and very loving, and her motivation and dedication intrigued me. "Why would she come all the way to this place?" I would ask myself. It fascinated me that despite their youth and beauty these women had sacrificed having families and living in comfortable surroundings and instead had committed themselves to God and had come to serve strangers in a remote part of the world.

I spent four years at St. Cecilia's and grew very fond of many of the sisters who helped shape my life there. One of the nuns, however, was quite different. Most of the sisters were relatively slim and tall, at least to me as a young girl, but this one was an exception—a strongly built nun who had come to Kenya from South Africa called Sister Christiana. She was a disciplinarian but as she went around to "put us straight," as she would say, she made us laugh and, though she thought she had us under her thumb, for the most part we still did what we wanted. The sisters were suspicious that girls were writing to boys, something the nuns considered distracting and completely unacceptable. The school did not have the services of a post office, so if you wrote or received a letter it had to go through a nun—and that sister more often than not was Sister Christiana.

On one occasion, a girl wrote a letter to a friend in which she included this piece of news: "Here in St. Cecilia's we are fine, still eating fire." Sister Christiana read the letter and was appalled and angry. The girl had lied and scandalized the school. "Now look at this girl!" she said. "No shame whatsoever: Telling lies that we are feeding them with fire!" That evening in the dining hall, all of the girls had food on their plates, except the girl who had written the letter. On her plate, she found pieces of charcoal. After we had said grace and sat down to eat, Sister Christiana explained that the girl had told a lie that the nuns were feeding us fire. "So that is fire," she thundered at the girl. "Eat!"

Well, we could barely stifle our laughs—even the girl herself found it funny. Quite obviously, Sister Christiana had missed a very important point: The girl in her letter had taken a Kikuyu saying (*no tūrarīa mwaki*) and given a literal translation into English. "We continue to eat fire" is a Kikuyu colloquialism meaning "we're having a great time." But given that our English skills were still rudimentary, the girl had rendered this expression in English, where it had no obvious meaning. Sister Christiana had taken it literally. The letter-writer got no food that evening and the rest of us could not wait to get outside where we burst into gales of laughter. I am quite sure that eating fire was a main topic of conversation at the nuns' dinner table that night, too.

Although this incident was funny at the time, you had to be careful what you laughed about because you could be punished, and nowhere was this more prevalent than with the matter of speaking or not speaking English. By this time, English had become the official language of communication and instruction in Kenyan schools. Those of us who aspired to progress in our studies knew that learning English well was essential. Many schools emphasized that students must speak English at all times, even during the holidays.

A common practice to ensure that students kept pressure on one another was to require those students who were found using a language other than English to wear a button known as a "monitor." It was sometimes inscribed with phrases in English such as "I am stupid, I was caught speaking my mother tongue." At the end of the day, whoever ended up with the button received a punishment, such as cutting grass, sweeping, or doing work in the garden. But the greater punishment was the embarrassment you felt because you had talked in your mother tongue. In retrospect, I can see that this introduced us to the world of undermining our self-confidence.

Not surprisingly, none of us wanted to be caught with the monitor and as a result we spoke English from the time we left church in the morning until we said our final prayers at night. This was remarkable given that everyone in St. Cecilia's had spoken only Kikuyu until then. But the system worked in promoting English: Even when we went home or met children from school in the village, we tended to speak English. The use of the monitor continues even today in Kenyan schools to ensure that students use only English. Now, as then, this contributes to the trivialization of anything African and lays the foundation for a deeper sense of self-doubt and an inferiority complex.

Years later, when we became part of the Kenyan elite, we preferred to speak in English to one another, our children, and those in our social class. While the monitor approach helped us learn English, it also instilled in us a sense that our local languages were inferior and insignificant. The reality is that mother tongues are extremely important as vehicles of communication and carriers of culture, knowledge, wisdom, and history. When they are maligned, and educated people are encouraged to look down on them, people are robbed of a vital part of their heritage. I am very glad I did not lose my desire or ability to speak Kikuyu, because this helped ensure that a gap did not open between my parents and me, as it has for some of our children for whom education became synonymous with Westernization.

As we became fluent in English, we were also shifting in other ways—moving from a life of traditional dancing, singing, and storytelling to one of books, study, prayers, and the occasional game of netball. When I wasn't in the classroom or playing, many of my friends and I were involved with a Christian society known as the Legion of Mary that instilled in us a sense of service and the importance of volunteerism for the common good. We visited the sick and eased the work of nuns and other staff in the hospital. We washed and ironed the church linen and were involved in prayer meetings. We worked in the school gardens and helped other students with homework. The idea was to serve God by serving fellow human beings.

During my time at St. Cecilia's, and after many lessons on Christianity, especially on the Reformation, I decided to become a Catholic. We were taught that the Catholic Church was the original church and held God's truth. I do not remember discussing this decision with my family. I just made it. On my next birthday, I was born again. To show my admiration for the Holy Family, Mary and Joseph, I took a new Christian name: Mary Josephine (in Anglophone regions no one would name themselves after Jesus). My friends called me Mary Jo through high school and college.

Many years later St. Cecilia's was transformed into a pastoral training center, but otherwise the Mathari Mission remains relatively unchanged. The hospital is still a major health center for the area and the buildings look much the same. The Chania River is still there, although when I used to cross it, it was very wide and roaring. These days, like so many rivers, the Chania is very narrow and much quieter. Deforestation in the Aberdare range is taking a toll on rivers and their tributaries downstream.

Toward the end of my first year at St. Cecilia's, in 1952, the Mau Mau rebellion against British rule broke out and lasted throughout much of the 1950s. Organized by members of the Kikuyu, Meru, and Embu communities, the Mau Mau struggle was fueled most immediately by the sense of betrayal felt by soldiers returning to Kenya from the Second World War. Not only did they not receive any recognition or compensation for their service, but, to add insult to injury, their British colleagues were being showered with honors and even allocated land, some of it taken from the Kenyan war veterans, who were forcibly displaced.

The roots of the Mau Mau movement, however, are found in an

older betrayal. In 1890, Captain (later Lord) Frederick Lugard arranged a meeting with Waiyaki wa Hinga, a Kikuyu leader, to establish station posts for the Imperial British East Africa Company on Kikuyu land and enable goods to be brought to and from Uganda. At their meeting, Lugard and Waiyaki swore an oath to allow the station posts on the condition that the British would not take Kikuyu land or other property. The agreement, however, did not last long, because Lugard's porters started looting the nearby settlements and raping women. The Kikuyus fought back in a series of battles that culminated in a standoff in 1892, when Waiyaki was captured, taken away, and eventually buried alive by the colonial administration.

The Kikuyus were stunned by Waiyaki's humiliation and death. In Kikuyu culture, everybody had a right to shelter and space: People who had land were expected to share with people who did not, who became like squatters, and were allowed to stay while they tried to purchase their own land. It was profoundly shocking that the British, when temporarily given such land under oath, would renege on their word and seize the land. Even though the oath was oral and not written, to the Kikuyus this was seen as a solemn pledge. But as the Kikuyus would learn, the newcomers had no time for verbal promises between themselves and the native population. Eventually the strangers simply acquired and distributed land to themselves and others, who began arriving in Kenya in numbers. The appropriation and redistribution of land became a feature of the British presence in Kenya.

In the early decades of the twentieth century, all the peoples of Kenya resisted colonization, and many were killed in the process. Eventually, they were all defeated, suppressed, and largely silenced. In the decades after the First World War, tension increased among settlers, the colonial government, and the native population, especially Kikuyus who occupied some of the highlands that the settlers had appropriated. Immediately after the First World War, the British established an identification system, called *kipande,* that required every male African in Kenya to carry a pass. The government introduced indirect forced labor and increased taxes. Local men began to organize to fight for better conditions, but after the British used violence to stop a peaceful protest in 1922, African associations and periodicals were either banned in Kenya, or their activities were curtailed.

Many of the organizers of the Mau Mau, also known as the Land and Freedom Army, were ex-soldiers who had fought for the British in Somalia, Ceylon, and Burma during the Second World War. Serving on the front lines to win a war for a colonial government raised their awareness about conditions in Kenya, while the insurgency skills they learned fighting on the side of the British in Burmese jungles gave them the expertise to resist a military assault. When these ex-servicemen returned to Kenya in the mid-1940s, they and others began organizing a coordinated resistance. In 1944, the Kenya African Union (KAU) was formed to campaign for independence. In 1946, Jomo Kenyatta, already a leader of the independence movement, returned from England to Kenya, and a year later he was elected to head the KAU.

In the early 1950s, frustrated by the slow pace of change, a guerrilla war for independence was launched: the Mau Mau. While there are many theories about the origin of the term "Mau Mau," the one I find most interesting is this: In Kikuyu, when beginning a list, you say, *"maūndū ni mau"*—"The main issues are . . ."—and then hold up three fingers to introduce them. For the Mau Mau, the three issues were land, freedom, and self-governance.

My family felt some sense of relief that at St. Cecilia's I would be protected from the violence of the insurgency and the efforts to suppress it. For the most part, I was insulated from the conflict, although I could not be completely so. There were very few Kikuyu families whose lives the Mau Mau rebellion did not affect. I had been sufficiently indoctrinated to believe that the Mau Maus were the terror group and that everyone else was trying to restore order.

The British propaganda kept us naïve about the political and economic roots of the conflict and was designed to make us believe that the Mau Maus wanted to return us to a primitive, backward, and even satanic past.

One night we heard gunshots very close to our dormitories. The sisters came in, woke us up, and told us that there were marauders in the mission and that we should start saying the rosary. The extent of the misinformation and brainwashing was such that we prayed that the Mau Maus would be arrested. I did not understand that the Mau Mau were our freedom fighters!

Through much of the 1950s, it was not uncommon to encounter British soldiers, Mau Mau fighters, or Home Guards in and around Nyeri. The Home Guards were mainly drawn from Kikuyus who collaborated with the British government. In addition to the fifty thousand or so soldiers the British deployed in Kenya during the Mau Mau insurgency, they also armed the Home Guards and gave them considerable freedom to move around the countryside. They often accompanied British soldiers—nicknamed johnnies—and sometimes uniformed men from other communities who did not identify with the aspirations of the Mau Mau movement, which they despised and sought to crush. They did not believe that the British Empire could be challenged.

As the Mau Mau period went on, more and more people were mobilized and people were forced to choose to support the Mau Maus or the British. All able-bodied men and boys, unless they were very young, were required to be part of the Home Guards and were expected to be at their posts by six o'clock at night. Gathering the young men at the posts was also a way to prevent their being abducted by the Mau Maus. Both of my older brothers participated in the night watch to protect Ihithe from Mau Mau attack and worked closely with the local Home Guards during the holidays. The violence came very close. Across the ridge from Ihithe, at Gatumbīro, the Mau Mau burned a Home Guards' depot to the ground, killing more than twenty of them. It was one of the worst local massacres by the Mau Mau and left many widows in the community. Such traumas have never been addressed. Indeed, there has almost been a desire to deny these atrocities took place. There is still need for healing, reconciliation, and forgiveness.

Young girls in particular were at risk of rape from Home Guards, johnnies, and policemen. Genuine Mau Maus did not harass or physically violate women. Instead, they abducted them to serve as cooks, porters, or spies. The Home Guards had a reputation for extreme cruelty and all manner of terror and intimidation. Initially, Mau Mau soldiers were respectful of women and did not abuse them sexually. Later on, however, when the war deteriorated into internal strife between the Home Guards and Mau Maus, and the barriers became blurred, the Mau Maus started using tactics that could punish even the innocent.

During the holidays, the protection available in boarding schools disappeared, so it was common for girls to sleep together in one house rather than being spread throughout the village. This way, if the Mau Maus, Home Guards, or soldiers came, the girls could be more easily hidden or evacuated altogether.

One night, when I was staying at my cousin Wangari's house in Ihithe with two other girls and a small baby, Wangari's mother heard the noise of a raid. We were quickly taken to hide in a nearby wood-lot of black wattle trees. The woodlot was thick and dark and full, and that night I remember the moon was very bright. We put the baby on the ground between us to continue sleeping and then the three of us kneeled and began to recite the rosary. "Hail Mary, full of grace," we prayed, hoping she would protect us. Then, suddenly, in front of our eyes, perhaps twenty feet away, a leopard passed in the moonlight. We prayed harder: "Holy Mary, Mother of God, pray for us sinners now . . ." "Especially now," I thought to myself. But the leopard did not so much as look in our direction. It just walked on and disappeared into the thicket. We looked at each other with much relief.

My family, like many other families at the time, was split between those who sympathized with the Mau Maus and those who supported the status quo. Even though I never heard much discussion in my family, I was old enough to know that division existed. My father had a special regard for Mr. Neylan and his family, and I know that Mr. Neylan trusted him. This presented my father with a dilemma, because those members of the family who supported the Mau Maus perceived him as a collaborator who should have been killed. For a time, my father stopped sleeping at his homestead and took temporary shelter at night in Mr. Neylan's compound. Mr. Neylan was allowed to carry a gun for self-defense.

The division within families also worked itself out in Nyeri, where my mother was attacked by men she assumed were Mau Maus. It happened at night, so she could not tell for sure. "They held the knife to my neck," she told us. "I thought they were going to kill me!" Although she only received a cut, which was not life-threatening, the fear and intimidation she felt lingered for most of her life. After independence, my mother discovered that her main assailant was a disgruntled member of our extended family who used the emergency situation to avenge grievances against my father but made it appear like Mau Mau terror. My mother never got over the fact that someone within the family would want to harm her. Such was the trauma that many families experienced during these times.

In October 1952, during the end of my first year at St. Cecilia's, Kenya's British governor, Sir Evelyn Baring, arrested Jomo Kenyatta and declared a state of emergency. By that time, the Mau Mau rebellion had succeeded in creating an atmosphere of panic and terror among the white settlers. The British took harsh measures, eventually interring nearly a million Africans in detention camps, effectively concentration camps, and "emergency villages" where women, children, and the elderly, in particular, were confined and where hunger and disease were common. Entry and exit were tightly controlled.

In April 1953, Kenyatta was sentenced to seven years' hard labor over his alleged role in the Mau Mau struggle. A year later, in one of the largest crackdowns of the rebellion, ten thousand Mau Mau fighters and suspected sympathizers were arrested and sent to detention camps where methods of interrogation were often iron-fisted and accompanied by torture. New historical research suggests at one point around 1954 three out of every four Kikuyu men were in detention. Land was taken from the detainees and given to the collaborators, while detainees were pushed into forced labor. Visitors arriving at Kenyatta International Airport in Nairobi today might not know that Mau Mau detainees laid the concrete foundation of the runways. Their suffering and their contribution have been deliberately forgotten.

My mother, like hundreds of thousands of others, was forced to live in an emergency village—in her case, in the center of Ihithe. Such relocation was costly in many ways, including monetarily. My mother had to abandon an almost-completed house on our land and build a new one within the confines of the emergency village. She stayed there for nearly seven years and was able to return to the site of a new home she'd built only in 1960.

I was detained only once, when I was sixteen or seventeen. It was during the school holidays, and I was on my way from my high school at Limuru to Nakuru to visit my extended family. Unlike most men, including my father, I was allowed to travel. Traveling for my mother would have been too dangerous, so during the whole Mau Mau period, my mother and father never saw each other. Instead, they communicated through us children, who were able to travel to and from school. When I reached Nakuru town, I was arrested. I do not know the cause, but I suspect that even though I had the required passbook, it indicated I was from Nyeri and, therefore, should not have been anywhere near Nakuru. Even though I was young, being a Kikuyu meant that I was in the wrong place at the wrong time. This was enough for me to be thrown into a detention camp, where Kikuyus belonged.

I was terrified. The conditions were horrible—designed to break people's spirits and self-confidence and instill sufficient fear that they would abandon their struggle. Sanitation was poor, food was minimal, and the camp was very crowded. Women and children, along with a few men, were everywhere—sitting, sleeping, talking, and cooking. I did not recognize anyone and slept where I could find a space. Because I arrived in my uniform, people in the camp immediately recognized me as a schoolgirl and asked what I was doing in the camp. I was questioned and after two long days the police took me to my father's homestead. I suspect that both my father and Mr. Neylan had been contacted and that Mr. Neylan had confirmed that I was a daughter of one of his workers, coming to visit during the school holidays.

I will never forget the misery in the camp. Nevertheless, it had its own strange calmness. In spite of the crowding, there was no disorder. I didn't even hear children crying, and made sure that I did not cry. I was also struck by the tenderness with which both men and women spoke to me. When they asked what I was doing there, I could see the concern on their faces and hear it in their voices. They knew I was an innocent schoolgirl, but by then no Kikuyu could be trusted.

New research indicates that in spite of the hysteria in the British press and the government, of the approximately four thousand people who died as a result of Mau Mau activities, a total of thirty-two were white settlers. In comparison, recent scholarship estimates that more than one hundred thousand Africans, mostly Kikuyus, may have died in concentration camps and emergency villages—on top of the humiliation, loss of property, and trauma that families suffered. It is clear that terrorism was not confined to one side. Interestingly, it is only very recently that the law in Kenya has been changed so that the Mau Maus are no longer described as *imaramuri* ("terrorists") but as freedom fighters.

Even though the Mau Mau rebellion undoubtedly hastened Kenya's independence in 1963, and the events of the Mau Mau period are now fifty years in the past, the struggle has left trauma among Kikuyus that remains unaddressed to this day. The social cost to families and children of the violence of the 1950s may be incalculable. Fathers, sons, and brothers were jailed. Rape was a weapon used to suppress the rebellion. The trauma of the colonized is rarely examined, and steps are rarely taken to understand and redress it. Instead, the psychological damage passes from one generation to the next, until its victims recognize their dilemma and work to liberate themselves from the trauma.

In one aspect, I was very lucky. I started at St. Cecilia's nearly a year before the Mau Mau insurgency began. If I had been born a few years later, there is a good chance that the insecurity of the countryside around Nyeri would have dissuaded my family from continuing my education beyond the village school in Ihithe. If this had been the case, my life would have been very different. I most likely would have stayed in Ihithe, married, had children, and continued to work the land. You would see me there now, cultivating the earth and carrying firewood on my back up the hills to my home, where I would light a fire and cook the evening meal. I would not tell stories, because they have been replaced by books, the radio, and television.

I did very well in my examinations at the end of Standard 8. In fact, I was the first in my class, and when I left St. Cecilia's in 1956 I received a place at Loreto Girls' High School in Limuru, just outside the capital, Nairobi. It, too, was Catholic, run by Irish sisters of the Loreto order. Loreto Girls' High School (known as Loreto-Limuru) was at that time the only Catholic high school for African girls in the country, and it drew students from all over Kenya. For the first time, I was studying with girls from many communities and regions. Of course, the rule was to communicate in English all the time.

At Loreto-Limuru, I had a very good teacher, Mother Teresia. During breaks, she would ask me to come and help her wash petri dishes and test tubes in the lab. Through our many conversations, she aroused and encouraged my lifelong interest in science—at that time, chemistry; later, biology. We stayed friends until she died. I was also close to Mother Colombière, the headmistress. Now retired, she still lives in Nairobi, and we keep in touch. The Loreto Sisters also ran an all-white school close to ours. At that time, I did not find the racial segregation strange. Nobody, least of all the nuns, discussed it. If someone had come and told my classmates and me, "You are being discriminated against," we would have been baffled. However, nobody ever did.

After my education by the nuns, I emerged as a person who believed that society is inherently good and that people generally act for the best. To me, a general orientation toward trusting people and a positive attitude toward life and fellow human beings is healthy— not only for one's peace of mind but also to bring about change. This belief came from a combination of my education and my Kikuyu heritage, which taught me a deep sense of justice.

When I was at Loreto-Limuru, I would go to Mass every Sunday, even during the holidays when I was visiting Ihithe or Nakuru. My father had a friend, an old man named Murango Kamau, who accompanied me to Nakuru town. On Sunday mornings, he would pick me up at four o'clock and two hours later we would arrive in Nakuru just as the sun was rising. Now, I don't care how much of an early riser you are, four o'clock is early for anyone! I was practically sleep-walking, so I would ask him to make sure I didn't walk into people. Sometimes, I would close my eyes as I walked and say to Murango, "Make sure I don't go into the bush."

Finally, we would arrive at Nakuru Catholic Church, now called Christ the King. At that time, an Irish priest served at the church, and one day after Mass he invited me to his house for tea. I was very appreciative, because we were not supposed to eat before Holy Communion, so I had not eaten since I had gotten up that morning. If I hadn't gone to his house, my first meal of the day would have been when, well into the afternoon, I arrived back at the farm—famished.

From that single tea came something lasting. It seems I convinced the priest that a school was needed for the children of the workers on settlers' farms around Nakuru, because my father's younger children and many other children of squatters on Mr. Neylan's farm were not in school because there were no schools in the area. I don't recall our conversation, but I must have been very bold! I later learned that the priest spoke to Mr. Neylan, who, I understand, was also a Catholic and attended church in Nakuru. When Mr. Neylan sold his farm in the early 1960s, he donated land so the church could establish a Catholic school, St. John's, where my younger half brothers and sisters were educated and which still operates today. It wasn't until a number of years later that friends reminded me of the impact my cup of tea with the local priest had had. "Not bad," I thought. Many children otherwise would not have gone to school.

Education, of course, creates many opportunities. In Kenya, for most people of my generation and after, a high school education or a college degree is a guaranteed ticket out of the perceived drudgery of subsistence farming or the cultivation of cash crops for little return. I, too, got this ticket out, but I never severed my connection to the soil. Throughout my years in boarding school, I saw my mother only on school holidays. She did not have the means (cash or a vehicle) to visit me and also had my three younger siblings to take care of. But a gulf never developed between us.

When I went home to see my mother during my time at Loreto-Limuru, if I found that the mud walls of my mother's house needed plastering, I would go into the cowshed, collect the dung, mix it with ash, and then plaster the walls, all with my bare hands. I cannot remember whether my mother asked me to do this or I told myself, "Do it." I never thought of not putting my hands in that dung just because I was a high school student. The results of my work looked good, and my mother was happy.

In the context of Ihithe, I was highly educated, one of the few girls in the area who had gone to high school. People never told me directly that they were pleased that I was educated and still helping my mother, and my mother never commented on it, either. Not giving compliments in public is common in Kikuyu culture. But later in life, I met women and men who would tell me, "When I was going to school my parents encouraged me to study hard and be like you." How I wished they had told me so!

But at that time in Kenya, 1959, the number of women who had completed high school was very small and their options for careers or higher education were relatively few. Women could become teachers or nurses while men could be teachers or clerks in an office. Being a clerk was a well-paid and highly esteemed job, because you would be in the mainstream of British Kenyan civil life. You would work in an office! You would be a member of the new elite class.

Although the nuns did not provide us with any career counseling, as graduation neared many of my classmates were signing up for training in teaching or nursing. That was the end of education for them. I did not want to be a teacher then and I never tried to be a nurse. I wanted to go on with my studies, which for a girl was unusual. Back when I was at St. Cecilia's, neighbors would say to my mother about me: "There's no need to keep her in school. She cannot even become a clerk. She's a girl, after all."

Even my teachers and friends asked me, "What are you going to do? Become a teacher or a nurse?" But my mind was focused elsewhere. "I am not going to be either of those. I'm going to Makerere University," I replied. Makerere was in Kampala, Uganda, and was then the only university in East Africa. Anybody who passed their high school exams and could continue their studies went to Makerere, which was the epitome of education—the Oxford of East Africa. But aspiring to go there was very ambitious. Even though I was a good student, I was more hardworking than naturally bright, so my gaining admission to Makerere was still a gamble.

"What if you don't pass?" my teachers and friends asked. "What do you mean?" I asked. "Of course I will pass!" As it turned out, an opportunity arose that was to take me much farther west than Makerere—in fact, all the way to the United States of America.

4

American Dream

By the time I graduated from high school in 1959, the colonial era for most of Africa was coming to an end: Ghana had become a sovereign nation in 1957 and three years later many French and Belgian colonies in West and Central Africa achieved their independence. In Kenya, too, freedom was in the air. Although Jomo Kenyatta was in internal exile and political activity was still limited, the "winds of change" that British prime minister Harold Macmillan said were blowing across Africa made Kenya's independence inevitable. In 1957, black Kenyans were allowed to vote in elections for the first time, and in 1959 the British government invited Kenyan politicians to London to negotiate over a new political order. In 1960, preparations for Kenya's independence had begun.

A newly independent Kenya would need educated men and women ready to fill key positions in the government and society once the British administrators departed. To that end, in the late 1950s the Kenyan politicians of the day, led by Tom Mboya, Gikonyo Kiano, and others initiated and encouraged contacts with political and cultural figures in the United States, led by then-senator John F. Kennedy, Andrew Young, and others. The aim was to provide scholarships for promising students from emerging African states to receive higher education in the United States. This would also open up the United States to these former European colonies, hitherto closed from the rest of the world.

Senator Kennedy agreed not only to fund the program through the Joseph P. Kennedy Foundation but also to fly all the students to the United States at the foundation's expense. Kennedy also pushed the U.S. State Department to expand its Africa scholarship program and make it possible to receive the African students (the State Department initially had turned down Mboya's request). So began what became known as the Kennedy Airlift, which eventually saw nearly six hundred Kenyans airlifted to study in different colleges and universities throughout the United States.

When the Catholic bishop in the Nairobi diocese learned about the proposed venture, he decided to have students from Catholic schools in his area join in. As fate would have it, I had just completed my education at Loreto-Limuru at the top of the class and was a favorite candidate for the bishop's proposal. I was in the right place at the right time. When I was informed of the opportunity to go to study in America, I did not hesitate: "Yes!" I said.

Thanks to the bishop and the nuns, I became one of about three hundred Kenyans selected for the "Lift" of September 1960. That was the fourth time my educational destination had been chosen for me and, as at my last two schools, I was to attend a Catholic institution: Mount St. Scholastica College in Atchison, Kansas, which was under the management of Benedictine nuns.

I was very excited about this new development: It would be so much fun to go to America. It was a great honor and privilege that people in both countries had such trust in me and had made this great opportunity possible. My parents supported me and were happy to hear that I had received a scholarship for further education in the United States. It was quite astonishing news, especially in my village, where girls' education was still not fully appreciated.

As had happened on my return to Nyeri in 1947, in September 1960 a whole new world opened up, one that reached for the first time beyond the borders of my own country. You can imagine what it must have been like when I, twenty years old, boarded a plane for the very first time. Indeed, everything I saw or did for the next few days was for the very first time. The propeller-driven aircraft took off at midnight and flew for days, crawling across the sky: northward to Benghazi in Libya, then on to Luxembourg, Reykjavik in Iceland, Newfoundland in Canada, and finally New York City.

As the Sahara Desert unfolded beneath me, I could not believe my eyes. You can look at an atlas or read about how large the Sahara is, but you don't realize its vastness until you have flown over it. I looked at the desert as dawn rose, fell asleep, and woke up hours later to see still nothing but sand. We were flying too high to make out people or animals or individual dunes. Instead, below were massive, fantastical formations of sand and the occasional green dot of an oasis.

It was fascinating to be in Luxembourg, because I had only read about Europe in books. I had never heard of this small country, whose name sounded so beautiful and memorable. Why we stopped in Luxembourg of all places is a mystery, but I loved feeling that the geography I had learned in school was coming alive with the names of places we arrived at or were near. All three hundred of us drove through the winding streets from the airport to town for dinner.

In Newfoundland, a name I fondly remembered from my geography class, we stopped for dinner, which consisted, so some students told me on the plane, of frogs' legs. I thought I'd eaten chicken and was shocked that it could have been frogs, since I'd never considered frogs edible before. Even before I had time to digest that piece of information, the pilot informed us that we were about to land in New York. Buses picked us up from New York International Airport (later renamed for President Kennedy) and took us to various hotels in Manhattan. As part of our orientation, we toured the United Nations, where dignitaries welcomed us to the United States, and we met other young Africans who had also just arrived to study.

Coming to New York City was like landing on the moon. Fortunately, I was constantly in the company of my friend Agatha Wangeci, with whom I had studied at St. Cecilia's and Loreto-Limuru. Both of us were to attend Mount St. Scholastica. Together we figured out this strange city and shared our experiences. As we walked the busy streets of New York, we were lucky not to be knocked over, since we spent most of the time staring up at the skyscrapers, which seemed to sway in the wind and touch the clouds.

Then there were the elevators! I had been in an elevator in Nairobi when I had received instructions on how to get a visa for the United States. But that elevator went only to the fourth floor. In New York I rode in elevators to the twentieth and thirtieth floors at lightning speed. I was convinced my stomach and heart would not arrive at the same time as the rest of me. How relieved I was when I reached the ground floor again and got out!

One of the things we had to do in New York was go shopping, of course. This led to my first encounter with an escalator. My initial reaction was to think of the *irimũ*—powerful and noisy, slithering between floors, coming from nowhere and returning to nowhere. "Well," I thought, sizing up the escalator, "everybody else is stepping on it, so I'd better do the same." While I made it safely to the next floor, one of my shoes didn't and I looked back wondering how I would recover it. I had no idea that there was another escalator going down on the other side. Luckily, a good old New Yorker realized my predicament and brought my shoe to me with a smile on his face. I have never forgotten that man's generosity and his warm welcome to the magic city. Neither have I forgotten that first encounter with a moving staircase. Even today, I'm a little circumspect when I get on an escalator.

Another aspect that amazed Agatha and me about New York was the presence of black Americans. We could not believe that these were Americans and that they were as dark as we were and didn't speak English with Kenyan accents! As a child in Kenya, I grew up thinking there were only three types of people in the world: black people, like me, pink people such as Europeans, and brown people such as Indians, Goans, and those from the Seychelles. I had assumed that all American Negroes, as we were taught to call them, were light-skinned. Therefore, to arrive in New York and see people as black as me going about their business was a shock. Agatha and I kept comparing some of them with people we knew at home: "Doesn't he remind you of so and so?" We smiled as we compared the likenesses.

How little I knew about the Americas apart from what I learned from my geography class: the Appalachians, the Rocky Mountains, and the Andes; the Amazon rainforest, the prairies and the pampas and the Great Lakes. I had also learned about the *Mayflower*, the Civil War, and the Indians (although probably more from the cowboys' point of view than theirs), and I knew that the Americans had fought a war for independence from the British in 1776. In those days in Kenya, there were few radios, no television, and very few films and little pop music to take America to every village. I found myself ignorant about simple things, such as knowing that Coca-Cola was an American drink and that Indians in Kenya and those in America are different.

We didn't spend long in New York City. Myself, Agatha, and a young Kenyan man called Joseph Kang'atu boarded a Greyhound bus with other students for our long journey to the Midwest, where we would spend the next four years studying. It would take us two days to get to Atchison on our bus, which was specially chartered to transport us to various colleges. We traveled through New Jersey to Pennsylvania and then to Ohio and Indiana. In the Midwest we began to pass miles and miles of flat land full of corn that was perfectly proportioned and ready for harvesting. I thought to myself, "Lord, have mercy! Where did they get all this corn?" When I found out that corn had come from the Americas and was not native to Kenya, I was stunned.

At each stop a few more students left the bus, and by the time we reached Indiana there were ten of us left. At one stop, we decided to get a drink at a local café. We saw a big sign for Coca-Cola, which, along with Fanta, was a very popular drink in Kenya—in fact, they were the only drinks we recognized. While we girls looked around the café for a place to sit, the boys went up to the counter to order the drinks. A few moments later, however, they returned, empty-handed.

"We can't sit down and have a drink," they told us.

"Why not?" we asked.

"Because we're black," they replied.

A lightbulb went on in my head. "Even here in America and even in a small, open café!?"

It was explained to us that we could have a drink but only outside. "Why should we drink outside?" we said, outraged. "Let's go. Let's get back on the bus." So we did—without a drink. That was my first encounter with racial discrimination in America. It was so shocking because it was unexpected in my newfound home.

Years of colonial education on the subject of America had somehow kept the African American part hidden from us. Even though we studied the slave trade, the subject was taught in a way that did not leave us appreciating its inhumanity. An African has to go to America to understand slavery and its impact on black people—not only in Africa but also in the diaspora. It is in America that words such as "black," "white," "Negro," "mulatto," "skin color," "segregation," "discrimination," and "the ghetto" take on lives of their own.

The Greyhound bus finally rumbled into Atchison, which is in the northeastern corner of Kansas. When we arrived we found a small town along the Missouri River, best known as the birthplace of America's pioneering female aviator, Amelia Earhart, and a one-time hub of several railroads, including the Atchison, Topeka, and Santa Fe line. Benedictines were among Atchison's first settlers, establishing St. Benedict's Abbey for men in 1858 and its sister college, Mount St. Scholastica, for women in 1863. The women's college was popularly known as the Mount and the students proudly referred to themselves as Mounties. The emblem for both colleges was the raven, which I used to see everywhere I turned.

The reception we received at Mount St. Scholastica was wonderful: nothing to compare with the one we had gotten at the café in Indiana. The other students had obviously been told that Agatha and I were coming. They were very welcoming, exhibiting the over-flowing enthusiasm typical of Americans. Throughout our stay, the girls embraced us so warmly that I do not remember ever being homesick or lonely. They truly made us feel at home.

We quickly became aware that election fever was sweeping the country and the campus and that the Nixon-Kennedy election was less than two months away. The students knew that we were part of the Kennedy Airlift and, even though I had no idea what Republi-cans or Democrats represented, they assumed we were for Senator Kennedy. The fact that he was a Catholic also added to the excite-ment. Visiting local Democrats urged us to join the campaign and asked us to speak at campus rallies supporting Kennedy. It was a great introduction to campus culture—even before we unpacked, we were plunged into the presidential campaign. We Kenyans on the two campuses celebrated with everyone else when Kennedy won.

Just like the nuns at school in Kenya, I found the sisters at Mount St. Scholastica very kind, and several became academic and personal mentors and friends. Among them Sister Imogene, the college dean, and Sister John Marie, my academic adviser and mentor in bio-logical sciences, were wonderful people to be with. They gave me a sense of belonging to the community and the feeling of being at home, even though I was thousands of miles from Kenya. Each Christmas, Sister Marcella, who taught me home economics, would make Agatha and me the most beautiful new dresses, taking great care with the design and the sewing. I have never forgotten that ges-ture or the times she and I would talk about my life in the United States and Kenya and what I hoped and dreamed of for my future.

My academic experience at Mount St. Scholastica was quite dif-ferent from what I had known in Kenya. The workload was demand-ing, although I made it to the dean's list several times. I enjoyed biology more than the chemistry I had focused on in high school, so biology became my major, and I minored in chemistry and German. The classroom presented challenges. Although the nuns were surprised that Agatha and I could understand so much English, we noticed the difference between speaking English as a foreign language and being surrounded by native English speakers. Critical analysis was not easy. We had little idea of English literature. The American students knew more about it than we did and could relate culturally to Shakespeare in a way we never could.

I worked hard at my studies and was pleased with the results. The sisters wrote each semester to my parents to update them on my progress. Since they couldn't read English, my brother Nderitu translated the letters for them. He saved some letters from that period, and I was amused to read so many years later what Sister Imogene had written at the end of one semester: "I am pleased to inform you that your daughter is doing highly satisfactory work. She seems well and happy and has made a most successful adjustment to life in the U.S. We are proud and happy to have students from Africa in our college and we want you to know that they are very fine representatives of their people."

In one of my own letters to Nderitu, dated February 28, 1961, I recounted my experiences of college life and my studies, as well as my responsibilities to him as my oldest brother and to the family. It is interesting to read this earnest, pious young woman's words: "Your description of the adventure to the Aberdares almost made me homesick," I told Nderitu. "This semester I am taking zoology, psychology, scripture, English composition, modern European history, and sports. It's quite a bit of work, enough to keep my little brain busy."

I assured Nderitu that the college was treating me well. "The nuns with whom I live are as nice as the ones I had at home. They have a big heart for Africans." The dean of the college was going to send Nderitu a report and I was clearly concerned. "She will tell you my behavior and such things as I should not do. Should you feel that there is some weakness I . . . ask you kindly to let me know and I will do my best to put it right." Finally, I sought to allay any concerns he and my family might have. "Don't worry about me, my dear. God is taking care of me. Give my best love to my mother and all the neighbors. . . . I am as sound as a bell."

I quickly realized that Mount St. Scholastica and St. Benedict's, although both Catholic schools, were very different from St. Cecilia's and Loreto-Limuru. The education was broad-based and, on reflection, quite liberal. I marveled at the freedom that the students had—young men and women kissing in public and watching films with romantic scenes. In high school, we had seen Westerns and other American and British films, but the romance had been blotted out or edited. It astonished me to see young men and women walking past the nuns holding hands and the nuns not making any comment. On the weekends, students held parties where men and women danced—*with each other.*

In this and other ways, America was incredibly liberating. It was also troubling. It made me think about what the nuns in Kenya had told us. I began to ask myself, "Why was dancing so wrong? Why was holding a boy's hand so atrocious?" I came to understand that my previous education had been very Victorian. I had been practically living the life of a nun, even though I hadn't taken holy orders.

When I arrived in Atchison I was a very strict and dogmatic Catholic. This was the time leading up to the Second Vatican Council (1962–1965) and support for reforms in the Catholic Church was growing. At the Mount, I began to look at religion differently and to examine the issues confronting people of faith. During Vatican II I began to question my faith: not to the extent of losing it entirely, as happened to some, but wondering why behavior we had been told was wrong was now deemed acceptable by church authorities.

In my schools in Kenya, for instance, we never ate meat on Fridays, and suddenly there were no food restrictions. It used not to be possible to take Holy Communion if you had eaten anything after six o'clock the previous evening and now that limit was three hours. Mass every Sunday had been compulsory, but now Catholics could attend services on Saturday evening instead. The Mass had always been said in Latin, but now services in vernacular languages were allowed. Even though Mass wasn't compulsory at the Mount, I found myself attending it quite often, partly out of habit and also because it was easy for me to get to the chapel. The Mass itself was much more personal, with fewer directed prayers. We could follow it in English in the prayer book rather than reciting the rosary ad infinitum. Though some of these changes were relatively minor, they made me think. Had God changed his mind? Was that possible? All this was strange and discomforting, and forced me to reflect on my faith.

The countryside in Kansas was also different from my home region, which is full of hills and mountains. By contrast, Atchison is as flat as a pancake. There were no hills for me to look up at in Kansas, but I did enjoy taking long walks along the Missouri River, known to me from maps but now very real. Unlike in Kenya, near the Equator, the seasons in Kansas are also very distinct. When we arrived in late September, we found leaves of green, yellow, gold, radiant red, and brown. Shortly after they dropped from the branches until each tree looked naked and dead. Although leaves fell from wild fig and acacia trees in Kenya, it was nothing to compare with the colorful leaves gathered in heaps, flying in every direction at the slightest breath of wind in Atchison. Never before had I seen so many leaves on the ground at the same time. No wonder the season is known as the fall.

And then there was the snow! I had seen the white ice on top of Mount Kenya and had not quite understood how it was frozen water, but I had never seen snow fall. And nothing could have prepared me for the cold weather when it finally arrived in earnest in January. I had never been as cold as I was during those winter months. Fortunately, the sisters made sure I was warmly dressed and, despite the cold, I do not remember being sick while I was in Atchison.

Another unforgettable experience of Atchison was the murmur of the winds, blowing through the branches of the leafless trees. I had seen trees sway and dance to the wind, but only in Kansas did the wind whisper in the dead of winter. At first it seemed eerie, but I soon learned to love that sound, which reminded me of violins. I had never heard anything like that whisper, and still haven't anywhere in the world.

Spring was also very new to my senses. It reminded me of the excitement of seeing seeds germinating after the rains fell at home. I would watch as plants emerged from the ground once the snow had receded. Buds appeared on twigs and branches and before you knew it trees would be clad again with beautiful green leaves, all at once. Back home leaves would grow and fall throughout the year, so there were never trees uniformly green or bare. What a miracle!

Summer in Kansas was hot and humid. That first summer, Agatha and I worked on campus. These must have been the days before air conditioners, because I remember Agatha and I trying to work with one hand while we were fanning ourselves with the other—waving hot air onto our faces and wishing for the cold highland air of home.

The Americans were baffled. "Why are you fanning yourself?" they asked me. "We thought that you'd enjoy this weather."

I looked at them askance as sweat streamed down my face and my back. "Let me tell you," I said. "I've never experienced such miserable weather anywhere in the world."

"Well, where else have you been?" They laughed.

"Well, you have a point," I replied, appreciating that this was only the second place outside the Kenyan highlands I had ever lived. Ever since then I have appreciated even more the near perfect weather in the Kenyan highlands. These seasonal changes also helped me understand why people outside the tropics like to bask in the sun even when their skin is peeling off!

In those days, it was not possible for us Kenyans to go home and visit: The journey took too long and it was very expensive. We resigned ourselves to the fact that we would go home only when we completed our studies and, in the meantime, we consoled ourselves with letters, although they could take as long as three to six months to reach Kenya or the United States. Since then, the revolution in communication has been extraordinary: telephones, including cell phones, computers, faxes, and color television have taken information technology to levels unthinkable forty years ago during my days in Atchison.

Luckily, I made some good friends at the Mount. On off-hours during the school year my friends and I would go window-shopping in Atchison. I couldn't afford to buy anything, but we enjoyed looking at the latest styles of clothes. One friend with whom I have stayed in touch is Florence (Conrad) Salisbury. She became a real sister. During most Christmases, Thanksgivings, and Easter holidays, Florence would take me to her family's house near Wichita.

I felt completely at home with Florence's many siblings and loving parents. I would spend evenings chatting with her father at the kitchen table as we sipped coffee and nibbled on biscuits that we all had participated in baking. The Conrads' house became like my second home in Kansas. If I was not there making Christmas cookies with Florence and her sisters, I was back on campus doing the same with the nuns in the kitchen. Or I would be packing books with my great friend Sister Gonzaga, the registrar, to send to her favorite schools in the Philippines.

Another friend was Margaret Malone from Texas. She was so fond of her state that she kept giving me presents decorated with the Yellow Rose of Texas, which was also the nickname I gave her, since she was a beautiful blonde. During my third year at the Mount another student from Kenya arrived to join us, Mary Paul Gakunga. Together, Agatha, Mary Paul, and I formed a great team and had a very happy life both on campus and off. We have remained friends and when we get together in Kenya we often reminisce about our experiences at the Mount.

Among my other friends at the Mount were fellow international students from China, India, and Japan. There was a certain bond among the foreign students and sometimes we would be interviewed by the local press and asked to speak about our countries at local schools and functions. We also put on an international night at the college so we could share our national heritage. I remember dressing up with a sheet over my shoulder to look like a typical Kikuyu girl and teaching some of my friends dances from back home as a way of sharing my culture with other Mounties.

We valued such events because they gave a sense of belonging to our adopted community even though we were many miles from our own. Although the alumnae office tried to keep us informed about one another, years of separation and the responsibilities of family made it difficult to keep in touch. In 2005, I traveled to Japan as a guest of Mainichi Newspapers. When I informed them that some of my college friends were Japanese and that the only name I could remember was Shoko, my contacts at Mainichi told me that Shoko was one of the most common first names in Japan. So I could hardly believe my eyes when at a special luncheon the newspaper organized in Tokyo I saw my fellow Mounties Shoko Komaya, Grace Mahr, Suzanne Tamura, Sonoko Takada, and Tuneko Shibuya, after a gap of more than forty years! We hugged, laughed, cried tears of joy, sang our favorite Mountie songs, and enjoyed a most memorable meeting.

During my time at the Mount, and especially during the national holidays, families would open up their homes to foreign students. I was impressed by their generosity to us Africans at a time when there was so much conflict between the races in the United States. On television we saw protests and black people being cruelly treated by policemen. Even then I did not quite absorb what was happening and the long-term impact of what I was watching. The Mau Mau struggle for justice in Kenya had led me to believe that education was part of the solution to many of the problems black people were facing everywhere. But I was not adequately conversant with the history, politics, and mind-set of American society.

I tended to bury myself in my books, but nonetheless I took an interest in the civil rights movement and learned a lot. I wanted to understand it, and America in all its intricacy, and to see where I as a Kenyan and a black woman fit in. I often wondered why I should come to America to see black people being treated as harshly as I had witnessed in Kenya as the British attempted to crush the Mau Mau movement. While Britain was a colonial power, America was "the land of the free and the home of the brave"! So how was I to explain such happenings?

Apart from the incident at the café in Indiana, I was saved from discrimination during the rest of my stay in America, partly because I did not move about much, preferring to stay on campus. Even when I visited my white friends and stayed with their families, I never experienced any form of racism. Nevertheless, during my time in the United States, when the civil rights movement was violently confronted, I became more aware of how institutionalized discrimination based on skin color existed in America. That I never encountered another direct experience of discrimination was an exception. Many of my fellow Kenyan students elsewhere experienced racism in finding jobs, places to stay, and friends.

Perhaps because the Mount was an almost all-white school and there were only two African American students I did not interact much with African Americans in Atchison. I never hit it off as friends with the African Americans in college, even though they were cordial. Much more friendly and approachable were two women support staff at the Mount. They took Agatha and me under their wings and were quite maternal. One of them, Mrs. Collins, was a short, hardworking woman who could have been my elder sister or young aunt. She always had a smile on her face and we exchanged niceties as we passed each other in the halls. Occasionally, we would meet off campus for friendly chats. Sometimes, Mrs. Collins and her coworker would take us to their neighborhood, where most of the black people in Atchison lived, not far from the campus.

At that time, Atchison was segregated. As the women took us around their neighborhood and the more affluent part of town, they pointed out to us the inequities in American society. The economic differences between the neighborhoods were stark but not surprising to us, because the same divide was evident in Kenya. We blamed our inequities on colonialism, while Americans blamed theirs on the legacy of slavery. However, whenever we visited the two women's two-story houses, I thought they looked positively luxurious compared to my mother's house.

On some occasions, with the handful of Kenyan boys studying at St. Benedict's, we'd go dancing at what I recall were cold, large halls mostly frequented by local black patrons. I was still learning to appreciate American music. I was also learning to dance, because we weren't allowed to dance at school in Kenya. As it turned out, we didn't dance much, and spent most of our time drinking sodas and chatting with the boys. Some of those young men had been in America for several years and thought we were inexperienced and conservative. They openly criticized us and encouraged us to change and become more like American girls. They were particularly critical of our kinky hair, which they said would be much better if treated with a hot comb.

Although none of us then was in a hurry to become a Kenyan American, the boys didn't have to wait long, since by the time we were in our third year, we could hold our place on the dance floor with twists, rock 'n' roll, and whatever else was in vogue. Even the hair got a touch of the hot comb. By the time we graduated, we were fully Americanized. That is the lure of America. What it did to me in Kansas, it continues to do to every generation around the world.

During summer vacations, the nuns would find us jobs in Kansas City, Missouri, so we could acquire experience and skills to complement our studies. One such summer, Sister John Marie got me a job in a tissue-processing laboratory at St. Joseph's Hospital. We moved to the big city and stayed in a house owned by the Benedictines that also hosted students from many other countries—Mexico, the Philippines, and India—as well as Puerto Rico. Like Agatha, Mary Paul, and I, these students worked in different places during the day but in the evening we all came together to form a pleasant international community.

At the hospital my task was to assist the laboratory technician responsible for processing body tissue so it could be observed under a microscope. This helped the doctors and other experts determine the ailments of their patients. The skills I learned in this laboratory later proved immensely valuable in my academic career in Kenya.

The technician was an African American who, by turns, was gentle and sarcastic. He thought me hopelessly naïve about America and African Americans and decided that I needed some educating to raise my consciousness. He suggested I attend a Sunday prayer group of the Nation of Islam, then led by the Honorable Elijah Muhammad. I invited Agatha. When we arrived at the meeting we immediately saw a large gathering of both men and women; the latter wore long white dresses and had their heads covered with equally white scarves.

Once the meeting began, much of what the speakers said contradicted what I had been taught in the course of my religious education at school. They said that Jesus was a black man and not a blue-eyed blond, that he had attended the University of Alexandria in Egypt, and had spent much of his early years in Africa. For me that was not only untrue but also sacrilegious. I had never heard anything so outrageous! I was so shocked by such misrepresentation that I believed that I should not even hear it, because hearing it alone must be a sin. So in the middle of the meeting I left the hall, found a pay phone, and called the priest at our residence for an immediate consultation.

"Father," I confessed. "You will never guess where I am at the moment, and I am not sure I should even be here. But I'm at a Nation of Islam meeting and you should hear what they are saying about Jesus!"

The priest laughed, perhaps to ease my anxiety.

"What are you doing there?" he asked.

"I know as a Catholic I shouldn't be listening to this," I replied, "but I'm here and I'm not sure what I should do. Should I stay and try to respond to them or leave? They need to be talked to because they're giving wrong information about Jesus."

To my surprise, the priest encouraged me to stay. "Just listen to what they're saying," he said. "You don't have to believe it, but it's good to listen. It will be interesting to hear what you think about it when you come back to the residence hall." Not only did I now have permission to listen but the mandate to speak my mind.

So we stayed. They continued to speak about many things I found contradictory and unbelievable. All these years I'd been taught that believers do not question faith, even when it does not make sense. One believed and the understanding came later. But here were people who were not teaching me but rather urging me to question.

Finally, I was given a chance to speak. "It's not true that Jesus went to the University of Alexandria," I said. "There wasn't even a University of Alexandria at that time. You are misinformed about the life and times of Jesus."

I continued and when I was through, the main speakers on the podium turned to the audience: "You see how indoctrinated this sister from Africa is! This is part of the problem and we must do whatever we can to educate her and others like her." I realized that I had probably wasted my breath but I felt extremely unsettled. I could see that they believed in what they were saying; but I also believed in what I was saying. After some time, Agatha and I decided that it was time to leave. It was also getting late and we had to get back to the residence hall before dinner.

The next day I reported to work, eager to tell my boss what had happened at the meeting and how I had informed the followers of the Nation of Islam that what they were saying was not true. "How are you so sure?" the technician asked, with a sly smile.

"I just know," I told him, emphatically.

"You mean," he replied, "you've been *taught* so. Why do you think that everything you've been taught is true?"

I looked at him with astonishment and asked myself, "Is he telling me that I may not have been told the whole truth?" I realized then that he also believed what I had heard at the meeting. "Perhaps he knows something I don't," I thought to myself.

I didn't discuss the subject any further with him and he never invited me to another prayer meeting. But from that time on I started to think more critically about religion and developed an interest in other faiths, including the oral faith traditions. I came to realize that my understanding of Jesus's life and of my faith and others' was rather superficial and narrow and that I needed to seek more knowledge. I gradually appreciated that the teaching I had received in Catholic schools might not have exposed me to everything I needed to know about my faith. That experience actually prepared me for the progressive steps taken by Pope John XXIII and later Pope John Paul II, who even entered a synagogue and a mosque for prayer and contemplation.

In hindsight I can see that my boss that summer in the lab must have wondered how I could have grown up in colonial Africa and yet have had no idea about the struggles of African Americans, the African diaspora, or any knowledge of history or religion beyond what my Catholic education had taught me.

We Kenyan students in the Midwest felt separated from the rest of the Kenyan community in the United States, especially from the majority who lived along the East Coast. Occasionally, however, we managed to travel and attend meetings with other Africans studying in the United States that were organized by a student body known as the East African Students' Association. Such opportunities and exchanges gave us a sense of life in Africa outside of Kenya and a sense of being Kenyans rather than British subjects, as well as of being Africans. This was important because our continent was emerging from a century of colonial rule and giving rise to new nation-states.

Then, as now, and despite the very modern forms of communication in the United States, we had little access to news about Kenya in any media, unless it was bad news. Fortunately, there was little bad news in Kenya at that time and we came to appreciate that no news was probably good news. We did get the big news that Kenya was going to become independent on December 12, 1963, and elections for representatives to the new government had been held in May 1963. To celebrate our independence, the Kenyans in Kansas got together with friends of Kenya, including many Americans, in the city of Lawrence, to eat, drink, sing, dance, and listen to speeches. Much rejoicing took place, both in Kenya and abroad, as Jomo Kenyatta became Kenya's first prime minister and, a year later, president.

Sadly, our celebration of Kenya's independence came only a few weeks after the trauma of President Kennedy's assassination on November 22. As news of his death reached the Mount that day, classes were suspended and, in great disbelief and remorse, we prayed for the peaceful repose of his soul. Shortly after, the college closed and students were sent home. Agatha and I stayed on campus and remained glued to the television, following the events as the presumed assassin, Lee Harvey Oswald, was himself murdered by Jack Ruby. And it all happened as the world watched on television!

The night that President Kennedy died, I wrote with great urgency to my brother about what had happened and how I felt. "I admired him as a leader," I wrote, "a lover of peace and a man who was very humanistic. I mourn with the Americans and with all those who know what it means to have an official shot dead." I told Nderitu that even as the television repeated the news of Kennedy's death over and over again, "We find it hard to believe and yet it is so true."

It was a momentous time for me, for many Americans, and for many around the world for whom President Kennedy will always remain the young, energetic, and charismatic leader who was not allowed to realize the dreams he had for America and the world.

Through the Kennedy Airlift I had become part of his dream, and now he was gone before I could realize it. I mourned him like a member of my family. I am lucky that later in life I was able to develop working relationships and friendships with members of the Kennedy family who helped me understand President Kennedy better. I am privileged to know and work with Kerry Kennedy, Robert F. Kennedy's daughter and one of JFK's many nieces. For many years she supported pro-democracy activists in Kenya by working for human rights and democratic institutions.

My four years at the Mount, and the experiences I had both on and off the campus, nurtured in me a willingness to listen and learn, to think critically and analytically, and to ask questions. These skills stayed with me wherever I went from then on. The Mount also provided me with a springboard to my next educational establishment. Some of the sisters suggested some of the American universities to which I could submit an application for graduate studies, which I was eager to pursue. Once I received my bachelor of science degree in 1964, I applied to and was accepted by the University of Pittsburgh in Pennsylvania to study for a master's degree in biology. The Africa-American Institute, which supported higher education for many Africans (and still does), gave me a scholarship that made this possible. I had visited the University of Pittsburgh on a scholarship in the summer of 1963 to attend a six-week course on leadership. My course paper was on helping women in rural areas work together and promote development efforts. Little did I know that I would be putting that theory into practice only a decade later, when I would be inspired by rural women to initiate the Green Belt Movement.

In 1990, when I returned to Mount St. Scholastica after more than twenty-five years, almost everything except the buildings had changed: The Mount had merged with St. Benedict's, become coeducational, and was rechristened Benedictine College. The monastery, which had been the exclusive preserve of the nuns, had thrown open its doors to the public and visitors could now mingle with the sisters in their dining room. The nuns, who used to wear long black habits and white flowing veils, now wore short dresses and skirts and even trousers. They also exposed their hair, which was cut short. This time, I was the one with the floor-length skirt and a headscarf! But Atchison remained the same old, pleasant, and welcoming flat midwestern town that was home for four of the most wonderful years of my life.

I entered the University of Pittsburgh in September 1964 and studied biological sciences under the supervision of Professor Charles Ralph, who became a good friend. Initially, he wanted me to research the life cycle of the cockroach, but I couldn't stand the thought of cockroaches crawling all over me! Instead, Professor Ralph gave me the chance to study the pineal gland, which lies deep in the brain just opposite the pituitary gland. He wanted to know how the gland develops and what its role is as animals go through life.

He chose to look at the gland in Japanese quails, because they are small birds and easy to handle. I incubated and hatched the quails' eggs and followed the development of the pineal gland in the brains from egg to adulthood. The study constituted my master's thesis and fulfilled the requirements of my master of science degree. It also further developed my skills in embryology, microanatomy, processing tissues, and microscopy, which proved pivotal less than two years later in Kenya.

Pittsburgh was much bigger than Atchison, a real urban center, and much more industrial, although its rolling hills reminded me more of home than the plains of Kansas. I had become used to big towns because of the summers I spent in Kansas City, and so adapted well. In the mid-1960s, Pittsburgh, like other manufacturing towns in the United States, was coming to terms with the legacy of pollution from a hundred years of the industrial revolution. This turned out to be my first experience of environmental restoration, because the city was already working to clean up the air. People from Pittsburgh would tell me that they had had to paint their houses each year because the soot made them look as dirty as the inside of a chimney, and that there was no point in hanging your washing out to dry because it turned black. Over the years, however, environmentalists' efforts have paid off: Today, Pittsburgh is no longer shrouded in smoke, but is one of the most beautiful metropolises in the land.

The university was much bigger than Mount St. Scholastica, and I interacted mostly with graduate students in my department, which was relatively small. I also spent a lot of my time with the other African students at the university. Except for going to the library or cafeteria or sporting events, I wasn't very involved with the huge campus. Nor, as far as I could tell, was it a hotbed of radicalism. During my years at the University of Pittsburgh, from September 1964 to January 1966, most people, including me, did not understand why America was in Vietnam and had not fully decided if they were for or against the war. (Although as a child of colonialism, the sending of troops to a foreign land was not wholly strange to me.)

An African American in my department was the only person I knew who was drafted. Unfortunately, he was killed soon after he arrived in Vietnam. That was my only personal experience of this conflict that was to have such a long-lasting impact on American society. When I visit the Vietnam Veterans Memorial in Washington, D.C., I think of him in particular, mourn his loss, and honor his memory.

By 1965, as I was completing my studies at the University of Pittsburgh, Kenya had been independent for nearly two years. The new government knew that many of us who were part of the Kennedy Airlift were just finishing our degree programs. In an effort to recruit personnel to take over positions being vacated by British civil servants, the Kenyan government sent officers to the United States to recruit young Kenyans about to graduate. As part of this process, I was interviewed by a group of people from the University College of

Nairobi (later the University of Nairobi), including the deputy vice chancellor. One of the positions available was research assistant to a professor of zoology.

Later, I received a letter from the college confirming my position. I would be involved with a project concerning the control of desert locusts. The letter instructed me to report to work on January 10, 1966. This was to be my first "real" job and I took it very seriously. I was so keen to assume my new position that I sacrificed marching at my graduation ceremony at the University of Pittsburgh and collecting my master's diploma.

When I left the United States, I was taking back to Kenya five and a half years of higher education, as well as a belief that I should work hard, help the poor, and watch out for the weak and vulnerable. I knew that I wanted to teach in a university and share what I had learned about biology. I wanted to see my family and to start a family of my own.

I also took America back to Kenya with me. When people think of America they think of a vast, powerful, confident country—a place where, especially in the big cities, people can be angry or brash. But there is something about the United States that I experienced in the early to mid-1960s and that I still see now. The country is an enormous juggernaut with many smaller systems in it, from the government to academic institutions to farming to transportation. In spite of everything that comes to rock that larger system, whether it be a hurricane, political controversy, or economic difficulty, the wheels of the juggernaut do not come off but, indeed, keep turning as if nothing else is happening.

There is a persistence, a seriousness, and a vision to America: It seems to know where it is going and it will go in that direction, whether you like it or not. In America, if you can find your place you can be treated very well, because its people are very generous. But you have to be tenacious, innovative, and strong. Besides, you have to keep moving, because the machine will grind on, whether you are on board or not.

I also returned to Kenya with a new name—my original one. When I was born, my parents gave me the name Wangari. When I was baptized as an infant, like other Christians in Kenya I was trained to consider my baptismal name, Miriam, as my primary name. Throughout my childhood I was known as Miriam Wangari, and my father's name was set aside. This was a legacy of the missionaries: Africans were taught to accept a certain amount of informality, in which surnames didn't feature. After I became a Catholic, I dropped Miriam and became Mary Josephine, or Mary Jo, Wangari, which is how I was known when I arrived in the United States. The way surnames were forgotten in Kenya struck me as similar to how many African Americans in the times of slavery and segregation were known only by their first names, yet had to address white people as Mr. or Miss, followed by their surnames.

At the Mount the sisters called me Miss Wangari. This began to seem absurd, since I knew the term "Miss" meant the "unmarried daughter of . . ." and I knew I was not the unmarried daughter of myself. I decided to put this right and began writing my name as Mary Josephine Wangari Muta, so I'd be called Miss Muta. I then reversed my primary and personal names, becoming Wangari Mary Josephine Muta, and later dropped Mary Josephine because the name had become too long. When I returned to Kenya, I was Wangari Muta. That was what I should always have been.

The United States prepared me to be confident not only in reclaiming my original names but to critique what was happening at home, including what women were experiencing. My years in the United States overlapped with the beginnings of the women's movement and even though many women were still bound to traditional ideas about themselves at that time, I came to see that as an African woman I was perhaps even more constrained in what I could do or think, or even hope for. This was to come into sharper perspective when I returned to Kenya in 1966, thinking that the sky was the limit for me.

It is fair to say that America transformed me: It made me into the person I am today. It taught me not to waste any opportunity and to do what can be done—and that there is a lot to do. The spirit of freedom and possibility that America nurtured in me made me want to foster the same in Kenya, and it was in this spirit that I returned home.

5

Independence–Kenya's and My Own

January 6, 1966. Nairobi International Airport. After a long, although considerably shorter than the one I took leaving Kenya in 1960, overnight flight, I step off the plane into the warm, dry air and descend the metal stairs to the tarmac. I see a group of people waving frantically from the observation bay. Even from that distance I recognize my father's towering figure. Thrilled that my family has come to greet me, I wave and walk faster toward them. They stretch out their hands and wave back, calling my name. I am home.

Tears roll down my face as I think of how much has happened to me and to my country since I last walked on the same tarmac. I hurry into the terminal. Then I see them: my parents; my father's youngest wife, whose Kikuyu name, Wanjiru, is the same as my mother's; Murango, my father's friend from Nakuru, and his son; my oldest brother, Nderitu, and youngest, Kamunya; and others. Even though I had sent a letter letting them know the date of my arrival, I had not expected anyone, let alone so many, to meet me at the airport. They have traveled a long distance to welcome me home. I am overwhelmed.

When I finally get through passport control, everything is a whirl of questions, hugs, handshakes, long embraces, and tears of joy. We have all changed, grown grayer, taller, or thinner. "Nderitu!" I cry to the young man I think is my oldest brother. The young man laughs. "No! I'm Kamunya!"

"Kamunya," I reply, embarrassed at mistaking him for my oldest brother, "you've grown so tall!"

My parents look at me. "What happened?" they ask. "You're so tall. And so *thin*! Didn't you eat enough?"

Even though they say this lightheartedly, I can sense the concern in their voices. "I'm all right," I assure them. It is true I was much thinner than when I left Kenya. But they didn't need to feel sorry for me. In the United States, I was considered just right: slender, but not skinny; the perfect size for the red hot, close-fitting, A-line dress I was wearing that day. To my family, though, I looked like I hadn't eaten enough in years.

We all somehow managed to fit into an old car borrowed from a friend and drove to Bahati Estate in Nairobi, where some of Murango's family lived. The car radio was playing a recording of one of Jomo Kenyatta's thundering speeches. I sensed that this was a historic moment: It was not only the first time I had heard his voice, but it was the voice of *President* Kenyatta. He was urging us to return to the countryside and create wealth from the land by growing coffee and tea and developing our agricultural industry. As all of us listened to the *Mzee* (Kiswahili for "respected elder," as Kenyatta was called) on the radio, nodding along with what he said, I almost felt like shouting back to him: "Here I am, Mr. President! I'm back and ready to join in the building of our free country." I felt a deep sense of pride at being a Kenyan.

I was buoyed by the enthusiasm and optimism I sensed around me. I could almost hear myself agree with the concluding words spoken by the great American civil rights leader Dr. Martin Luther King Jr. at the Lincoln Memorial in Washington, D.C., on August 28, 1963: "Free at last! Free at last! Thank God Almighty, we are free at last!" These thoughts dominated my mind in the days and months that followed as I reconnected with my country and my people.

We were welcomed warmly at Bahati Estate and enjoyed lunch with friends and neighbors. Because Bahati was typical of the crowded, one-bedroom houses assigned to Africans in the days when Kenya was a colony, there was not enough space for all of us to sleep there. So that afternoon my brothers and I drove to the high-class New Stanley Hotel in downtown Nairobi and I stayed there for several nights. This would have been unthinkable before independence because of the color bar then in effect that stratified society into three racial layers: white, brown, and black. As black Africans, we would not have been allowed to eat or drink, let alone sleep, at the New Stanley.

While I was at the Stanley, family and friends came to visit. They were as excited as I was to be in the hotel, and I shared with them how the color bar was practiced in the United States and the progress of the civil rights movement there. After a few days in Nairobi, my family returned to the countryside: my father to Nakuru, my mother and Kamunya to Nyeri, and my older brothers to their places of work outside the city.

After all the troubles that Kenya has had since independence, it is difficult to convey how exciting that time was. We felt that Kenya's destiny was in our hands. It truly was a whole new world, and yet, forty years on, in some ways the potential of political independence and the elimination of racial barriers have yet to be realized. My generation and those that followed failed fully to appreciate and take advantage of the great opportunities that that breakthrough presented. Instead, Kenyans have often engaged in retrogressive and destructive practices that continue to frustrate and retard the realization of the promise of that time.

In those early days of 1966, of course, I had no inkling of what would happen in the coming decades. I simply got ready to report to work that Monday, January 10. With great enthusiasm, I presented myself to the professor of zoology, my new boss. To my dismay, without blinking an eye, he had the audacity to inform me that the job had been offered to someone else. I was shocked. "But you wrote me this letter," I protested, showing him the handwritten letter of appointment on official university letterhead and signed by him. "I've come all the way from the United States of America."

The professor was immovable; I might as well have been speaking to a stone. In my desperation I went to the office of one of the professor's superiors to plead my case, but he supported his colleague. "Because the professor wrote the letter to you on the letterhead of the Department of Zoology rather than the office of the chancellor," he replied without shame, "and because it is hand-written, the letter is not official." I was devastated. I couldn't understand how someone— and a professor at that!—could be such a hypocrite. How could the college claim no responsibility for that decision? What was I supposed to do?

I decided to pursue the matter in different offices. I found out that the zoology professor had indeed offered the job to someone else, and that that person was someone from his own ethnic community. To add insult to injury, that person was still in Canada. It was the first time I had encountered that form of discrimination. Was it also because I was a woman? Perhaps not, but it wasn't long after that, when seeking another job at the same institution, that I encountered sexism from the same men. Both ethnic and gender barriers now were placed in the way of my self-advancement. I realized then that the sky would not be my limit! Most likely, my gender and my ethnicity would be.

What I did not know then was that tribalism and other forms of corruption were going to become some of the most divisive factors in our society, and they would frustrate the dreams of the Kenyan people after independence. What I suspected then, and I know for sure today, is that the letter I received from the University College of Nairobi was official. But the professor of zoology practiced tribalism and sexism and denied me the job. There was nothing I could do about it; such issues were neither admitted nor discussed. The official verdict was that there was no vacancy because the position had been filled. I was left to find another job, if I could.

Anyone who has lost a job knows that it's not easy to find another one, especially when you are desperate. In my case, it took several months, during which I first stayed with two old school friends, Agatha Wangeci and Miriam Wanjiru, in Westlands. This was a lively, predominantly Indian area, then opening up to different races as the color bar came down and the ability to pay became the determining factor in where you could live and what luxuries you could enjoy. It was during one of my job-hunting expeditions that I ran into a brother-in-law called Nderitu Mathenge, who invited me to stay with his family in Nairobi.

Nderitu was an assistant dean at the very recently established School of Veterinary Medicine at the University College of Nairobi and his wife, Elizabeth, was, like me, a graduate of Loreto-Limuru. Nderitu must have seen how vulnerable I was as a young woman just returned from America, because he not only invited me to live with him and his wife but was very protective and reassuring. "Don't worry," he would tell me, "You'll get a job."

It was while I was living with Nderitu and Elizabeth that I met Professor Reinhold Hofmann, who had been sent by the University of Giessen in Germany to establish Kenya's own Department of Veterinary Anatomy in the School of Veterinary Medicine. Professor Hofmann was looking for an assistant to help in the microanatomy, or histology, section. I had an interview with Professor Hofmann and he offered me a job, precisely because of the particular skills in processing tissues and using microscopes I had developed in the lab in Kansas City and refined at the University of Pittsburgh. At that time, University College of Nairobi was a constituent college of the University of East Africa at Makerere in Uganda, so I had indeed, after six years, finally fulfilled my high school ambition of getting to Makerere University.

As fate would have it, the Department of Veterinary Anatomy was separated from the Department of Zoology only by a beautiful courtyard lined with layers of colorful bougainvillea plants. From my window, therefore, I could see those who could have been my colleagues in the study of locusts a few months earlier. I'm sure by then they had forgotten our early encounters, but I hadn't. To this day, I wonder how my future would have unfolded had the professor of zoology been fair and honest.

Initially, I was disappointed I had not joined the Department of Zoology because anatomy is a very specialized science and I had wanted to study something more general. However, I gradually found that working with tissues and studying them under the microscope was very interesting. Not surprisingly, given Professor Hofmann's background, some of my colleagues were German and we used some German textbooks. Even though the work was completely new and very challenging, the German I had studied at Mount St. Scholastica proved useful, and I quickly became engrossed in my studies. I virtually forgot about the locusts.

The university's main campus is in Nairobi's city center, while the departments of veterinary anatomy and biological sciences were and still are on the Chiromo campus, a mile away. The campus was comprised of low-rise, L-shaped buildings, open staircases, and many windows, organized around a grassy courtyard. In the years that followed, the Chiromo campus became my second home as I buried myself in books, microscopes, and slides. I progressed in the Department of Veterinary Anatomy and eventually became part of the research and teaching team.

I registered for my Ph.D., for which I would be required to use an electron microscope. At that time, the University College of Nairobi had only one electron microscope, in the Department of Human Anatomy, so that is where I did my work. Professor Mungai, the head of the department, allowed me to use the microscope in their department and visit their laboratories. They were amused by my interest in human anatomy. Occasionally, I would steal into their department and have a look at their specimens. It was very different to look at and handle the remains of a human being. It reminded me of my own vulnerability and insignificance, and that we should value our short time on this planet. I did not have the same reaction to the animal specimens.

I loved working with the students during their first years in their pursuit of doctorates in veterinary medicine. They came to us young, eager, and vibrant. When I began teaching, all the students were male and they found it difficult to believe that I had the qualifications to be their instructor in anatomy. I was a woman, after all, and in my mid-twenties, so not much older than them. It wasn't always easy to deal with the students or my male colleagues. The latter would often tease me: "Do you really have a master's degree in biology?" they would ask. I knew deep inside they doubted my capabilities, but I also knew I was better qualified than they were. As for the students, they quickly learned who was boss and to take their work seriously. A failing grade from me counted as much as it did from my male colleagues, and that was a language they understood.

Soon after I began working with Professor Hofmann, I made a decision that enhanced my independence but was not very smart. I decided I needed a car. Nderitu and Elizabeth lived far from the center of Nairobi and had only one car, which made our commute into work complicated. One day I said to Elizabeth, "Let's go and buy a car. I have money." So I went to the bank, withdrew all my money, and bought a tiny, white, brand-new Toyota, with cash. I didn't even know how to drive! In many ways, I wasn't a very good investor then. If I knew then what I know now, I would have invested the money in a house.

But I was young, it was the swinging sixties, and now that we had a car, my friend and I could truly be mobile young women around town, together or separately—once I learned how to drive. This gave me a deep sense of independence. I also received a university flat, next to the women's dormitory on campus, and became a warden for the women's hall. It was very safe and close to town, so to me it seemed perfect.

Nairobi in the 1960s was known as the Green City in the Sun. It was a pleasant place and very livable, and had many open spaces, although a number of them have since been built on. Nairobi National Park, a piece of wild grassland that still sits on the edge of Nairobi, was much larger then and the grasslands weren't far from the city center. Nairobi then had fewer than half a million people, a sixth of its population today.

In the early years of independence and through much of Kenyatta's time, most of the development in the country was concentrated in Nairobi. Eventually, if you had nothing, you went to Nairobi, but in the 1960s it was the professional class that came to the city. Although Nairobi was relatively small compared to, for example, New York, it was along with Johannesburg and Cape Town a main hub in sub-Saharan Africa and we were proud of it.

There were no street children and no slums. Even Kibera, which is now the largest slum in Africa, had few inhabitants. Its land was still covered in trees and vegetation, although then, as now, there was little infrastructure. (Even today, Kibera's half a million residents have limited access to electricity and running water.) Nairobi's buses then were seldom overcrowded, garbage collection was regular, and the whole city was clean. My women friends and I would regularly stroll among the small shops and cafés in the city center without fear of being mugged or raped.

My friends and I also enjoyed Nairobi by night. We went out to clubs, chatting and dancing to the British and American rock 'n' roll, rumba, and all the dances then in fashion. In the 1960s, you didn't dance alone! So a number of young men, many of whom had also studied in America, went out with my friends and me. We had a comradeship based on our shared experiences in the United States. Nevertheless, while we were enjoying ourselves, we were also being constantly reminded by our close friends who were getting married that this freedom was probably not going to last forever.

While my family never put pressure on me to find a husband, my aunt Nyakweya the storyteller always made it her business to declare that a woman's biological clock ticks constantly. Any time I attended a wedding in Ihithe, she would remark on the importance of a woman marrying in good time—not waiting for too long and not paying her debt to society. She would look at me out of the corner of her eye and hope I was listening to her every word. I would smile back at her playfully, but I got the message!

In April 1966, I met Mwangi Mathai, the man who would become my husband, through mutual friends. He was a good man, very handsome and quite religious. He had grown up in Njoro in the Rift Valley, not far from Nakuru, where his parents had relocated from Nyeri. He had also studied in the United States and worked for various corporations in Kenya before he entered politics. He was always a very good businessman, and in many ways he introduced me to the business world, even though I really felt more at home with books and blackboard chalk at the university. When I eventually let my family know I was going to be married, Aunt Nyakweya could not hide her urge to celebrate. As tradition demanded for a woman, she ululated four times in my honor. I could see that my mother and aunt were genuinely happy for me and knew that I was happy, too.

That first year back in Kenya was a busy one. In addition to starting my job at the university and meeting my husband, I also needed to assist my family. To that end, I brought my two sisters Beatrice and Monica to Nairobi. My idea was that since neither of them had gone to university, they should learn a trade, such as typing, to make them more competitive in the job market and able to support themselves. They also needed a place to stay and something to do. So I rented a small shop on the corner of Second Avenue in the Eastleigh area of Nairobi and established a general store that sold milk, soft drinks, vegetables, grains, snacks, and other general provisions. When they weren't studying in the secretarial college, my sisters worked in the shop and lived in an apartment at the back.

I did not have much capital to build the business (it was all tied up in my car!), but I did my best. I would wake up very early in the morning and go to Marigiti, the city's largest food market, where I would buy vegetables and bring them to the shop. Then I would report to the university looking so professional that they'd never imagine I had spent the morning out buying vegetables. At least twice a week I would replenish the supplies from wholesale shops in the center of town. In time, Beatrice excelled at typing and found secure employment as a secretary in a government office. Monica became very interested in the business and ultimately became the shop's manager.

Early in 1967, Professor Hofmann told me that he anticipated the arrival of many more electron microscopes in Kenya and asked me to consider deepening my knowledge of electron microscopy and carrying out some of my Ph.D. research at the University of Giessen. I assured him of my interest in doing this and left for Germany later in 1967. Before I did, though, I asked Mwangi to help my sisters manage the shop and look after my car. As it turned out, while I was away my small business flourished, so much so it needed more space. Mwangi sold my car to raise some capital for the shop, created a company out of it, added more capital, bought the building, and made himself a minor partner. When I returned to Nairobi, I hardly recognized the place: The original business had been incorporated into Mwangi Investment Ltd., which eventually became a huge operation.

I stayed in Germany for about twenty months. I missed my family, friends, and Mwangi, but going to America had made me adaptable. When I get into an environment, I tend to take it as it is. I don't presuppose what it should be like, so I'm therefore not disappointed if it is not what I expected; instead, I'm excited by its newness and difference. I knew I would not be in Germany forever, so I tried to enjoy my time there and apply myself. In the United States, everything had been new: I was twenty years old, it was my first time living in another country, I was in college and far from home. But when I went to Germany I was twenty-seven, more mature, more focused, and working on my doctorate. I also felt stable in my personal life; I was, after all, engaged and looking forward to getting married. Unlike Mwangi, however, I was not in a huge hurry. He was obviously worried I might stay in Germany longer than was good for his plans. Therefore, he wrote me many letters and sent emissaries to persuade me to return to Kenya so we could start our family.

Although I was formally registered with the University of Giessen, I spent most of my time at the University of Munich, in Bavaria, where I did the bulk of my dissertation research under the supervision of Professor Peter Walter. This entailed frequent travel back and forth between Munich and Giessen, which took about half a day on the train. However, as you might expect, the German trains were reliable and punctual and traveling through the countryside was a delight because it was clean, green, and fresh. Professor Walter was very supportive, and I made some wonderful German friends.

In Munich I lived in a *Studentenhaus* (student house), close to the university in a neighborhood full of little restaurants, theaters, and places to drink German beer for those who preferred beer to wine. I loved German wine. I loved Munich, too, and particularly enjoyed the English Garden, which was next to the School of Veterinary Medicine. It is Europe's largest park, nearly two and a half square miles, and lies alongside the Isar River. In summer, the garden was full of brightly colored flowers, green trees, and expansive lawns. In winter, my friends and I walked there and enjoyed the snow and the quiet. The park was very safe, even at night. It was a wonderful place for me to escape and reflect on the journey I was on in Germany.

I supplemented my knowledge of German with courses at the Goethe Institute and found it relatively easy to speak or listen to German in classes or in the world outside the universities. Being in Bavaria was very interesting, especially with respect to language. One of my friends was a veterinary doctor, Fräulein Koch, who was a lovely young lady. When we were at the university, she always spoke to me in High German, which I could follow. But as soon as we stepped into the streets, Fräulein Dr. Koch would speak to her friends in Bavarian dialect and completely lose me!

The countryside in the southern highlands of Germany was beautiful and very green. Occasionally I would go with friends from the university into the mountains. I also vividly remember the annual carnival, or *Fasching*. Traditionally, *Fasching* represented the two-month period before Lent when people would indulge in pleasures forbidden to them once Lent began. During this time, a good deal of drinking and dressing up in elaborate disguises took place. Sometimes I couldn't even recognize my friends in the costumes they spent hours and lots of money creating. Today *Fasching* is a time for fun and laughter, whether you are going to observe Lent or not.

Having been in America made it easier for me to have fun in Germany. My exposure to Europe, which had brought Christianity to Kenya, helped me see that there should be no conflict between the positive aspects of our traditional culture and Christianity. After all, Europeans were themselves very close to their culture: How could it be bad when Africans held on to their culture even as they embraced Christianity? This was important to me because my culture was ruthlessly destroyed under the pretense that its values and those of Christianity were in conflict. I watched in awe and admiration as Westerners embraced their culture and found no contradiction between it and their Christian heritage.

In the spring of 1969, I returned to Nairobi and rejoined the University College of Nairobi, now as an assistant lecturer, and continued to do research for and write my dissertation. I also resumed teaching. Mwangi and I were married in May. He was thirty-four and I was twenty-nine. Reflecting our lives in both worlds, we had two different ceremonies—a traditional one, held on my father's farm in Nakuru, and a Catholic wedding at Our Lady Queen of Peace Church in Nairobi, for which I wore a long, white Western-style wedding dress with a veil and carried a bouquet of white flowers. I also wore a beaded necklace with nine strings, which represented the married daughters of Gikuyu and Mumbi, the primordial parents of all Kikuyus. It had been made especially for me, for that day.

By this time, Mwangi had decided to run for a seat in Parliament in that year's election, the second since independence, and had started his political campaign. Rather unexpectedly, I found myself part of this campaign. It was very demanding since I had to combine my teaching and dissertation with politicking. Sometimes I would work all night, even though I was also pregnant with our first child.

I was expected to be a superwoman, which I wasn't, and consequently the campaign was both trying and tiring. I hoped my partner appreciated what I was sacrificing for him.

I was very conscious of the fact that a highly educated woman like me ran the risk of making her husband lose votes and support if I was accused of not being enough of an African woman, of being "a white woman in black skin." This meant that competitors and detractors would visit our home with a double agenda: Some would claim to be supporters and want Mwangi's guidance, while others would look for gossip that could be used in public rallies to embarrass him and lose him votes. I treated everyone the same, even when it was obvious they were detractors. They were often surprised that I spoke Kikuyu, as well as the national (Kiswahili) and the official (English) languages, and that they were received warmly and treated with respect and dignity by a woman they all knew was a lecturer at the University College of Nairobi.

Like any woman without my academic credentials I attended to my home, personally received and served guests, and made them feel welcome. It was important for me to demonstrate to people that they *were* welcome in our home. What they encountered was very different from what they expected. I served them personally with food no matter the time of day or night or whether they were hungry or not. Once a woman had fulfilled these obligations, she could sit and talk with the guests. This wasn't a problem for me. I did it naturally and still do, even though I'm no longer a politician's wife. The training I got as "a good African woman" during the campaigns still serves me well: If you come to my house, I still get the urge to rush to the kitchen and make you something to eat, never mind how worn out I feel at the end of the day!

This attitude of many of our people was curious given that Kenyan politicians were part of the elite. Like Mwangi, many had been educated abroad, spoke English at home and in their workplaces, wore European-style clothes, and lived in European-style houses. But they wanted to project their "Africanness" through their wives, both at home and in society. Women are commonly described as carriers and promoters of culture. Yet men are also carriers of culture: Why in these instances couldn't they express it?

Another reality of being a politician's wife was that I was constantly in public, whether with Mwangi on the campaign trail or, as often was the case, representing him at forums where I was the featured speaker. This experience led me over the next few years to develop the style I maintain to this day. It became important for me not to wear clothing that might put me in a compromising situation because it was too tight-fitting or short. Therefore, long dresses and skirts became practical as well as comfortable and stylish. I gradually abandoned the short dresses (even my nice red one!), trousers, and high heels I had accumulated and loved to wear in America when I was single and independent.

Nineteen sixty-nine was a challenging year in many ways. My second brother, Kibicho, died at the young age of thirty-nine of pancreatitis. Although my oldest brother, Nderitu, had been more influential in my life, I was closer in age to Kibicho and we grew up together. It was a great shock to see him pass away so young and for his children to be left without a father.

There was also another death that greatly affected me: One late afternoon in the middle of the campaign, Mwangi came home with a terrible look on his face. "What's happened?" I asked, worried.

"Mboya has been killed," he replied, agitatedly. It was stunning news. This was the same Tom Mboya who had been instrumental in the Kennedy Airlift and who had become minister for economic planning and development in Jomo Kenyatta's postindependence administration.

Mboya was a member of the Luo community (Kenya's second-largest ethnic group) and had been seen as a successor to Kenyatta. His death, supposedly at the hands of a Kikuyu, roiled the country and has since caused much mistrust and suspicion between the two communities. It was also a watershed in the short history of independent Kenya. Soon after Mboya's assassination and the 1969 elections, Kenyatta banned the Kenya People's Union (KPU), an opposition party founded in 1966, and arrested its leader, Oginga Odinga, another prominent Luo. This effectively brought an end to the multiparty system in Kenya, a system that would not be revived for another twenty-three years.

Unfortunately, when the elections were held in early December, Mwangi narrowly lost. He returned to work at the Colgate-Palmolive Corporation and began planning his second run for 1974. Happily for us, a few weeks later our first child, a boy, was born. I had had a good pregnancy and the delivery, at Nairobi Hospital, went well. In line with Kikuyu tradition, we named our son Waweru, after Mwangi's father. I took a few weeks off from the university but went straight back afterward. I hired a nanny to take care of Waweru during the day, although at lunchtime I came home to nurse him, even though these were the days when African women were being advised not to breastfeed but instead to give their babies formula.

I enjoyed being a mother and had a wonderful time during those early years with Waweru and then with our two other children, Wanjira, our daughter, whom we named for Mwangi's mother, and Muta, our second son, named for my father. (If we had had a second daughter, she would have been named for my mother, Wanjiru.)

In 1971, I completed my Ph.D. on the development and differentiation of gonads in bovines, which deepened my understanding of how sexual organs develop to become female or male. I spent hours at the microscope, studying tissues and describing the developmental anatomy of these organs. The degree was awarded by the University College of Nairobi, which was still a constituent college of the University of East Africa. I was among the last students to be awarded a degree by that university. The University College of Nairobi was dissolved shortly afterward, and the constituent colleges became full-fledged universities—of Nairobi, Dar es Salaam, and Makerere. The University of Nairobi was Kenya's first national university.

With Mwangi accompanying me, I walked up to the dais to receive my diploma from President Kenyatta, who as the head of state was also the university's chancellor. I was the first woman in East and Central Africa to receive a doctoral degree—a significant achievement that went largely unnoticed. It didn't even make the media headlines, probably because I was not the president, or his daughter, and my husband wasn't famous. It is funny how such things can be conveniently ignored. By that time, I was expecting Wanjira and it was only a matter of a few months before she arrived, the day after Christmas.

When I received my Ph.D., the university's School of Veterinary Medicine was in full swing. More and more Kenyans were taking over positions from retiring professors who had established and then led academic departments in the years after independence. After the completion of my Ph.D. work, I was made a senior lecturer. I enjoyed teaching. I have heard that students thought me to be a serious and dedicated teacher. None of them complimented me then but I also know that I wouldn't have gotten away with less.

My classes consisted of a lecture that took place in the lab, after which the students would try to see for themselves under the microscope what I had just taught them. Once the students started looking at slides under the microscope, I would go around to each one and make sure they had really understood. "That looks right," I would say or "That doesn't look quite right. You have to work more on that." To check in individually with each student in the class was natural to me.

In America as well as in Germany professors were very engaged with their students, as was Professor Hofmann, under whom I learned how to teach. I may have picked up this style from him and others I worked with. I also learned to distinguish when students were listening and understanding and when they were lost—that was the time to ask, "Anybody listening?" Going to class unprepared or facing students in a compromised state was completely unacceptable in those days.

Ironically, this approach and method of communication was useful on the political campaign trail because I could engage the public and discuss *with* them rather than preach *to* them. Today, when I meet my former students, it is always very satisfying to hear them express appreciation for the valuable times we shared at Chiromo.

What I did not enjoy at the university was the discrimination I and my fellow female colleagues faced. Bearing in mind my first encounter with the professor of zoology in early 1966, it became important to ensure that female members of staff were accepted as equal members of the university's academic staff and received the same benefits as their male colleagues.

Before Vertistine Mbaya and I arrived, there had never been an African woman among the academic members of staff in the faculty of veterinary sciences at the University of Nairobi, and the number of women on the academic staff of any faculty at the university was at that time tiny. Vertistine, an African American who had come to Kenya in the early 1960s and was married to a Kenyan, Simon Mbaya, taught in the Department of Biochemistry and was qualified to get all the benefits due to academic members of staff. So was I. (A woman married to another member of the academic staff complicated the issuance of benefits such as housing, health insurance, and a pension, because it would mean duplicating benefits. Neither of our husbands, however, enjoyed that status.) I met Professor Mbaya, or Vert, as she is known to her friends, in the second-floor corridor outside our offices at the Chiromo campus. Only three offices separated us and we hit it off immediately. She has been a wonderful and trusted friend ever since.

Vert and I waged this first fight for equality together. Many of the benefits given to male professional staff at the university were legacies of the colonial era, when young male teachers from Britain were encouraged to work in Kenya and other colonies and were provided with incentives in addition to their salaries. These included housing, free tuition for their children's education, and paid holiday time. When Kenya became independent, we took over most of these systems completely intact. The university also had a number of incentives that, taken together, amounted to a large increase of one's salary.

However, the university's full benefits accrued only to men. At that time, only single women or widows on the professional staff could receive university housing. Married women were expected to be housed by their husbands and it was argued that they therefore did not "need" a housing allowance or insurance coverage or a pension. I argued with the university that this was completely unacceptable and that terms of service must be equal. Professional women, I said, could not be discriminated against just because during colonial times no women professionals came to work in the colonies. This seemed a completely reasonable proposition. It never occurred to me that Vert and I would have to *fight* this battle. That I or other women should be paid less than our male colleagues of equal standing was very irritating to us. Because of that type of discrimination, junior male staff took home more than we did, despite our senior academic positions.

We went to the university officials and demanded an explanation for the gender discrimination. "You are married," they informed us, shrugging their shoulders. "You should just take the basic salary because the rest of the services that men get you don't need. Your husband is getting those services from his place of work and he should have you benefit from them. If he does not, too bad." We were outraged by the arrogance and what appeared to be men refusing to accept that a woman can be a professional in her own right. "Well, my husband doesn't help me teach," I argued, raising the alarm for battle.

Our complaints fell on deaf ears. That only made us more determined. The members of the academic staff operated the university Academic Staff Association. When Vert and I were elected association officials, we decided to engage the university authorities using the official positions we now occupied. Unfortunately, the association could not negotiate with the university over salaries and benefits, which is what we wanted, because its legal status did not allow this. We therefore decided to turn the association into a union, which could negotiate. This was controversial for many reasons, not least because the chancellor of the university was also the president of the country. Therefore, when we tried to make the association into a union through the courts, it was tantamount to taking the president to court. I need not tell you how easy it was for this case to be dismissed.

In the end, however, the university must have decided that to maintain peace the two of us should be given what we were asking for. From then on, although women colleagues continued to be paid less than their male counterparts and did not receive equal benefits, Vert and I were treated like honorary male professors! We continued to campaign, urging women—especially those married to academic members of staff or civil servants (all of whom received superior terms and incentives)—not to sign discriminatory terms-of-service contracts that would, for example, deny their children the medical insurance coverage and deny them the pension granted our male colleagues.

However, the women refused to join us. Many said they'd been advised by their husbands not to be part of that struggle. Perhaps it is not surprising. Those women opposing our campaign were portraying us as women who didn't want to live with our husbands, which of course was not true. Fighting battles with women can be very difficult and sad, because both society and the women themselves often make it appear that most women are happy with the little they have and have no intention of fighting for their rights. I am often confronted by women who have waited until that security called "man" is no longer available to them to remember that they should have protected their rights, irrespective of the men in their lives. That is when women will say, "You know how men are!"

Since then, things have changed quite a lot. Now there are quite a few women members of the academic staff at the university and the terms of service have greatly improved for everyone, including women.

This experience was an eye-opener for me. I had never anticipated that I would be discriminated against on the basis of my gender as often as I was, or that I could be belittled even while making a substantial contribution to society. I did not want to accept that one human being would deliberately seek to limit another, and I found myself challenging the idea that a woman could not be as good as or better than a man.

What the struggle for equality at the university also taught me was that sometimes you have to hold on to what you believe in because not everybody wishes you well or will give you what you deserve—not even your fellow women. Indeed, I found myself wanting to be more than the equal of some of the men I knew. I had higher aspirations and did not want to be compared with men of lesser ability and capacity. I wanted to be me.

To their credit, I never heard any criticism from the male colleagues with whom Vert and I raised these issues. Many of them were involved in our advocacy for a staff union and would have agreed that there was no reason on earth that I should receive less money than my technician. I dare say that some men probably didn't like the idea of their wives being independent in terms of housing, medical coverage, or bringing a larger portion of salary or benefits to the household. Fortunately, Mwangi was not bothered. We were already living in a university house on a leafy street in an upscale area of Nairobi.

In retrospect, Mwangi was a beneficiary of our struggle. Once Vert and I won, she and I each received a considerable sum of money as arrears to cover the period when we did not live in university houses. Using that money, Mwangi and I bought a house in Nairobi on Lenana Road, but only his name appeared on the title deed. I could have insisted that my name also appear on the deed, but I chose to let that sleeping dog lie. In retrospect, I should have insisted—some years later, when I resigned from the university and was suddenly without shelter, I could not lay claim to that house.

Despite Vert's and my activism for equal wages and benefits, my career did not stall at the university. In 1974, I was named senior lecturer in anatomy, then, two years later, chair of the Department of Veterinary Anatomy, and finally, in 1977, associate professor. Even though my colleagues and I did not make a big deal out of it, I was the first woman in all of these positions. I was quite set on an academic career, and looked forward to being named a full professor and, after that, perhaps dean of the School of Veterinary Medicine. Aspiring to be the university's head, the vice-chancellor, would have been considered too ambitious for a woman in the 1970s!

The strange fact is that throughout my career at the university, I was at the School of Veterinary Medicine and yet I was not a vet. So I would have had to have been extremely good for my colleagues to agree that I could be the head of the faculty. Of course, even if I had been a vet, some of the men at the university would probably have fought me, but it would have been harder for them if my qualifications were in veterinary sciences. For that reason, I knew that the way to the top of the School of Veterinary Medicine would always be an uphill battle.

The reality that I was not a vet was lost on many people I knew, including my friends. I had been in that faculty for so long that many people believed that I must be a veterinary doctor. I'd get calls and they'd say, "My cat is sick. What should I do?" or "The dog isn't feeling well. What can you do for him?" Sometimes my friends even brought their sick animals to my office! I would also go to parties where a goat would be slaughtered for that night's meal. Before they are eaten, goats are supposed to be inspected by a vet, so when I arrived, my friends would say, "We haven't started. We were waiting for you to inspect the goat." I would reply, "I'll inspect the goat, but you eat it at your own risk!"

6

Foresters Without Diplomas

A great river always begins somewhere. Often it starts as a tiny spring bubbling up from a crack in the soil, just like the little stream on my family's land in Ihithe, which starts where the roots of the fig tree broke through the rocks beneath the ground. But for the stream to grow into a river, it must meet other tributaries and join them as it heads for a lake or the sea. So, when people learn about my life and the work of the Green Belt Movement and ask me "Why trees?," the truth of the matter is that the question has many answers. The essential one was that I reacted to a set of problems by focusing on what could be done. As it turned out, the idea that sprang from my roots merged with other sources of knowledge and action to form a confluence that grew bigger than I would ever have imagined.

In the early 1970s, in addition to my work at the University of Nairobi, I was involved with a number of civic organizations, including the Nairobi branch of the Kenya Red Cross of which I became director in 1973, and the Kenya Association of University Women. Many of these organizations had been founded by the British and staffed almost entirely by the wives of colonial officials. After independence, Africans gradually replaced the white women. Educated Kenyan women, of whom there were still very few in the early 1970s, were often asked to volunteer their time in positions of leadership.

I was invited to join the local board of the Environment Liaison Centre. The Centre had been established in 1974 by a group of international environmental organizations to ensure the participation of civil society groups (also known as nongovernmental organizations, or NGOs) in the work of the United Nations Environment Programme (UNEP), whose headquarters were established in Nairobi. UNEP, the first (and only) UN agency devoted to environmental issues and the only one headquartered in the developing world, was launched following the first United Nations global conference on the environment, held in Stockholm in 1972. The Stockholm conference helped raise awareness of the realities of environmental degradation in Africa and other regions, even though many developing countries' governments didn't agree with the solutions to the environmental crisis put forth by the industrialized nations, which they viewed as seeking to inhibit the development of poor countries.

Most of the originators of the Environment Liaison Centre (now called the Environment Liaison Centre International) were from Europe, North America, and Asia, and felt it was important for local people—Kenyans—to serve as "alternate," or local, board members. I was one of the few women members of the local board and became an alternate for Huey Johnson of the Resource Renewal Institute in California. Huey became a good friend and supporter and remains so to this day.

For me, a biologist who had grown up in a rural area where our daily lives depended on the health of the environment, the issues raised at the Liaison Centre were not completely strange. For example, when we discussed biological diversity, my study of genetics was relevant. But a great deal of the information I was exposed to through meetings at UNEP, books and articles, and discussions with people working in environmental NGOs in different countries was new to me. Much of it dealt with natural sciences from a holistic perspective. Through the Liaison Centre, a whole different world opened up to me. In time, my colleagues elected me chair of the local board, a position I was to hold for more than ten years. I became so preoccupied with my voluntary work with the Liaison Centre that it almost became my second full-time career!

Another stream that contributed to my growing environmental

awareness was academic. In the early 1970s, Kenya was the best pro-
ducer of livestock products in East Africa. At the university I participated in research in veterinary medicine in an effort to keep domestic
animals healthy and productive, not just in Kenya but throughout
the region. Consequently, I undertook postdoctoral research on the
life cycle of a parasite responsible for East Coast fever, a disease fatal
to imported hybrid cattle that is spread through brown ear ticks.
Local bovines are almost immune to the disease. I collected hundreds of the ticks from the cattle, incised them through the salivary
glands (where the parasite lodged), cut them up for microscopic observation, and produced thousands of slides.

While I was in the rural areas outside Nairobi collecting the ticks,
I noticed that the rivers would rush down the hillsides and along
paths and roads when it rained, and that they were muddy with silt.
This was very different from when I was growing up. "That is soil
erosion," I remember thinking to myself. "We must do something
about that." I also observed that the cows were so skinny that I
could count their ribs. There was little grass or other fodder for them
to eat where they grazed, and during the dry season much of the
grass lacked nutrients.

The people, too, looked undernourished and poor and the vegetation in their fields was scanty. The soils in the fields weren't
performing as they should because their nutrient value had been
depleted. It became clear to me through these observations that
Kenya's and the whole region's livestock industry was threatened
more by environmental degradation than by either the ticks in the
cows' ears or the parasites in the ticks' salivary glands.

When I went home to visit my family in Nyeri, I had another indication of the changes under way around us. I saw rivers silted with
topsoil, much of which was coming from the forest where plantations of commercial trees had replaced indigenous forest. I noticed
that much of the land that had been covered by trees, bushes, and
grasses when I was growing up had been replaced by tea and coffee.

I also learned that someone had acquired the piece of land where

the fig tree I was in awe of as a child had stood. The new owner perceived the tree to be a nuisance because it took up too much space
and he felled it to make room to grow tea. By then I understood
the connection between the tree and water, so it did not surprise
me that when the fig tree was cut down, the stream where I had
played with the tadpoles dried up. My children would never be able
to play with the frogs' eggs as I had or simply to enjoy the cool,
clear water of that stream. I mourned the loss of that tree. I profoundly appreciated the wisdom of my people, and how generations
of women had passed on to their daughters the cultural tradition
of leaving the fig trees in place. I was expected to pass it on to my
children, too.

Whatever the original inspiration for not cutting these trees, people in that region had been spared landslides, as the strong roots of
the fig trees held the soil together in the steep mountains. They also
had abundant, clean water. But by the early 1970s, landslides were
becoming common and sources of clean water for drinking were
becoming scarce. Ironically, the area where the fig tree of my childhood once stood always remained a patch of bare ground where
nothing grew. It was as if the land rejected anything but the fig tree
itself.

Another tributary of knowledge consisted of the women themselves, who brought the urgency of the situation home to me. By the
early 1970s, I was a member of the National Council of Women of
Kenya (NCWK). The NCWK was founded in 1964 as an umbrella
organization to unify women's groups, both large and small, throughout Kenya, with membership drawn from urban and rural areas. The
leadership consisted of women who were successful in their business, professional, or religious lives and they gave one another moral
support in whatever sphere they were involved.

At a seminar organized by the NCWK, a woman researcher presented the results of a study she had done, which found that chil-

dren in the central region of Kenya were suffering from diseases associated with malnutrition. This was an eye-opener for me, since that is where I come from and I knew from personal experience that the central region was one of the most fertile in Kenya. But times had changed. Many farmers had converted practically all of their land into growing coffee and tea to sell in the international market. These "cash crops" were occupying land previously used to produce food for people to eat.

Consequently, women were feeding their families processed foods like white bread, maize flour, and white rice, all of which are high in carbohydrates but relatively low in vitamins, proteins, and minerals. Cooking these foods consumed less energy than the foods I had eaten as a child, and this made them attractive and practical, because available firewood for cooking was limited due to deforestation in the region. Instead, women were using as fuel materials left over from the harvest, such as corn stems and husks. This shortage of firewood, the researcher concluded, was leading directly to malnutrition as people's diets changed in response. The most vulnerable were children and the elderly.

These facts troubled me, not least because they seemed so contrary to my experiences as a child—when there was more than enough food, the food itself was nutritious and wholesome, people were healthy and strong, and there was always enough firewood to cook with. I remembered how the colonial administration had cleared the indigenous forests and replaced them with plantations of exotic trees for the timber industry. After independence, Kenyan farmers had cleared more natural forests to create space to grow coffee and tea. Until now, however, I had not fully appreciated the multiple costs of these activities.

Although the leadership of the NCWK was generally elite and urban, we were concerned with the social and economic status of the majority of our members, who were poor, rural women. We worried about their access to clean water and firewood, how they would feed their children, pay their school fees, and afford clothing, and we wondered what we could do to ease their burdens. We had a choice: We could either sit in an ivory tower wondering how so many people could be so poor and not be working to change their situation, or we could try to help them escape the vicious cycle they found themselves in. This was not a remote problem for us. The rural areas were where our mothers and sisters still lived. We owed it to them to do all we could.

At the same time, women in other countries throughout the world were recognizing the need to make changes in their own communities and bring their perspectives and experiences to the global arena, and their political leaders were giving them increasing space to do so. In June 1975, to coincide with the International Women's Year, 133 governments and about 4,000 women from around the world gathered in Mexico City for the first UN conference on women.

In the two years leading up to the women's conference, at both the Environment Liaison Centre and the NCWK, we were asking ourselves what our agenda should be for Mexico City. The NCWK held a number of seminars at which we heard from various constituencies, including women from the rural areas. These women confirmed what the researcher's study had suggested. They didn't have enough wood for fuel or fencing, fodder for their livestock, water to cook with or drink, or enough for themselves or their families to eat.

As I sat listening to the women talk about water, energy, and nutrition, I could see that everything they lacked depended on the environment. These women were laying out their agenda. When the representatives of the NCWK returned from the Mexico City conference (I was unable to go because there were not sufficient funds), they carried the same message: We needed to do something about water and energy. The conference participants had also concluded that the world needed to address the realities of rural women, their poverty, the overall lack of development, and the state of the environment that sustained them.

It suddenly became clear. Not only was the livestock industry threatened by a deteriorating environment, but I, my children, my students, my fellow citizens, and my entire country would pay the price. The connection between the symptoms of environmental degradation and their causes—deforestation, devegetation, unsustainable agriculture, and soil loss—were self-evident. Something had to be done. We could not just deal with the manifestations of the problems. We had to get to the root causes of those problems.

Now, it is one thing to understand the issues. It is quite another to do something about them. But I have always been interested in finding solutions. This is, I believe, a result of my education as well as my time in America: to think of what can be done rather than worrying about what cannot. I didn't sit down and ask myself, "Now let me see; what shall I do?" It just came to me: "Why not plant trees?" The trees would provide a supply of wood that would enable women to cook nutritious foods. They would also have wood for fencing and fodder for cattle and goats. The trees would offer shade for humans and animals, protect watersheds and bind the soil, and, if they were fruit trees, provide food. They would also heal the land by bringing back birds and small animals and regenerate the vitality of the earth.

This is how the Green Belt Movement began. The rest of it perhaps was sheer luck: If I'd picked something other than trees my efforts might have failed, and I may have remained at the University of Nairobi as a professor and now be retired and enjoying my pension. But that wouldn't have been half as interesting. When I reflect on the years leading to the creation of the Green Belt Movement and the years of its emergence and growth, it also seems no coincidence that it was nurtured during the time the global women's movement was taking off, or that it flourished during the decade for women (1976–1985) the United Nations declared in Mexico City.

By 1975, I already had an idea of how I might go about encouraging the planting of trees because of events that were happening simultaneously in my personal life. In spite of his defeat in 1969, my husband's appetite for politics had not diminished. In 1974 he decided to run for Parliament again for the same constituency, Lang'ata, that he had contested five years earlier. I supported this decision and worked very hard to make sure that this time he won. This was a tall order since I was still working full time at the university and we now had three children, including a newborn, Muta. Nevertheless, we worked together and separately on the campaign trail, visiting people and talking to them about their aspirations. We were a young and highly educated couple, and I could see how much hope people were investing in us. They believed we could make a difference in their lives.

By this time, unemployment had become a major issue for Kenya and lack of jobs was one of the voters' main concerns. In the course of the campaign, Mwangi promised that he would create more employment for people if they voted for him. This worried me a lot. When I make a promise, I expect to keep it, and if I cannot deliver something, then I do not promise that I will. But Mwangi kept on saying that jobs would be found. "Where will he get these jobs from?" I thought to myself. "There are no jobs these days." We couldn't simply knock on doors and ask people to give the voters jobs. Many of them had no academic qualifications or marketable skills and were illiterate. It simply wasn't possible.

But I have never been interested in what is not possible. "I'm going to plan," I said to myself. "I'm going to make sure these people have jobs, or they will never vote for us again, because we've broken our promise." When Mwangi won the election, I was proud of his achievement. I was in the speaker's gallery when he took his oath of office and was genuinely happy for him. I knew that he was happy, too; he was now an honorable member of Parliament. After he had taken his oath of office, I raised the issue of his promises. "What are you going to do with all the people you promised the jobs to?" I asked. "That was the campaign," he replied. "Now we are in Parliament."

"But they might not vote for us the next time," I urged him to remember.

"Don't worry, they won't remember."

I couldn't believe what I was hearing. "Excuse me?" I cried. "Of course, they'll remember! How can we face these people in another campaign? How can we walk around asking for their votes? Don't you think they'll ask, 'Where are those jobs you promised?' " Mwangi told me not to worry. But I did. I refused to accept that we should break our promises so easily. Soon after, I launched a business that I hoped could provide many jobs and would incorporate the planting of trees. I called it Envirocare Ltd.

Now, Lang'ata constituency contained many of the richest as well as some of the poorest parts of the city, including a section of the expansive Kibera slum. The wealthy areas consisted of huge estates with many large and luxuriant gardens. To me these gardens never looked well maintained, even though the owners of the estates employed servants to look after them throughout the year. I thought that I could change that. My idea was simple: Why not bring a whole army of men and women into these gardens and let them do everything that needed to be done, in one day? The owner of the house would come home to find his garden looking perfect and he would need only to call us again when his hedges needed trimming or his flowerbeds required tending or new trees needed to be planted. Furthermore, the owner could enjoy his garden by himself, without having servants wandering around it each day.

Envirocare would employ people from the poor part of Mwangi's constituency, who needed jobs, to keep happy the richer members of the constituency, who could afford to employ them. They would also plant seedlings in parts of the city that were bare of trees. In the process we would create a beautiful Nairobi! It seemed to me a perfect solution, and I thought the wealthy people would support it. Envirocare would be located in our house, and my idea was that, in addition to providing employment, it would become a forum through which Mwangi and I could listen and respond to the concerns of his constituents.

During the campaign, a family friend who had campaigned for

Mwangi with me introduced me to Kimathi wa Murage, a forester in charge of Karura Forest to the north of Nairobi—the site twenty-five years later of a standoff between myself and government forces. The friend explained to Mr. Murage that I wanted to establish a tree nursery so that the people in Lang'ata who needed jobs could plant seedlings. Mr. Murage told me I could start a tree nursery right next to his government nursery. So I hired a young man, Charles Githogori, to look after it and this became my first tree nursery. It gave me the confidence that I might be able to fulfill the promises made to the Lang'ata constituents.

Unfortunately, Envirocare met with numerous problems. The rich residents of Lang'ata didn't seem to want lots of poor people wandering around their gardens, if only for a day or so. They seemed to enjoy their gardeners being around. In addition, when Envirocare was hired, the homeowners would not pay me in advance. This posed a problem since the people I was employing were so poor they needed me to pay them at least half of the fee Envirocare charged the homeowner and couldn't afford to wait to get their money at the end of the month.

Whenever they were employed, I also had to cover the costs of transporting the workers to and from Kibera, where they lived. All of this meant I had to pay out of my own pocket, and I was not a wealthy woman. My husband thought my idea wasn't very bright and saw no reason to help me with the expenses. So I wasn't getting support either from the people I was trying to help or from the man whose promises I was attempting to keep.

Still, I kept on trying to find a way to make it work. I decided that I could raise awareness and money for Envirocare by selling seedlings. As part of seeking a market for the seedlings, I decided to attend the five-day-long annual International Show that took place in Nairobi in 1975. The show is organized to highlight innovative approaches to agriculture and raise awareness of its importance to Kenya as a whole. I brought all the seedlings from the Karura Forest nursery and arranged them in the shape of a map of Kenya, drawing attention to the regions of the country where trees were desperately needed to regenerate the land.

After the show, because I had no proper place for people to collect the seedlings, I used our home address as the location for people to pick them up. This meant that I had to keep all the seedlings in our compound, then on Kabarnet Road near Kibera. That's when my husband really thought I was crazy, because there were trees all over the house and yard. But while some people at the show expressed interest in tree planting, particularly on their farms outside of Nairobi, they did not buy any seedlings. Neither did they come to my home for them. So the trees just sat there in the compound.

As you can imagine, this was dispiriting, but I still thought planting trees was a good idea and that people were interested in doing it, if I could just find a way to make it take root. Several things happened that enabled me to break through the obstacles I had encountered. By this time I had become good friends with Hanne Marstrand, who was then a friend of Maurice String, then the executive director of UNEP. Like me, Hanne was interested in the work of the Red Cross and she and I worked together to address the needs of Nairobi's growing population of street children. Hanne and Maurice later married and settled in Canada. When I discussed Envirocare with Hanne and Maurice, they both thought that planting trees in Kenya was a good idea. "That's what *we're* trying to encourage at UNEP," Maurice said.

As a result of our conversations and my work with the Environment Liaison Centre, UNEP made it possible for me to attend the first UN conference on human settlements, known as Habitat I, in Vancouver, Canada, for two weeks in June 1976. Habitat I examined the spread of cities around the world and the problems associated with this, including the creation of concrete jungles and air pollution from vehicles. One of the solutions the conference participants pointed to was "greener" cities that had more trees and vegetation in them. Among the speakers at the conference who most impressed me were noted anthropologist Margaret Mead, Mother Teresa of

Calcutta, and the British economist and journalist Barbara Ward. This was the first time I had been to a global meeting of this kind and listened to such inspiring women leaders.

The beautiful surroundings of British Columbia and the engaging with people who shared my evolving concern for the environment were just the tonic I needed after the disappointment of Envirocare. I returned to Kenya reenergized and determined to make my idea work. Sadly, I also returned to a water shortage in Nairobi. Most of the seedlings died and the tree nursery collapsed. My husband also had had quite enough of living with trees everywhere he looked. Envirocare had run its course.

The concept of tree planting, however, remained alive. In 1977, two years after the women's conference in Mexico City, the National Council of Women of Kenya invited me to talk about my experiences at the Habitat I meeting and shortly afterward elected me a member of its Executive Committee as well as its Standing Committee on Environment and Habitat. Within this setting I again proposed planting trees as an activity the NCWK could take on to assist its rural members and so meet the women's needs. The membership agreed and encouraged me to put my idea into action.

A name was needed for this new venture. I wanted to place tree planting within the spirit of Jomo Kenyatta's idea of community mobilization, which he popularized in the national slogan *Harambee!* (Kiswahili for "Let us all pull together"). I suggested to the NCWK that we call our project Save the Land Harambee. My vision was that, instead of fund-raising for this initiative, the harambee spirit would inspire Kenyans, both wealthy and poor, to plant trees to protect our country from desertification. In so doing, Kenyans would also safeguard the livelihoods of millions of small-scale farmers from the Sahara Desert's spread southward and the drying out of land as forests were cleared.

My father had also planted many trees on his land in Nakuru and

Nyeri, so I may well have inherited my affinity for trees! Planting trees for the public good also echoed the work of pioneering organizations such as Men of the Trees, founded by senior chief Josiah Njonjo and the Englishman Richard St. Barbe Baker, which since the 1920s has tried to promote planting of trees in Kenya. This organization continues to flourish in Australia and Britain, but unfortunately failed to take off in Kenya.

On June 5, 1977, Kenya marked the worldwide celebrations of World Environment Day with a procession and tree-planting ceremony organized by the NCWK's new initiative, Save the Land Harambee. Hundreds of us, led by a boys' marching band, walked two miles from the Kenyatta International Conference Centre in downtown Nairobi to Kamukunji Park on the outskirts of the city. There we planted seven trees. Joining us at the ceremony were the mayor, Margaret Kenyatta, the daughter of the president, government ministers, local officials, UNEP's deputy executive director, and the NCWK's then chair, Eddah Gachukia, a nominated member of Parliament. A message from President Kenyatta was read and news about the celebration made the front page of the *Daily Nation*, one of Kenya's main newspapers.

I thought that we should have a theme each time we planted trees, to enhance the meaning of our actions. Kamukunji was where Jomo Kenyatta and other leading politicians held rallies, and it was used for public gatherings. I felt that Kenyans of my generation had not adequately honored our forebears and tended to idolize the leadership then in office. This was partly the result of colonialism's trivialization of those who had been leaders before the British arrived or those who had resisted the colonial administration and fought for the restoration of our land and political and economic freedom, and whom the current leaders ignored.

Therefore on that World Environment Day we planted trees in honor of seven people from different ethnic groups, all of whom were community leaders in the late nineteenth and early twentieth centuries: Wangu wa Makeri, a woman chief from Murang'a, not far from Nairobi; Waiyaki wa Hinga, the Kikuyu leader betrayed by Captain Lugard in the 1890s; Madam Ketilili from Kilifi on the north coast; Masaku Ngei, after whom the town of Machakos is named; Nabongo Mumia, a visionary chief during the early colonial period; Ole Lenana, an outstanding Maasai leader; and Gor Mahia wuod Ogalo, a Luo hero. Among the tree species we planted were the nandi flame, broad-leaved cordia, African fig tree, and East African yellow wood. These seven trees formed the first "green belt."

Sadly, since that day in 1977 the fate of Kamukunji has mirrored the way independent Kenya treated its history and potential. Slums have overtaken the park and the grounds are no longer as clean or well maintained as they once were. Although the Green Belt Movement still has a nursery there, the trees we planted that day fell victim to vandalism and the surrounding population's need for firewood. Only two trees survived, but both of those have thrived and are now more than thirty feet tall and their canopies provide shade for local people selling goods and resting.

In August–September 1977, during the United Nations Conference on Desertification in Nairobi, the NCWK organized delegates to plant our second "green belt" on a farm northwest of Nairobi in Naivasha that was owned by eight hundred women. Among those who planted trees that day were Josiah Njonjo and Richard St. Barbe Baker.

We tried to establish the Green Belt Movement in many places in Kenya. After Naivasha, we went to Nyanza near Lake Victoria in the west of the country, and then to Ukambani in Machakos and Kitui, and Kajiado to the south of Nairobi—places that receive little rain, unlike the central region. None of these projects lasted for long. I learned that if you do not have local people who are committed to the process and willing to work with their communities, the projects will not survive. For instance, the Business and Professional Women's Association wanted to start a Green Belt group in Isinya, in Maasailand, the traditional lands of the Maasai people. Generally, this area is very dry. Since the rainfall would not be sufficient for the seedlings as they grew in the nursery, we gave the community two donkeys to use to carry water for the trees. But as soon as the Business and Professional Women's Association and I left Isinya, the project faltered. This happened not only because the people initiating it were not grounded in the community, but also because of the prevailing culture.

Traditionally, donkeys were used by the Maasai to transport their household goods from place to place, not to carry water. So to suggest that donkeys be used to cart water—and to relieve the women of some of the burden of this work, which was also one of our aims— didn't make sense to the local people. Not long after we returned to Nairobi, I learned that the members of the community had decided that the donkeys could be better used and that the women could continue to collect the water! I knew that without the donkeys there would never be enough water to sustain the trees. This showed me that we needed to make local people feel invested in the projects so they would mobilize themselves and their neighbors to take responsibility for sustaining them. It also demonstrated to me that aspects of people's lives such as culture are very important: You may think you are doing the right thing, but in the local context, you are completely off track.

By late 1977, news of the tree-planting initiatives had spread throughout the NCWK networks and soon farmers, schools, and churches were eager to set up their own programs. That was the beginning of communities themselves taking ownership of Green Belt Movement initiatives, and I have insisted on working this way ever since. It was gratifying that after so many disappointments, my idea was taking off. But it was still an extracurricular activity for me, on top of my job at the university, my other affiliations, and raising my children.

Luckily, I enjoyed using my potential and I had a lot of energy: Then, I could move like a gazelle; nowadays my legs are giving way. I also had a woman who helped me take care of the children and worked around the house. It was, nonetheless, difficult for me to be in so many places: I was organizing and instructing and, when we decided to establish our own tree nurseries, I went out in the field with the foresters and created them.

With the tree planting taking root, work and expenses increased. I was constantly asking friends and others to sponsor trees. Luckily, we were beginning to get support from institutions. I managed to get some money from the NCWK, and the Canadian ambassador to Kenya gave us a car for the project activities, while Mobil Oil (Kenya) was one of the few companies that responded to my requests for funds. It provided a grant that allowed us to establish another tree nursery in Nairobi.

Within months, the tree-planting program became so popular that the NCWK was overwhelmed by the demand for seedlings. So I paid a visit to the government's chief conservator of forests, One-simus Mburu, and told him our plans. We were thinking big: We wanted to plant a tree for every person in Kenya—at that time, a total of fifteen million. We even had a slogan: "One person, one tree."

Mr. Mburu burst into laughter. "You can have all the seedlings you like," he replied. "And you can have them free of charge." Now it is obvious that he didn't believe that we would ever exceed his supply of seedlings. However, only a few months later, this is exactly what happened. "You'll have to pay for them," he told me when I asked for more. "You are taking too many seedlings from the forest-ers." Then it was my turn to laugh. We could not possibly afford to pay for as many as we needed. We still needed the trees, however, and it was getting increasingly difficult to get them from the Depart-ment of Forests. Although the foresters had been supportive at the beginning, I sensed some professional jealousy creeping in as the women became more efficient at planting trees.

Initially, we had distributed seedlings through individual farmers and groups of women who went to the nearest forester in their region to take seedlings, and the NCWK would compensate the Department of Forests for them. However, we soon had to change this policy, partly because the foresters raised fast-growing exotic species and not native trees, which grow more slowly but are better for long-term environmental health. Many of the sites from which women had to collect the seedlings were far from their farms and they usually needed a way to bring their seedlings home. Complicating things further was the fact that the foresters didn't have money or vehicles to transport the women to and from the nurseries to collect the trees. In addition, when the trees were taken from the nurseries they lost a lot of soil because they were virtually uprooted. This meant a lot of seedlings died before they could be planted.

Our solution was to create our own supply of trees. Most of the seedlings we grew were indigenous, although a few communities did plant exotic species, which they liked because they grew very quickly. We organized meetings where foresters talked to the women about how to run their own nurseries. But these were difficult encounters. The foresters didn't understand why I was trying to teach rural women how to plant trees. "You need a professional," they told me. "You need people with diplomas to plant trees." But, I learned, professionals can make simple things complicated. They told the women about the gradient of the land and the entry point of the sun's rays, the depth of the seedbed, the content of the gravel, the type of soil, and all the specialized tools and inputs needed to run a successful tree nursery! Naturally, this was more than the women, nearly all of whom were poor and illiterate, could handle or even needed.

What the foresters were saying didn't seem right to me. You might need a diploma to understand a tree's growth and what the content of the seedling was, but I didn't believe the women needed all the technical knowledge the foresters were dispensing to plant trees successfully. All they needed to know was how to put the seedling in the soil and help it grow, and that didn't seem too hard. Anybody can dig a hole, put a tree in it, water it, and nurture it.

In any case, these women were farmers. They were putting things in the ground and watching them grow all the time. Like them, I too had seen and planted seeds ever since I was a child. So I advised the women to look at the seedlings in a different way. "I don't think you need a diploma to plant a tree," I told them. "Use your woman sense. These tree seedlings are very much like the seeds you deal with—beans and maize and millet—every day. Put them in the soil. If they're good, they'll germinate. If they're not, they won't. Simple."

And this is what they did. The good ones germinated and the bad ones didn't, and the ones that did looked exactly like the trees planted by the foresters! This showed us we were on the right track. Soon the women started showing one another, and before we knew it tree nurseries were springing up on farms and public land around the country. These women were our "foresters without diplomas."

As we went along, we constantly examined what we were doing, looking to change what didn't work as well as it could and refine what did and make it even more effective. At first, we gave the women seeds, but that made the women too dependent on us. It also meant that we'd be growing the same kinds of trees around the country. Just as we did not want exotic species instead of native trees, we also wanted, as in nature, a diversity of species and not millions of the same trees spread across Kenya. So we told the women to collect seeds in the forests and their fields and try to grow trees native to their area. We also encouraged them to experiment with different ways of ensuring the seedlings' survival. In addition, we gave the women containers to retain the soil around the seedlings as they grew and when they were transplanted.

Not surprisingly, the women were incredibly resourceful. They used the technology they had available and they used it well. Sometimes they laid their seedbeds on the ground and sometimes they filled broken pots with soil and placed them in a high spot out of reach of their chickens and goats, who might eat the growing trees. The women also used old pots or cans with holes punched in them to water their seedlings. I encouraged this innovation and constantly asked them to think of new ways to do things and not wait for some "official assessment" to take place.

We also gave the women an incentive. "Whenever a seedling that you have raised is planted," I told them, "the movement will compensate you." This was a small amount—the equivalent then of four U.S. cents a tree—but it provided a lot of motivation. After all, these were poor women who, even though they were working all the time—tending crops and livestock, gathering firewood, carrying water, cooking, taking care of their children—had few options for paid employment.

To help the women progress in a way they could handle, we developed a procedure with ten steps, from forming a group, locating a site for a tree nursery, and reporting on their progress to planting trees and following up to make sure they survived. "Do the first step," I said. "If you do the first step and you succeed, let us know. Then move to the second step and the third. By the time you get to the tenth step we'll bring you your money. You'll have done a good job."

After the women had planted seedlings on their own farms, I suggested that they go to surrounding areas and convince others to plant trees. This was a breakthrough, because it was now communities empowering one another for their own needs and benefit. In this way, step by step, the process replicated itself several thousand times. As women and communities increased their efforts, we encouraged them to plant seedlings in rows of at least a thousand trees to form green "belts" that would restore to the earth its cloth of green. This is how the name Green Belt Movement began to be used. Not only did the "belts" hold the soil in place and provide shade and windbreaks but they also re-created habitat and enhanced the beauty of the landscape.

Although I was a highly educated woman, it did not seem odd to me to be working with my hands, often with my knees on the ground, alongside rural women. Some politicians and others in the 1980s and 1990s ridiculed me for doing so. But I had no problem with it, and the rural women both accepted and appreciated that I was working with them to improve their lives and the environment. After all, I was a child of the same soil.

Education, if it means anything, should not take people away from the land, but instill in them even more respect for it, because educated people are in a position to understand what is being lost. The future of the planet concerns all of us, and all of us should do what we can to protect it. As I told the foresters, and the women, you don't need a diploma to plant a tree.

FROM LEFT TO RIGHT: My mother, Lydia Wanjiru;
my aunt Nyakweya, the storyteller; and me outside
my mother's home in Ihithe about 1993.

Overlooking the valley near Ihithe where we had our farm.
In the time since I was a child, the valley has been largely
deforested and planted with tea and coffee.

Ihithe Primary School (building in foreground) today.
I began studying there in 1948. Tea fields have since been planted in front.

Consolata Missionary Sisters at St. Cecilia's in the late 1950s.
On the far right is Sister Germana, one of the nuns
I grew close to during my four years there.

The end of the path I used to walk on from Ihithe to St. Cecilia's
boarding school at the Mathari Catholic Mission
and back home again during school holidays, as it looks today.

My yearbook photo in 1964, when I graduated from Mount St. Scholastica. Quite a '60s look!

In Kansas in the early 1960s. FROM LEFT: Elaine Klaas (DeWulf), Florence Conrad (Salisbury), Agnes Wangeci, and me at Mount St. Scholastica.

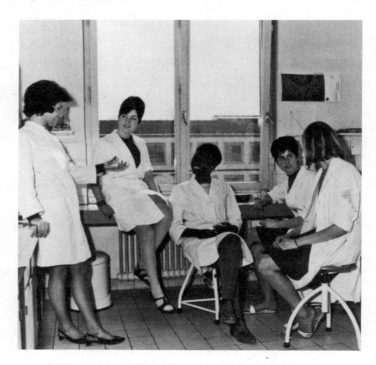

At the University of Munich, 1968. On the far left (standing) is my friend Fräulein Dr. Koch, whose high German I could follow but whose Bavarian dialect was beyond me.

ABOVE: Mwangi's and my wedding reception at the United Kenya Club, 1969. Mwangi is to my right; my father is standing to my immediate left and my mother next to him. Next to her are my father's youngest wife and then my brother Kibicho.

RIGHT: On honeymoon at the Gedi ruins near Mombasa, Kenya, 1969.

With Mwangi on November 8, 1971,
the day I received the diploma for my doctoral degree.

My children, Muta, Wanjira, and Waweru
(left to right), in the late 1970s.

1979: The Canadian ambassador hands over the keys to a car to support the Green Belt Movement, which was launched under the auspices of the National Council of Women of Kenya (NCWK). I am fourth from the left.

Planting trees in Kibwezi, southeast of Nairobi, on May 26, 1979, with the then director of the National Environment Secretariat of Kenya.

Leaving the office of the Deputy Supervisor of Elections
in January 1982, after a ruling that I would
not be allowed to run in a parliamentary by-election.

In Uhuru Park, Nairobi, 1989,
when the "park monster" was still set to be built.

February 22, 1992. The fence around the work site for the
Kenya Times complex in Uhuru Park is finally dismantled.

Freedom Corner in Uhuru Park in 2005.

The reinforced door at my home in South C, Nairobi. The police broke it open in 1992 to get me out. The door and door frame still bear the marks.

Rev. Timothy Njoya (center) of the Presbyterian Church of East Africa talks to journalists at my front gate, having been refused entry to the house by police, January 1992.

FROM LEFT TO RIGHT: Me, Vertistine Mbaya, and my mother at my mother's homestead in Ihithe.

Marching to protest illegal logging in Karura Forest
with members of the Green Belt Movement and Kenyan civil society.

Rallying supporters at the gates to
Karura Forest after contractors fenced off
the work site, October 1998.

En route to a meeting in a parliamentary constituency
on October 8, 2004, I receive a call from the
Norwegian ambassador asking me to keep the
line open for a phone call from Oslo.

I plant a tree at Freedom Corner in Uhuru Park with Gordon Brown,
Chancellor of the Exchequer of the United Kingdom, in January 2005.

In Nairobi, shortly after being awarded
the 2004 Nobel Peace Prize.

7

Difficult Years

When we go through profound experiences, they change us. We risk our relationships with friends and family. They may not like the direction we have taken or may feel threatened or judged by our decisions. They may wonder what happened to the person they thought they once knew. There may not be enough space in a relationship for aspirations and beliefs or mutual interests and aims to unfold. For a couple, this is particularly so because most people marry young and are bound to grow and change in their perceptions and appreciation of life. This is probably what happened with Mwangi and me.

We were a young couple, both well educated in America, and society expected a lot from us. We both had demanding jobs (he in Parliament, me in the university) and we were raising three young children. We were under a lot of pressure. I was also facing the challenge of venturing into what was considered a man's world. Nobody told me that men would be threatened by the high academic achievements of women like me. But Kenyan society idolizes education and considers it a panacea for all other problems. Traditionally, society also puts more value on boys than on girls: Boys are provided education before girls and boys are expected to be greater achievers than girls. Therefore, it was an unspoken problem that I and not my husband had a Ph.D. and taught in the university.

That societal attitude toward me in regard to my husband shaped Mwangi's view of me: He saw me through the mirror given to him by society rather than through his own eyes. He was a product of the times and felt toward educated women the way most men in Kenya did then. Society's perception was part of the problem. It placed constant pressure on men to behave in certain ways. Even if their wives had more education or more achievements, they were expected to demonstrate that they were in control of their households and were not henpecked by and under the control of their wives.

People have ways of asking a man whether he is the one "wearing the pants at home," and having to prove that he is in charge can put a lot of pressure on a man. Such pressure can intensify to the point where it eventually wreaks havoc on a young couple and a young marriage. But nobody warned me—and it had never occurred to me—that in order for us to survive as a couple I should fake failure and deny any of my God-given talents.

I did not recognize the source of our discontent, but looking back, I can see that tensions began early and they were often precipitated by trivialities. For instance, when we were married, I did not want to change my last name to his and continued to use my surname. This was because, besides the fact that I had a number of important documents in my surname, traditionally a Kikuyu woman retained her surname after marriage and I was aware of that. She would be called her father's daughter or by the name of her children—that is, "Mama Waweru" or "Mama Wanjira" or "Mama Muta"—to emphasize the value given to motherhood.

The practice of using the title "Mrs." after marriage, followed by the husband's surname, was introduced by the British and I didn't see why I had to adopt it. True, that is what everybody else in the emerging elite class did, and not doing it seemed to suggest that I did not quite love Mwangi and his family. Largely to demonstrate that this was not the case, I agreed, but put a hyphen between the two surnames. Eventually I stopped using the hyphen and even dropped my maiden name for day-to-day correspondence.

When marriages fail, maturity and thoughtfulness take a backseat and emotions drive you forward. Even though I held out hope we could make it work—at least for the sake of the children, who were very small at the time—by the mid-1970s I knew that our marriage was not going well and that we could be facing difficult moments ahead.

But all marriages have challenges and I thought that we would find our balance.

Then one day in July 1977, I came back to the home we shared and, although I was used to Mwangi's going away on long business trips and not coming home at the end of each day, the minute I walked into the house, I could tell that things were different: There was packing material on the floor, some of the paintings on the walls were missing, and curtains, the record player, the television, and other furnishings were gone. I walked through the house and, sure enough, saw that Mwangi had taken many of the material possessions he brought to the marriage, including his clothes and special gifts from his friends.

"What happened?" I asked the woman who cared for the children and assisted with the housework. "Papa Mathai packed all his things in his car and left," she replied.

I was stunned. This was real: Mwangi had made a decision to leave me. I sat down to listen to myself and reflect on the hurricane of emotions now quickly building inside me. In an instant, I ran through our life together: our courtship and wedding, the joys when the children arrived, the laughter, the quarrels and tears and now . . . this! I replayed the past like a film, my eyes fixed on nothing in particular.

Then a strong force pulled me out of my chair to look for a broom. "Sweep!" an inner voice ordered me. I obeyed and walked to the kitchen, found a broom, and started sweeping the rubbish Mwangi had left behind. I swept in the kitchen and moved into the living room and then the bedroom. I swept the corridors, and out the main door I swept the dust that had been laid bare when Mwangi packed his things. As I swept, I began to realize that this might be it, that he had gone and that he might not come back. And if he did come back, what would I do?

As I swept the last bit of dust, I made a covenant with myself: I will accept. Whatever will be, will be. I have a life to lead. I recalled words a friend had told me, the philosophy of her faith. "Life is a journey and a struggle," she had said. "We cannot control it, but we can make the best out of any situation." I was indeed in quite a situation. It was up to me to make the best of it.

The days that followed were very lonely and sad. I searched my soul constantly for reasons that Mwangi had decided to leave me. I knew that he would blame me for the failure, even as the public, too, would blame me: It is always the woman's fault. I thought I had done everything: humbled myself, helped with his public role, served him, and loved him. I had tried to be a good mother, a good politician's wife, a good African woman, and a successful university teacher. Is it that those were just too many roles for one person to excel in? Did I miss something I should have paid attention to? Where did I go wrong? Because of the nature of our work, did we spend too much time apart? How could I have done so much for somebody, only to find it had not been enough to keep him with me? How was I going to cope with three children by myself? These thoughts ran over and over through my mind.

The children did not realize a tornado had just passed through our home. I told them nothing and very little of the turmoil going through me revealed itself to them. They went through their routine that night and then I tucked them into their beds. As I did, I looked into their innocent eyes and saw them searching mine. They had so much trust in us! "Everything will be all right," I remember telling them as I bid them good night, trying not to reveal my feelings of insecurity and loneliness. The day was finally over. It had been only a few hours since my ordeal had started, but it seemed like an eternity. I went to my bedroom, turned off the last light, lay my weary body down on what was a big, cold, and lonely bed, and cried myself to sleep.

The following morning I felt as if a close relative had died. You know your loved one has gone, but a part of you wants to believe that perhaps you are dreaming and the person is still alive. When you think about it, however, you realize it is clear that he or she has indeed passed away and you are overwhelmed by sadness. You step out of your house and you expect everybody to be sad and mourning like you, but you find that nobody else is. The sun has risen, as it always does, cars are rushing down the streets, and people are going about their business as if nothing had happened. You want to call out and ask them why they don't know your loved one has died or that your husband has left you, but you know you can't. You wonder how they can be so unaware that such an important event has taken place in your life. "They should stop everything and cry with me!" But they don't. They have no idea what you are going through. Indeed, nobody knows or even cares.

I faced such a wilderness and an uncharted path. Yet I was not the first woman to face this loss, and I will not be the last. I thought about my mother—and how she had pulled through her own challenges, with no education or financial security and without the exposure I had had to wider experiences. She had spent many years apart from my father, especially during the Mau Mau conflict. If anything, I owed it to her to carry on.

One aspect that helped me was that I had become a very independent person during the course of the marriage. Due to the nature of Mwangi's work and mine, and indeed due to my own sense of responsibility, I was making many decisions independently both at the university and at home. So when he left, very little of my daily routine changed, apart from what I did for him and with him. I still woke up in the morning and went to work. What I did at work stayed the same. At the end of the day, I'd come home and cook for the children, help them with their homework, make sure they had baths, and put them to bed. I kept busy. I didn't have to ask myself or anybody else, "What am I going to do now that my husband is not here?" I did what I always had.

What also helped me during that time was an approach I developed through my work with the Green Belt Movement. "Look," I would say to the people working with me, "we are on a track that has not been explored before. We are on a trial-and-error basis. If what we did yesterday did not produce good results, let's not repeat it today because it's a waste of time." Trying to think this way helped me a lot when Mwangi walked away, because I could have been devastated—completely destroyed. But I had that attitude: If you have given something your best shot and it is still not working, then what else can you do? Nothing. In my marriage, I felt I had done everything there was to be done. I had not succeeded, but I had to stop blaming myself for the failure. I also had to steel myself not to accept the inevitable recrimination from the public. Besides, as I like to tell people, "Failing is not a crime." What is important is that if you fail you have the energy and the will to pull yourself up and keep going.

I did make one big change, however. In the house we had shared I found myself thinking too much about Mwangi. The family photographs on the walls, the chair where he sat, and his favorite cup all reminded me of him. I decided it would be good to start anew. The children and I relocated to another university-owned house on Rose Avenue. It was in a quiet, leafy neighborhood of Nairobi not too far from State House, the president's official residence. The house had a large garden where the children could play and the property had several trees, many of them already mature fruit trees. The children were happy there and enjoyed climbing the trees and eating the fruit straight from their branches. They also found wonderful friends among the local children and spent many hours playing in the compound.

I sometimes wonder what I would have become if Mwangi had not left me—whether I would have followed the path I have. In some ways, his leaving allowed me to choose to take the direction I did. If he had stayed, things might have been very different: The path I would have taken would have been ours and not my own. There are opportunities even in the most difficult moments.

. . .

In 1979, the estrangement between my husband and me led us to the courts. I was not ready for a divorce and had hoped for reconciliation. I wanted a family and didn't want another husband. But Mwangi did not share my feelings. What came next took me by surprise. Mwangi could have chosen to keep our divorce proceedings private, as I expected and preferred. But he decided to make them public, which meant that our dirty laundry—a member of Parliament and his wife divorcing—would be aired in the press and our problems would become material for speculation and gossip. I was not ready for that, either. It was devastating.

Western-style divorce, like many other practices that were legacies of Kenya's colonial heritage, presented a contradiction in our lives. The legal process of divorce was foreign to our society and uprooted us into an alien sphere. It forced us into a modality of working through the courts while the community outside had very different norms surrounding marriage and family structures. We had to deal with both of these worlds.

The court system then in place to deal with estranged couples made the situation more awkward and negative than it should have been. Divorces were granted only on grounds such as cruelty, adultery, mental torture, or insanity. Not surprisingly, such a system encouraged wild accusations and, at times, outright lies. But did the lies have to be so extreme, so deliberate, and so hurtful? Mwangi accused me of adultery, of causing his high blood pressure, and of being cruel. I denied all the charges, so we had to go through a mandatory trial.

The trial lasted for about three weeks, but it seemed like years. Throughout, the press recounted details of the proceedings like it was a popular soap opera. With every court proceeding, I felt stripped naked before my children, family, and friends. It was a cruel, cruel punishment. My greatest claim to fame and press attention was that I was married to a man who was getting rid of me! As I went through the trial I swore to work for laws that would protect couples and their families from destroying each other. I cannot claim much credit, but such courts are now in place and it is a source of pride that the government of which I became a member appointed the first woman family judge when it came to power: Justice Martha Koome.

During the trial, Mwangi was quoted as saying that he wanted a divorce because I was "too educated, too strong, too successful, too stubborn, and too hard to control." This statement made it into the press and later went around the world. I don't recall his saying anything like that. It was the press's expression of what they perceived his sentiments to be. As it was, there was very little sympathy for me in the press: The reporters and editors, like many others, assumed that if a marriage fails it is the woman who is not doing her job properly and obeying her husband. As far as they were concerned I deserved to be whipped publicly for challenging the authority of my husband. And since I was an educated woman, being publicly humiliated would also serve to warn other such educated women that if they also dared to challenge such authority, the same fate would befall them.

At one point it became clear I was being turned into a sacrificial lamb. Anybody who had a grudge against modern, educated, and independent women was being given an opportunity to spit on me. I decided to hold my head high, put my shoulders back, and suffer with dignity: I would give every woman and girl reasons to be proud and never regret being educated, successful, and talented. "What I have," I told myself, "is something to celebrate and not to ridicule or dishonor."

One moment in the courtroom encapsulated the situation I found myself in. I was on the witness stand and Mwangi's lawyer had asked me a question. In court when you are asked a question you are supposed to answer yes or no and the atmosphere is designed to be very intimidating. But in that moment, I felt that I was addressing just another person who had asked me a question. I wasn't intimidated. Instead of answering, I posed my own question: "Why did you ask me that question?" The lawyer should have replied, but he turned to the judge and said, "Your honor, did you hear what she asked me? If she dares ask me a question in court what do you think she does to my client at home?" I realized that I had just put a rope around my neck.

I knew then that I would lose the case. I realized that because of that exchange the judge would be persuaded that I was indeed a stubborn, unyielding, and difficult person who dared to ask questions and seek explanations in a court of law. The judge would use that to show that, therefore, I was giving my husband hell at home! It did not surprise me either that the evidence I had with me to prove some of the lies that were being told in court—such as my causing Mwangi to have high blood pressure—was stolen from my car outside a restaurant where my lawyer and I were having a quick lunch before returning to court for more questioning. When the ruling was handed down, it went against me. I was now divorced. I felt cheated, betrayed, taken advantage of, and misused. I walked away in pain. I was in pieces, and worse was yet to come.

To add insult to injury, after our divorce Mwangi did not want me to continue using his surname and let me know it through a letter from his lawyer. I remember thinking to myself, "I'm not an object the name of which can change with every new owner!" And I had resisted adopting his name in the first place! As a way to deal with my terrible feelings of rejection, I got the idea of adding another "a" to "Mathai" and to write it as it is pronounced in Kikuyu. And so I became "Maathai." The extra syllable also signified that although a part of me would always be connected to Mwangi and his surname, I had a new identity. Henceforth, only I would define who I was: Wangari Muta Maathai.

A week or so after the trial, Salim Lone, then the editor of *Viva* magazine and an advocate for free expression, interviewed me about the case. When he asked me about the judgment, I told him that the only way the judge could have granted a divorce on hearsay was that he was either incompetent or corrupt. The truth of the matter was that there was not enough evidence to dissolve our marriage.

Although it was not considered grounds for divorce, incompatibility would have been a fairer reason.

My statement to *Viva* set off a chain reaction that astonished me. Apparently, my comment so angered the judge that I was threatened with contempt of court—a serious crime. "People," he said (and I suspect women in particular), "can't go around slandering judges." When I refused to retract it, the government hauled me before another judge, and I was actually charged with contempt of court. Once again I needed very competent lawyers to rescue me from the jaws of the judge and the courts. I argued that I hadn't actually called the judge corrupt or incompetent, but had rather concluded that he would have had to be one or the other to render the decision he had.

Unfortunately, the court did not see it my way. Salim was offered a jail term of six months or a fine of some forty thousand Kenyan shillings, which was a lot of money at the time. I, however, was given no such option to pay a fine, and was instead sentenced to six months in jail. I was immediately arrested and taken to Lang'ata Women's Prison in Nairobi.

This turn of events was so rapid and unexpected that I had little time to sort out what had happened and how I had come to be in this predicament. I had never come face-to-face with the law before, and imagine my astonishment as I confronted jail time as an outcome of my divorce. Not only had I lost my husband but I had also lost my freedom. I had no idea then, of course, that this was only the beginning and that I would eventually visit jail on many occasions in the course of the years that followed—almost earning the reputation of being a jailbird.

This time, as on many other occasions, I would not have the opportunity to go back home to say good-bye to my children or to explain my predicament. They were at home with the woman who helped around the house, and would learn from relatives or friends about my fate and deal with it the best way they could. How well they understood or appreciated the matter I could not tell. However, I was worried that they were too young to understand what was going on but old enough to have their sense of security threatened by it.

Thankfully, whenever I have been imprisoned, the stints have been short, generally a matter of days. But being in jail is never easy. Prison is crowded, filthy, cold, and dehumanizing. This first time was no different. The very afternoon I was due in court on the contempt charge I attended a lunch party. I had just had my hair done and the fashion at the time if you wore braids, as I did, was to have a lot of beads in your hair. I remember that I had beads all over my head, and I'd dressed carefully. At the lunch, I joked with some of the other women: "I better eat a lot because I don't know when I'll eat next," I told them. "Ah, don't worry," they replied, "they'll probably just give you a heavy fine and let you go."

As it turned out, it was a good thing that I'd eaten well since, once the judge had passed his judgment, the police didn't waste any time. There were so many of us in custody that we were all squeezed in together in the police cell and then the van that took us to prison. At first we were taken to the remand cell. It was raining and the cell had nothing that could be called a roof: Rain fell all over us and I felt wet and cold. There I was, dressed to kill with all my beads in a cell that was cold, dank, filthy, smelly, and crowded, with no room to sit down. Water was everywhere. Most of the other women were there for petty crimes, such as brewing illegal alcohol. This was strange company, very different from the elite crowd with whom I had shared a sumptuous lunch only a few hours before.

Finally officers came to transport me from the remand cell to the jail cell. I was taken in a police van down a long, dirt road lined with small market stalls to the prison proper: a large, squat building surrounded by high walls and barbed wire, not too far from the home Mwangi and I had shared on Kabarnet Road and within sight of the Kibera slum. When we got there one of the guards looked at my clothing and hair and said, "And where did this one come from?" I did not find this funny and at that point had no desire to respond.

I was put into a concrete, maximum-security cell with four other women and given a uniform, a pan to use as a toilet, and a blanket. The women wardens also cut off my braids. The situation was extremely depressing, to say the least, but the other women prisoners, no matter what had landed them in jail, treated me very kindly. They showed me how to fold my blanket properly. "You don't use it to cover yourself," they said, "you use it as a mattress so you can sleep on the concrete." They also told me to sleep between them in a huddle on the floor so I wouldn't feel cold.

"Why are you here?" one of the women asked me. I am sure she was surprised to see an educated woman, a member of society's elite so to speak, next to her in the cell. "I told a judge he was corrupt," I replied.

"But they are!" she cried. Another woman said, "We have to pray for the judges so they will judge fairly and justly tomorrow." For the very first time in my life, I heard people pray for judges. I prayed, too, because I knew I was in the deepest trouble I'd ever been in. I will always remember the generosity, gentleness, and kindness of those women.

The next morning, however, I discovered that my friends outside had been working hard because the fact that I'd been sent to jail was all over the newspapers. Details of my case had obviously made it inside, too, as a result. After we had cleaned the cell and the guards, who were also women, had assigned all the women additional jobs, one guard gave me the task of holding the baby of a prisoner. I knew then that the guard was sympathetic because I could have been given a job that was much worse. I sat and took good care of that baby.

The effect of the jailing on my children also weighed heavily on my mind. They were still young (ages ten, eight, and six) and I couldn't spend six months in prison away from them, especially for something I found absurd. I worried a lot about the children, because it was difficult for them to handle the public exposure and criticism, and they were still too young to understand what was going on.

It was also the case that while some among the public were happy with the punishment given to me, others felt that jailing me and with such a long sentence was not right. People knew that many of the judges were, in fact, corrupt, which helped build pressure for me to be released. After three days in prison, my lawyer developed a formulation whereby I provided a statement to the court that they found sufficient to set me free.

My experience in jail was a turning point. Until that time, I had had no problems with the law. Even afterward, though people accused me of deliberately courting arrest or acting arrogantly with Kenya's legal authorities, I always tried as far as possible to stay within the letter of the law. But after the divorce and my time in jail I could see that certain people were jealous and wanted me to be taught a lesson and put in my place. They took pleasure in what they perceived as my comeuppance. The message was clear: Every other woman who contested her husband or the (male) authorities was being told, "If you try to be anything but what you ought to be, we will treat you exactly the way we have treated her. So, behave, women!"

Far from beating me down, however, this message gave me strength. I knew I'd done nothing wrong. I had not acted maliciously, arrogantly, or criminally. And look what had been done to me! Despite my wrenching experience, something positive may have come out of it for other women who faced divorce in future years. Because many men saw that I remained resolute in the face of the pressure put on me, they realized that if they wanted to divorce their wives it would be best, for themselves as well as for their children and families, if they did it fairly and respectfully.

Throughout this difficult time, my children were the reason I got up in the morning and continued working. Each day I would look into their eyes and want to do something for them. They kept me focused: I still had to get them to school, make sure they had food to eat and clothes to wear, and pay their school fees. If I hadn't had the children I would have been left with an enormous vacuum in my life.

Vertistine Mbaya also helped me enormously. She was a wise and kind friend. In 1976, she experienced the trauma of her husband's death in a car crash, leaving her a widow with four children to raise. Having just gone through deep emotions herself, I think Vert could understand what I was experiencing. She knew I needed to forget what had happened and not dwell on it. She and I rarely talked about the divorce and the aftermath. Instead we discussed all other manner of subjects under the sun. By not sharing what she heard, Vert also protected me from any comments my colleagues at the university might have made to her about my situation. She helped me cross that valley.

Money, however, remained a problem. There was no legal requirement for Mwangi to help support me, and, in any event, I had decided not to seek any of his wealth or property, since the loss of him as a friend and companion far outweighed any money he could give me. But I was in debt, with very few savings, and hiring the lawyers to handle the divorce had cost a lot. They had also demanded their fees up front, because they didn't think I would be able to pay once the divorce was finalized.

I wanted to protect the children as much as I could from what had happened between their father and me. They were still too young to fully understand the pain and struggle I was experiencing. But at times I could not hide the realities of my situation or the financial hardship I faced. I remember one occasion vividly.

During the hot weather, I would take Waweru, Wanjira, and Muta to a nearby pool we frequented in one of Nairobi's hotels. Waweru and Wanjira were happily swimming in the main pool and Muta, their younger brother, wanted to join them. But I had to keep telling Muta to stay where he was in the kids' pool. The older children had inflatable plastic water wings (readily available and fairly cheap) that allowed them to swim safely in the big pool. Then, though, I could not afford to buy Muta a pair. He looked at me with his big eyes, leaving me with no doubts about what he wanted. I felt terrible that I couldn't buy him the wings.

Another time we were at the pool and the children wanted to eat sausage and chips from the pool's snack bar. I didn't have enough money to buy them each a plate of chips, so I ordered one plate and asked the children to share. But Waweru understandably wanted for each to get their own chips. He was the oldest and had been swimming hard and was hungry. "I don't have any money," I told him. I have never forgotten that day. I was without money and my children wanted chips and I couldn't buy them. They didn't understand how I couldn't have the money. There was nothing I could do. When people tell me they can't afford to put food on the table, I know how they feel because I experienced it myself.

It was clear that the salary I was drawing from the university was simply not enough to sustain the children and me. Soon after the divorce, an opportunity arose to supplement my income. Vert told me that the United Nations Development Programme was looking for someone to take a six-month assignment with the Economic Commission for Africa to explore the constraints on improving the region's livestock industry.

Even though I needed the money, I had to think very hard about this consultancy because I would have to be based in Lusaka, Zambia. I knew I couldn't take the children with me. They were in school, and the job required me to travel throughout Africa. Besides, the lawyers were asking for their money and I didn't have any. If I turned this consulting job down, the children and I could literally be out in the streets. I considered who could take care of the children in my absence. My mother? Another relative living in Nairobi?

Then one day I realized that if anything were to happen to the children in my absence, the person most likely to be called would be their father. Although Mwangi and I had no formal arrangement regarding the custody of the children or visiting rights, I knew he was the right person to care for them. "If there's anybody who loves them, it's him," I thought to myself. "If he can't take care of them, nobody else can." So I put Waweru, Wanjira, and Muta in my little Volkswagen Beetle and told them, "We're going to Daddy."

I drove the short distance to his house. I knew Mwangi wouldn't talk to me, but I also knew he wouldn't send the children back. Mwangi's niece, also named Wanjira, who was living with him, opened the gate and we greeted each other. "I'm bringing the children for a short time," I said. "I'm coming back soon." What I didn't say is that it would be six months before I returned to Nairobi to live full-time. Then I watched those little children turn and walk into the compound.

I thought then, and still do, that it was important for Mwangi, as it is for all fathers, to have a close relationship with his children. I deliberately tried to ensure that. I told the children, "You will be all right with your father." During the next few months, while I was in Zambia, I kept in touch with the children and tried not to let this disrupt their lives with their father. While I worked at the consultancy, I would pass through Nairobi regularly and hear how the children were. I was pleased to learn that Mwangi was taking very good care of them, and I was not surprised.

The children ended up staying with Mwangi for a number of years. When they eventually came back of their own accord to my house, around 1985, I was very happy they were back and that that chapter had ended. But I encouraged them to keep in touch with Mwangi and, when they were studying outside of Kenya, to write and call their father.

Now that my children are grown, I realize how lucky I've been. No one comes through divorce untouched—neither the wife, nor the husband, nor the children. That said, many children grow up in unbroken homes but are destroyed by the tensions they experience. Of course, there are many, many children who emerge from a broken family situation who are very strong. If the parents help their children and protect them, they come out all right. In spite of everything that happened between Mwangi and me, I am very pleased that our children have a positive relationship with both of us.

Around the time the children returned to live with me more or less for good, I was running into serious problems with the government. So it was a blessing that when they completed high school,

Waweru and Wanjira, followed a few years later by Muta, went to college in the United States, with my encouragement. I wanted them to experience what I had and to see another world. I did wonder sometimes whether it would have been better for them to see the daily struggles of their mother and not to have to worry from afar whether I'd be all right. But I also knew that, if something were to happen to me, they would be more likely to be able to take care of themselves in the United States than in Kenya. I believe that my children now understand the struggle I was going through and how important it is to live your life with self-respect and dignity.

The later 1970s and early 1980s were hectic years for me. I was being pushed and pulled in many directions and I pushed and pulled myself, too. As the Green Belt Movement took off under the auspices of the National Council of Women of Kenya, its activities attracted some favorable attention in the Kenyan press. We began to be noticed overseas, too, and a Danish schoolchildren's group began raising money to support our work. Soon, the Green Belt Movement was seen as one of the NCWK's most successful initiatives.

With the encouragement of colleagues in the NCWK, I decided to run for the post of NCWK chairman in 1979. I lost by three votes in an election that had a measure of ethnic politics in it. Many in Kenya, including the new president, Daniel arap Moi, an ethnic Kalenjin, wanted to reduce the influence Kikuyus were perceived to have in the country, including in the leadership of voluntary organizations, one of which was the NCWK, which was quite influential at that time. This is the only way I could understand why the NCWK's organizational members would not have elected me chairman, but overwhelmingly voted for me to be vice-chairman, a position in which I would be the immediate assistant to the chair. (In the NCWK it was the organizations that cast votes, not individuals.)

We used the term "chairman" and not "president" because Parliament had passed a law soon after President Moi took office that decreed that Kenya could have only one president. From then on, heads of organizations or private enterprises had to use another term, which most often was "chairman."

In 1980 I ran again for the post of chairman, and there was still considerable infighting among NCWK members about which candidate to support. This time, it wasn't only my ethnicity that generated opposition, but it appeared that elements in the government took an interest in the election, especially through one organization, Maendeleo Ya Wanawake. I realized I was involved in a political game, even though I believed I was not in politics.

Maendeleo Ya Wanawake (Kiswahili for "Progress for Women"), a prominent national women's organization set up to assist rural women to develop their skills and generate income, was one of the NCWK's members. Its chairman was always a rural woman and the leader at that time was very close to the president. My understanding is that elements in the government encouraged Maendeleo Ya Wanawake to take control of the NCWK from the elite women running it. They knew that if the chairman of the NCWK declared, "We support the new president," it would carry a lot of weight in the country. The president could then say, "See, the women of Kenya support me."

President Moi, who had been vice president, succeeded President Kenyatta when he died in office in 1978 at the age of eighty-six. Constitutionally, a contested election for the presidency should have been held within ninety days of Kenyatta's death, but instead, President Moi had run unopposed. Many civic groups in Kenya had gone along with this, including the NCWK, which had congratulated the president. There is even a photo of me shaking the new president's hand. Once securely in office, President Moi moved quickly to consolidate his power, including by co-opting civil society organizations.

Another factor against me becoming the NCWK chairman in the

government's eyes was my education. At this time in Kenya, the number of highly educated women was still tiny and we were viewed with suspicion by many people in authority.

Most women who gained prominence in society did so because their husbands were important—ministers, members of Parliament, or leading businessmen—not because they themselves were educated or successful. Likewise, the elite of Kenya (businessmen, politicians, and the civil servants) were also relatively few in number and all knew one another. This situation was tailor-made for corruption. Despite my marriage to Mwangi and my position at the University of Nairobi, I was not part of this group. Nonetheless, because of my academic achievements, my work with the Green Belt Movement, and the circumstances of the divorce, I had made some headlines. Now I was known to the authorities and they didn't like what they saw—an educated, independent African woman aspiring to leadership.

I was intrigued by this apparent opposition to my candidacy, which I knew was due in part to my ethnicity, in part to my education, and was again partly due to my marital status. For me, what was most important was the ability to fulfill the objectives of the position. Our refusal to acknowledge and reward ability and performance are among the reasons that Kenya finds itself in a state of underdevelopment. I eventually learned that these are some of the games people in politics play.

The forces opposing my candidacy had a problem. They and their surrogates could not, of course, simply come out and say that the government wanted to control the NCWK by installing its own candidate. The reason they gave for objecting to me, and presumably they thought it a good one, was closer to home: I should not be elected head of a national women's organization because I was divorced, so didn't set a good example for Kenyan women. The fact that I'd been elected vice-chairman in 1979, the year the divorce was granted, and my marital status had not been mentioned, was conveniently forgotten. Not only was this rationale unfair and insulting, I felt as if I was being punished again for the divorce, like beating a dead horse.

Some women in the NCWK asked me to abandon my candidacy. "You don't want the divorce to be in the headlines all over again," they said. "Save yourself and your children from the embarrassment."

"But I have nothing to save," I replied. "Everything has been lost, and you cannot use that to punish me."

Some even said they had been cautioned by their husbands not to vote for me. I realized I had to fight as a matter of principle. It was one thing for the women not to elect me, but quite another to withdraw before they'd had a chance to vote. I also knew that on a level playing field I would win.

When pressure is applied to me unfairly, I tend to dig in my heels and stand my ground—precisely the opposite of what those applying the pressure hope or expect. At that time in Kenya, if you thought the government didn't want you to take on a certain position, you generally withdrew. Yet the interference of outsiders struck me and many others as petty, verging on the ridiculous. Why should who led the NCWK become a matter of state? A week before the election, the opposition saw I would not stand down, so they tried a different tactic. Apparently, as I understood it, certain groups were told that they should leave the National Council of Women of Kenya. Sure enough, several organizations, chief among them Maendeleo Ya Wanawake and the Girl Guides, withdrew.

This was devastating to the NCWK because Maendeleo Ya Wanawake, especially, represented a majority of Kenya's rural women, while the professional organizations were largely comprised of elite women and therefore deemed not "African" enough. Indeed, the groups that left the NCWK made the serious charge that we did not understand or care about the problems of women in the rural areas, even though many of us were working hand in hand with rural women and later would fight for their rights, something the government most certainly did not like. When these groups left, those who had been officers signed checks for every penny in the NCWK's bank account, leaving it virtually bankrupt.

The controversy over the election attracted the media's attention. Some outlets supported me, while others that were aligned with the government, formally or informally, not surprisingly did not. For the second time in two years, my character, my actions, and my suitability were being openly discussed in the national media—a spotlight I had not sought. Thankfully, my friends stood by me and when the votes were cast I was elected chairman unopposed. Believe it or not, even some of the newspapers celebrated my victory.

Because of my defiance, however, for the next twenty years, the government ignored the NCWK and promoted Maendeleo Ya Wanawake, which received the bulk of support for "women's programs" in Kenya from international donors. Later, Maendeleo changed its constitution to become the "women's wing" of the ruling party, the Kenyan African National Union (KANU).

As a result, those of us in the NCWK had to become ingenious about raising money and making our presence and work known. One way we did this was to increase our focus on the environment through the Green Belt Movement and a water initiative. While this strategy opened up new sources of funding, we never had oceans of resources. For much of the 1980s, the NCWK and the Green Belt Movement struggled to survive, while from that time on, the regime labeled me "disobedient," and sought to curtail my activities and my voice. Back in 1980, newly elected the NCWK chairman, I had no idea that my path and the government's would cross repeatedly in the future and with far more explosive consequences.

On a more personal level, the election had brought to the national arena the issue of power and gender. Soon after I became chairman, some of my friends and supporters came to me to say that my election was causing them trouble with their husbands, many of whom were influential in the government. They asked me to step down and allow someone else to lead the NCWK. This saddened me, but I was not wholly surprised. "Some of you have supported me for a long time and I won't ever forget that," I told them. "But I can never withdraw from the chair after women have given me their support and their confidence. I must stay." I completely understood the pressure they were under to not be seen as supporting a divorced woman, but I couldn't change my mind.

That election helped me cross the river. Once I got to the other side, I could keep going. As it turned out, I was reelected chairman of the NCWK each year through 1987, when I retired.

The struggle over the chairmanship of the NCWK only intensified my feelings about what those in power had said during this episode and the divorce trial. They had abused and vilified me and I had had no recourse to defend myself: What could I say?

I knew that the only way to hold them accountable for their abuse and vilification of me and further the cause of women in general was to meet them on their own ground. An opportunity arose that could have enabled me to do this—a by-election for a seat in Parliament in early 1982.

In spite of my connection to politics through Mwangi, I had never considered politics as a career, although over the years others had suggested it. During Mwangi's 1969 and 1974 campaigns, many people told me, "You know, you could easily be elected on your own." If I represented Mwangi at an event, people who had heard me speak would say to him, "Oh, she did so well. We'd vote for her any day." It made me aware of my speaking skills. In standing for Parliament, I would not be directly competing with Mwangi, who had lost his seat in the 1979 elections to Philip Leakey, the brother of paleontologist and conservationist Richard Leakey.

Very few women were in Parliament at that time. Between 1980 and 1988, only two women were elected MPs. President Moi appointed a handful of other women as parliamentarians, but none wielded real power in that male-dominated assembly. The seat that opened up was in my home region, the constituency of Nyeri. Due to the fact that Kenya had been a de facto one-party state for more than a decade by that time, I could only be a candidate of the ruling party, KANU.

Standing in the election would also mean giving up my job at the university. Parliament had passed a law that said that if you worked for the government or any parastatal organization and wished to be a candidate for office you had to resign your position. This made getting involved in politics risky, since there was always the chance you could lose an election.

I had been at the University of Nairobi since 1966, so becoming a candidate and giving up my job to join politics was a major decision for me. In January 1982 I took a big leap, without a safety net below me. Imagine my disgust when, after I had submitted my official letter of resignation to the university, the authorities cooked up a technical reason why I couldn't run. The committee charged with overseeing the election told me I was not registered to vote. I was as certain my papers were in order as I was that the law required a citizen to register as a voter only once in the same constituency. According to the committee, however, I should have reregistered in the previous national election, in 1979. And because I hadn't, I wasn't eligible to run.

It soon became obvious that politics was at play again. The ruling party didn't want me in Parliament and had figured out a way to stop me from getting there. Once again, I decided to fight by taking the authorities to court and challenging their reason for disqualifying me, which I knew to be completely illegal. The court sat at nine o'clock on a Saturday morning, but I was required to present my candidacy papers by noon that same day in Nyeri, which is nearly a three-hour drive from Nairobi. Seeing that it would be impossible for me to meet the noon deadline if I drove, some friends had hired a plane to take me to Nyeri as soon as the court rendered its verdict.

By the time the judge made his final ruling, disqualifying me from running for Parliament, it was nearly midday. Even with the plane and a favorable ruling, I would have arrived in Nyeri too late. My case, like many others, demonstrated a miscarriage of justice that was frequent at that time in Kenya and that led me, later, to be involved in the pro-democracy movement. Once again, I had lost in court. I would not be able to run.

The blows kept coming, one after the other. When I returned to the university, explained what had happened, and asked for my job back as chair of the Department of Veterinary Anatomy, the university refused to reinstate me. I had presented my letter of resignation to the university on Thursday afternoon. By Friday morning, the university had given my job to someone else. I was stunned: After sixteen years of service, I had been replaced in fewer than twelve hours. I couldn't have had a clearer indication that the university did not want me anywhere near the place! The cloud that was to hang over Kenya for two decades was now beginning to be felt, and the university's vice-chancellor, whose superior was the president himself, didn't want to ruffle any more of the government's feathers. I had fallen afoul of the regime and it was easier for him if I did not return to my post.

As if that wasn't enough, because I had resigned my position and not been fired, I was ineligible to receive any of the benefits that normally accrued to university professors. I hadn't been fully aware of this when I'd made the decision to resign, but I felt the full consequences nonetheless. I walked out of the university with virtually nothing. I had no pension and no health care.

I didn't even return to my office to pick up my belongings. I asked my secretary to do that for me. (I've been told that some of my belongings to this day remain locked in a university storage room.) Although in the intervening years since my abrupt departure from the Chiromo campus I have visited Vert at her office, I have never returned to the Department of Veterinary Anatomy. Life is funny, though: The wheel sometimes comes full circle. After I was awarded the Nobel Peace Prize, the university of which I was an alumna, which was pleased to see the back of me in 1982, and which ignored my achievements during the ensuing years, awarded me an honorary doctorate in science in 2005, with full honors and all pomp and circumstance.

The day after I resigned, as I was preparing to go to court to contest the electoral commission's decision, officials from the university arrived at my door to tell me I had to vacate my house immediately. Housing, they said, was provided only to academic staff. I was incredulous. "I can't leave now," I told them. "I'm going to court." When I returned later that afternoon, the officials were still there, insisting that I vacate the house. Eventually they left, but said they would return on Monday with their eviction order. I had a miserable Sunday wondering what would happen to me next.

On Monday, I woke up and was confronted with the question of what to do with my life. I had no job and no salary. I had no pension and very few savings. I was about to be evicted from my house. Everything that I had hoped for and relied on was gone—in the space of three days. I was forty-one years old and for the first time in decades I had nothing to do. I was down to zero.

8

Seeds of Change

None of us can control every situation we find ourselves in. What we *can* control is how we react when things turn against us. I have always seen failure as a challenge to pull myself up and keep going. A stumble is only one step in the long path we walk and dwelling on it only postpones the completion of our journey. Every person who has ever achieved anything has been knocked down many times. But all of them picked themselves up and kept going, and that is what I have always tried to do.

So, while I was down, I was not out. For a time that miserable Monday morning I just sat and thought. Then I began moving, literally. I combed the newspapers looking for a suitable place to live that was reasonably priced. Even as I searched, I packed up the contents of my home. Luckily, I saw an advertisement for a house available for six months and, when I called the number listed in the newspaper, I found the cost was within my means. I moved into that house with all of my belongings the same week. I didn't unpack, because I knew it was only going to be for six months.

After those six months, I moved into a small house I had bought in 1975 but had never expected to live in. I purchased it when I was still married to Mwangi but paid the full cost myself and put my name on the title deed. Maybe I wasn't such a bad investor after all. The house was in South C, an area of Nairobi near Wilson Airport that had been developed in the early 1970s from grassland that once was part of Nairobi National Park.

It wasn't—and still isn't—a fancy part of town. The homes are relatively small and close to the street, the roads are pitted with pot-holes that fill with muddy water during the rainy season, and small market stalls crowd the sidewalks. My bungalow-style house was at the end of a cul-de-sac, so it was relatively quiet, and it ended up being a good place to live and work. I planted many trees and shrubs there and it became the greenest house in the vicinity. I love that house because it saved my life. I lived in it for nearly twenty-five years.

During those first months after I left the university I spent a lot of my time reflecting on what had happened and what I would do next. This was good, because for many years I had not had the time or space to think. While I was going through the divorce and feeling under a lot of pressure, I embraced a philosophy that has given me strength in difficult times ever since. Every experience has a lesson. Every situation has a silver lining. Each person needs to raise their consciousness to a certain level so that they will not give up or succumb. If your consciousness is at such a level, you are willing to do what you believe is the right thing—popular opinion notwithstanding.

We do the right thing not to please people but because it's the only logically reasonable thing to do, as long as we are being honest with ourselves—even if we are the only ones. I felt this statement was so important that I included it in one of the first pamphlets I wrote about the Green Belt Movement.

Although my marriage was over, my chance to run for Parliament ended, my job and my home gone, at least one part of my life had not been lost: I was still the chairman of the National Council of Women of Kenya and I was still developing the Green Belt Move-ment. At that time, the NCWK was a relatively poor organization and everybody was a volunteer, but visiting the offices gave me a sense of purpose. The Green Belt Movement was still a relatively small effort that I had worked on outside the hours I was at the university. Now, I started thinking hard about what the Green Belt Movement could become and the impact it could have if it was nurtured and grew and had sufficient funding and direction.

By then I knew that to be successful, an organization and the person heading it had to have plans and carry them out; they could not just talk. You also had to be willing to be something of an activist. You had to tell people, "This is not being done," and explain why the current situation needed to change. If you didn't, you could easily become irrelevant. I had also seen by then how important it was to make the Green Belt Movement's work of interest to the Kenyan press, since they helped spread the message about what we were doing and why it was valuable.

Generally, during those months that followed my leaving the university, I was in good spirits, although I still needed employment. I knew that I would never get another position inside the University of Nairobi, which was then still the only university in Kenya. It was controlled by the government and I had rubbed the establishment the wrong way. In order to be employed by the United Nations, for example at the UNEP headquarters in Nairobi, the government would have had to endorse me and it was obvious that that was not going to happen.

I began to fill out applications for positions in the private sector. The replies I received were not promising. "You are overqualified," one said. "We will get in touch with you as soon as we have an opportunity," said another, not very helpfully. It dawned on me that no one would employ me because they saw me as an enemy of the political system. I had been in a direct confrontation with the government.

Fortunately, an opportunity presented itself within that year that was to change the course of my life and the future of the Green Belt Movement. Some of the seeds of this were sown earlier. In August 1981, Kenya hosted a UN conference on new and renewable sources of energy. This was an issue high on the international agenda at the time and the Green Belt Movement's work fit well with the conference's goals. For two weeks, government officials and members of environmental, energy, and appropriate technology organizations met and agreed on a plan of action to promote new sources of renewable, "green" energy and good management of forests.

As chair of the local board of the Environment Liaison Centre, I coordinated the efforts of local NGOs to prepare for the conference and we formed an umbrella group for all the organizations then dealing with issues of renewable sources of energy. We set up a booth opposite Nairobi's City Hall near where the delegates were meeting at the Kenyatta International Conference Centre and established a woodlot, now called Global Forest, where dignitaries continue to plant trees.

We also organized a march in support of the conference. Hundreds of us wound our way from Uhuru ("Freedom") Park, down Uhuru Highway, past the New Stanley and Hilton hotels, and in front of City Hall, before arriving at the conference center. Many NGOs, both Kenyan and international, participated, including the World Conservation Union (IUCN), the Chipko movement from India (which had pioneered the hugging of trees to protest rampant logging), and, of course, the Environment Liaison Centre. I had arranged for a number of children to carry tree seedlings in the march. When we arrived, the children handed their precious packages to the dignitaries who had gathered on the conference center's spacious steps to meet us. It was fantastic to see all these important people from around the world holding tiny trees—and the press was there to cover the entire event.

That conference on new and renewable energy sources was also important in other ways. I interacted with a number of people working with NGOs in both industrialized and developing countries who were very interested in what the Green Belt Movement was doing. By this time I had sent a proposal for funding to the United Nations Voluntary Fund for the Decade for Women, which was established after the Mexico City conference. The Voluntary Fund, which later became the UN Development Fund for Women, or UNIFEM, was headed by Margaret Snyder, who had lived in Kenya and knew the work of the NCWK.

I kept my fingers crossed that the proposal would be well received back at the Voluntary Fund's offices in New York.

One afternoon in 1982 I was in the NCWK office, carrying out my usual activities, when a tall white man walked in. "I'm looking for Wangari Maathai," he said. "That's me," I replied. He explained that he was Wilhelm Elsrud, the executive director of the Norwegian Forestry Society. "We have heard about the Green Belt Movement and we want to find out more about what you are doing," he added. "We want to see if we can partner with you." This was music to my ears!

Wilhelm and I discussed the Green Belt Movement's work, and I showed him several of the tree nurseries. He was interested in what he saw and asked if I could think of how Green Belt and the Norwegian Forestry Society could work together. Since I needed to find employment I told him I wasn't sure how much time I could spend on the collaboration. "We'll need to employ someone," I said.

Within a few months Wilhelm returned from Norway with some funding and an idea. "Since you still don't have a job," he said, "why don't you take the position of coordinator we were talking about?" He confirmed that there was not much money, but said he could provide me with a small allowance that would help me manage as I looked for a full-time position. I thought about it: I didn't have another job and I wanted to focus more of my attention and energy on the Green Belt Movement. So I accepted his offer.

The rest, as they say, is history. I never looked for another job, since strengthening and expanding the Green Belt Movement as its coordinator became my work and my passion. As it turned out, though, the first substantial funds the NCWK received for the Green Belt Movement came from the UN Voluntary Fund for Women, which decided toward the end of 1981 to provide "seed money" to expand our work. The grant they approved was significant: $122,700 (U.S.). That was more money than I'd seen in my life!

The funds were given to the UN Development Programme office in Nairobi to administer. I would ask for money as I needed it, account for how I spent it, and then ask for more. This arrangement worked very well. If the funds had landed all at once on the Green Belt Movement, it probably would have overwhelmed us and we might not have been as efficient as we were in how we used the money. As part of the grant, there was an emolument for me of around $600 (U.S.) a year. That wasn't much, but I hadn't had a salary since I'd left the university, so anything was welcome. I have never needed a lot of money to live on, so I didn't feel deprived.

The Voluntary Fund's grant was crucial because it let me expand the Green Belt Movement's activities. Coming from a UN agency, that grant gave the Green Belt Movement a certain legitimacy that helped other funders feel secure as we sought support from them. More directly, the grant allowed me to hire people. Until then, the only staff had been me. Now I employed a handful of young women who had recently completed high school to serve as "monitors." They worked in Nairobi and in the field to assess what the community-based groups were doing. They also provided technical assistance as required, verified the number of surviving seedlings, and paid the women their compensation.

The funds also alleviated my near-constant worries about the Green Belt Movement's survival, at least for a few years. Many people have wonderful ideas, but if they don't get seed money to develop them, they can never germinate. Because of the grant, the vision I'd had back in the early 1970s was transformed from some talk and a few tree nurseries into the planting of literally millions of seedlings and the mobilization of thousands of women. It would be several years before I met Margaret Snyder, who became my dear friend Peggy. I am forever grateful to her and the Voluntary Fund. They were truly midwives to the Green Belt Movement's birth.

Now all I needed to worry about was work, and I worked like a donkey. I think I became a workaholic, but I enjoyed watching the activities expand, and in the process seeing people in the communities getting excited, too. The work was challenging as I applied the knowledge I had gained through my academic career in a whole new way. It was rewarding to see tree planting having an impact and actually changing conditions on the ground.

Our partnership with the Norwegian Forestry Society also got off the ground. One of our earliest collaborations began at Karũgia Primary school in Murang'a, about an hour's drive north of Nairobi on the way to Nyeri. President Kenyatta had planted a tree in the school compound. The tree had died and been replaced, but the school authorities approached me about the Green Belt Movement's planting more trees in the school compound. I agreed, but thought an opportunity existed to establish a larger program with the community. As it happened, a young man, Kinyanjui Kiuno, with whom I had been working in a nursery at the University of Nairobi, came to the NCWK office and said he was interested in planting trees. He no longer worked at the university and was looking for a job. "Do you want to go to Murang'a?" I asked him. When he agreed, I sent him to start doing outreach in that area. He still works for the Green Belt Movement, especially as a trainer.

The project in Murang'a, fortunately, went extremely well. We had adequate money and community acceptance from the outset. When the Norwegian Forestry Society exhausted its resources, it encouraged the Norwegian Agency for Development Cooperation (NORAD), the government's overseas aid agency, to support us, which it did for many years. We were able to expand our efforts in Murang'a and it became one of our most successful programs. To this day, as you drive along the main road that connects Murang'a with Nairobi, you can see thick groves of trees stretching from the valley into the hills that have been planted by Green Belt Movement groups.

I was learning on the job. I asked myself constantly whether something could be done differently or better. For instance, at first I encouraged groups of women to cultivate their seedlings together at large nurseries. This system was easier for me, because when I would visit a nursery I would see a lot of groups planting trees together. However, I began to realize that this didn't work well for the women. The nursery may have been several miles from some of the women's villages and they had no transport apart from their feet. So they found it difficult to travel to the nursery each day to water their trees. In addition, the fact that the nurseries served communities in a wide radius meant that the seedlings would often be planted on farms very far from the women's homes. This made it hard for the women to ensure that their seedlings had been planted and had survived.

My solution was to encourage women from groups whose members were walking more than three miles each way to one of these large nurseries to establish nurseries in their own villages instead. This not only increased the number of nurseries but also the number of communities that benefited from them, because the trees were more readily available closer to people's homes. It was also easier for people to come and pick up trees for their farms, and for the women to check on the trees once they had been planted.

I also decided that to make the Green Belt approach truly effective, the incentive system we had in place had to be refined. We weren't going to meet our objectives if we simply raised seedlings and put them in the ground. To restore degraded lands, we had to make certain those trees thrived. So I told the women: "You have to make sure that the people you give your seedlings to have planted them, and that they have survived for at least six months. *That* is when we will compensate you." This is still the way the Green Belt Movement operates.

I saw other ways to improve our effectiveness. While we wanted the women to spend time on tree planting, we also knew they had many other daily responsibilities that took up their time, from cultivating to cooking to caring for their children. One of the requests the women had was help in looking for the seeds on the ground from which they grew their trees. Since many of the women could not read or write, they also needed someone to maintain the records we required the groups to keep: how many seedlings they had cultivated, how many had been planted, and, most important, how many had survived after six months.

When I asked the women who they wanted to take on these tasks, they almost always chose one of their husbands or sons. These became what we called "nursery attendants." Hiring them created employment for many men, who would otherwise have had few options to earn additional income. It also made sense to hire men in these roles since the job required someone who was able to travel within a radius of several miles and convince farmers, schools, and others to plant trees. Only a young man would have the freedom to go knocking on people's doors.

Since these young men were educated at least through high school, we taught them about the different tree species, how to treat seeds and plant the trees, and why it was important to keep accurate records so the women would be paid. We made it a policy that the nursery attendants speak and write in their local language as well as in English. We knew the government would want to see proper records and that keeping them in English would confer more legitimacy and transparency.

The sight of these men was always a surprise to those who came to evaluate the Green Belt Movement's work. "We thought this was a women's organization," they would say, "but there are men here!" To my great disappointment, over the years we discovered that many of these young men turned out to be dishonest. They padded the numbers of seedlings the women cultivated and the number of trees that survived. What the men didn't realize was that our ten-step process allowed us to detect where, along the way, fraud had been committed. This dishonesty was very disturbing, and highlighted for me the challenge facing the larger society. If corruption like this existed at the grassroots, I could only imagine what it was like in the higher echelons of government and society in general.

As the Green Belt Movement developed, I became convinced that we needed to identify the roots of the disempowerment that plagued the Kenyan people. We had to understand why we were losing firewood; why there was malnutrition, scarcity of clean water, topsoil loss, and erratic rains; why people could not pay school fees; and why the infrastructure was falling apart. Why were we robbing ourselves of a future?

Gradually, the Green Belt Movement grew from a tree-planting program into one that planted ideas as well. We held seminars with the communities in which Green Belt worked, in which I encouraged women and men to identify their problems. As they spoke, I would write. Sometimes the list they generated would grow to 150 items. "Where do you think these problems come from?" I would ask. Almost to a person they put all the blame on the government.

It was partly true: The government was selling off public lands to its cronies and allowing tree farms for the timber industry to be established in national forests, and so destroying watersheds and biodiversity. In many ways the government continued the policies of the colonial era, but made sure the benefits went only to the small elite it favored. In turn, of course, this elite strongly supported the government and helped it stay in power.

However, I felt strongly that people needed to understand that the government was not the only culprit. Citizens, too, played a part in the problems the communities identified. One way was by not standing up for what they strongly believed in and demanding that the government provide it. Another was that people did not protect what they themselves had. "It is your land," I said. "You own it, but you are not taking care of it. You're allowing soil erosion to take place and you could do something about it. You could plant trees." I would also remind them that they had stopped growing their traditional foods that provided good nutrition. Instead, they were cultivating exotic crops that often didn't do well in the local soils. I urged them to look at their problems and the solutions more deeply. "Even though you blame the government," I said, "you really should also blame yourself. You need to do something about your situation. Do whatever is within your power."

In this way, communities where the Green Belt Movement worked began to develop personal responsibility for improving their quality of life, rather than waiting for the government, which wasn't very interested in the welfare of either Kenya's people or its environment, to do it. This personal responsibility became collective as communities managed their environment better. It was wonderful to see ordinary women and men speaking confidently in the meetings, in their own languages, and so honestly and openly.

Our insistence on people being able to speak their local languages was revolutionary. Many other organizations in Kenya that worked at the grassroots level would communicate in Kiswahili or English, but many people in rural areas, especially those who have had no schooling, do not fully comprehend English or Kiswahili, and their lack of fluency causes them to be shy in meetings. I wanted to hear what they had to say, and to know that they could fully understand us. In communities where we needed translation, we would ask someone locally who knew their mother tongue as well as Kiswahili or English to interpret.

Over time, this approach evolved into the "civic and environmental education" seminars that became part and parcel of the Green Belt Movement's work. In the early 1990s, the seminars expanded in scope to include an examination of the recent history of Kenya and how forests and land had been used and distributed in the colonial era and after independence. We also looked at issues of democracy, human rights, gender, and power.

In addition, I saw how important culture was to the larger goals of the Green Belt Movement and to managing our natural resources efficiently, sustainably, and equitably. Many aspects of the cultures our ancestors practiced had protected Kenya's environment. Before the Europeans arrived, the peoples of Kenya did not look at trees and see timber, or at elephants and see commercial ivory stock, or at cheetahs and see beautiful skins for sale. But when Kenya was colonized and we encountered Europeans, with their knowledge, technology, understanding, religion, and culture—all of it new—we converted our values into a cash economy like theirs. Everything was now perceived as having a monetary value. As we were to learn, if you can sell it, you can forget about protecting it. Using this analysis, we integrated the question of culture into our seminars and eventually wondered whether culture was a missing link in Africa's development.

By the mid-1980s, the Green Belt Movement had grown significantly and I had never been busier. I was working up to eighteen hours a day. By now, nearly two thousand women's groups were managing nurseries and planting and tending trees and more than a thousand green belts were being run by schools and students. Together, we had planted several million trees. Eventually, the Green Belt Movement would help establish more than six thousand nurseries, managed by six hundred community-based networks; involve several hundred thousand women, and many men, in its activities; and, by the early years of the twenty-first century, have planted more than thirty million trees in Kenya alone.

In Nairobi in July 1985 the UN convened the third global women's conference celebrating the conclusion of the Women's Decade.

Given the fact that the Green Belt Movement had been conceived at the start of the Women's Decade, it would have been nice if Kenya, as the host country of the conference marking the decade's completion, had chosen to highlight what we Kenyan women had achieved. It did not, and despite my participation in the preparatory meetings, it was clear the government's animosity toward me now extended to the Green Belt Movement. We were assigned an exhibition area for the conference near the National Museum, far from where hundreds of other NGOs had their stands and far from the official venue at the Kenyatta International Conference Centre. So as usual we had to make our own arrangements to share what we had done.

I arranged for rural women to talk about their experiences with the Green Belt Movement, and organized seminars to share with conference delegates what we were doing and why. Despite the distance—traveling halfway across town—many hundreds of participants in the conference visited our booth. I also took conference delegates to visit Green Belt groups outside Nairobi, see the nurseries, talk to the women, and plant trees.

One of the people who attended the conference was Terry Tempest Williams, a young American writer who was interested in our work. When she returned home to her native state of Utah, she established a Green Belt Movement of Utah that collected funds for us and also tried to mobilize her community to plant trees. Over the years, Terry also wrote about us and supported and publicized our work through her writings.

The Environment Liaison Centre, whose local board I still chaired, also organized a series of workshops on women and the environmental crisis, as part of the conference's official NGO forum (called Forum '85). The Green Belt Movement cosponsored several of the panels. Nearly thirty women from Asia, Latin America, the United States, Canada, Europe, and Africa, including me, spoke about the environmental challenges in their countries and the work they and other women were doing to address them.

During the conference, I also finally met Peggy Snyder, the head of UNIFEM, and she and I planted a tree together. I began to realize that the Green Belt Movement was becoming widely respected in Kenya and a number of other countries as well. At the women's conference in Nairobi I also met Helvi Sipilä, who was the first woman appointed a UN assistant secretary general, a post she held from 1972 to 1980. She had overseen the UN's women's conference in

Mexico City in 1975. After she retired from the UN, Helvi returned to Finland. I took Helvi to some of our tree nurseries close to Nairobi and explained to her how we were mobilizing women, supporting them to be innovative in how they raised seedlings, providing them with a small income, and encouraging the planting of "green belts" on farms and school compounds. She invited me to come to Finland to meet the network of women with whom the Finnish National Committee on UNIFEM, which Helvi had established, was working. I visited them the following year. As a result of my time there, UNIFEM-Finland began to raise funds to support the Green Belt Movement's work.

In 1986, with funding from UNEP, we expanded our work to other countries in Africa, many of which were also facing desertification, deforestation, water crises, and rural hunger. Over the next three years, UNEP supported four workshops that brought forty-five representatives from fifteen African countries to Kenya to learn from us. We provided a two-week training session that included seminars and time in the field with Green Belt groups. This led to the formation of the Pan-African Green Belt Network. Through the workshops and follow-up training, groups in Ethiopia, Tanzania, Uganda, Rwanda, and Mozambique, among other countries, launched tree-planting projects or brought the Green Belt Movement's approach to their work.

The press's interest in Kenya and abroad also increased and I found myself invited to address meetings and conferences on the environment. The Green Belt Movement and I also began to be honored with some prestigious awards, which was unexpected and very gratifying. It is impossible to list all the awards, but every one brought joy and a sense of validation after so many disappointments, so much pain, and feelings of rejection and abandonment. In 1983, I was named Woman of the Year in Kenya by a civic group in the entertainment industry. In 1984, I received the Right Livelihood Award, founded by the Swedish writer and parliamentarian Jakob von Uexküll, and often called the "alternative Nobel prize." In

1986, the Better World Society, a foundation initiated by U.S. media entrepreneur Ted Turner, conferred on me a medal; the following year, I was named to the UNEP Global 500 honor roll for environmental achievement. In 1988, I received the Windstar Award, founded by the late American singer and environmentalist John Denver.

In 1989, the U.K.-based group WomenAid, established to support women and children affected by war, natural disasters, and poverty, gave me one of its Women of the World Awards at a ceremony in London. I was delighted to be honored along with Mother Teresa and Mildred Robbins Leet, an American who founded a program called Trickle Up, which provides microgrants for women in developing countries to start their own businesses. We received our awards from Diana, Princess of Wales. I was pleased to meet this fascinating woman, who in person was gracious and down to earth. I asked her if she would sign my name card. Instead, she smiled and said, "I'll sign mine for you," and gave it to me, a souvenir I still have. When, now, I think of Princess Diana's life, I can understand something of what she went through: public recognition accompanied by moments of private loneliness and disappointment.

These awards brought international attention to our efforts, as well as making news at home. Both helped protect me from the increasing criticism and threats I experienced in subsequent years from the Kenyan government. The awards had other benefits. Some included financial remuneration, which helped with the Green Belt Movement's budget, and they sometimes attracted attention from the media in the countries where I received the awards. In addition, since people tend to hear only bad news from the African continent, these awards allowed me to explain what we were doing, and people who supported our work could say, "The Green Belt Movement is an example of something good that is happening in Africa."

Unfortunately, despite the Green Belt Movement's growing recognition by the international community, far from being supported by the authorities at home, we were under attack. In 1985, the government sought to dilute our strength through direct intervention by a cabinet minister, who came to the NCWK's annual meeting and demanded that the NCWK and the Green Belt Movement separate. He wanted the Green Belt Movement to focus on the environment and the NCWK on women's issues, not seeing (or not wanting to see) that they were intertwined. My reading of the situation was that the government wanted to reduce the attention the Green Belt Movement was getting in the press and its support from donors.

The government may also have thought (and hoped) that without the NCWK the Green Belt Movement would sink. This was similar to what it had expected to happen to the NCWK in 1980, when Maendeleo Ya Wanawake withdrew. But the National Council hadn't died, partly because the Green Belt Movement's activities kept it afloat and also drew public attention and media interest to the NCWK.

Although the government's directive that we separate the two was not given with a clean heart, I thought separation might be advantageous for both organizations. For one, if the Green Belt Movement was independent of the National Council, the government might be less inclined to interfere with our work. The Green Belt Movement could then focus on the environment and the NCWK on its traditional mandate. In addition, I had been chairman of the NCWK for seven years and felt it was time for a change. The parting, which took place in 1987, was amicable. I did not run for reelection as chairman and Vertistine Mbaya, who had been the NCWK's treasurer all the years I served as chair, became treasurer of the Green Belt Movement. The Green Belt Movement was registered as a separate NGO. Not only did both organizations survive, but the Green Belt Movement kept its office at the NCWK headquarters, although we soon found ourselves outgrowing the space.

As long as the Green Belt Movement was perceived as a few women raising seedlings, we didn't matter to the government. But as soon as we began to explain how trees disappear and why it is important for citizens to stand up for their rights—whether environmental, women's, or human—senior officials in the government and members of Parliament began to take notice. They soon realized that unlike some other women's organizations in Kenya, the Green Belt Movement was not organizing women for the purposes of advancing the government's agenda, whatever that might be. We were organizing women (and men) to do things for themselves that, in most cases, the government had no interest in doing.

This unsettled the authorities, and they began to come up with reasons to curtail our activities. They invoked an old colonial law that made it illegal for more than nine people to meet in one place without first obtaining a government license. Most of the Green Belt groups had between fifteen and thirty members. We asked the officials, "Why can't we meet? Why do we need a license to discuss with other women in the neighborhood how we plan to provide firewood for ourselves?" Those who wanted to prevent the groups from gathering would stonewall and make life difficult. I assured the women that they had every right to gather without seeking the permission of the authorities.

Fortunately, by this time, thousands of women had planted trees through the Green Belt Movement, and they had seen the value and the benefit of it. They were not going to be dissuaded by the government from participating. In addition, some members of the government at the grassroots level were beginning to appreciate the positive impacts of planting trees. In some cases, the wives of local chiefs and subchiefs were Green Belt group leaders or members.

In the last years of the 1980s, corruption became the culture of those in power in Kenya. Many people almost began to feel foolish for having a lot of money in their hands and not misusing it. In addition, the atmosphere became increasingly repressive as the regime ignored the needs of the people and hastened the destruction of the democracy we had created since independence two decades earlier.

The government clamped down on dissent and used heavy-handed tactics to consolidate its power and that of the sole political party, KANU. People were detained and sentenced to prison for voicing political views in opposition to the government line. Police shot live bullets into crowds of demonstrators, killing some, and the judicial system's independence was severely curtailed. Kenya had become a dictatorship, ruled, like many postindependence states in Africa, by a "strong man" president who kept an iron grip on power.

Some of the closing of democratic space after the end of colonial rule had begun in the later years of the Kenyatta administration. In 1975, J. M. Kariuki, then a member of Parliament from the Kikuyu community, publicly attacked what he perceived as a Kikuyu misuse of power in President Kenyatta's government. As a result, Kariuki was arrested and a few hours later found murdered. Many people suspected that senior members of the government's security forces had been involved. His death led to student demonstrations and a government select committee for investigation, but his assassins were never found. Like the killing of Tom Mboya in 1969, Kariuki's death made many Kenyans realize that all was not right with the postindependence political system.

When he came to power in 1978, President Moi released all of the twenty-six political prisoners then held by the government. However, any hopes invested in him were soon dashed. Kenya had been a de facto one-party state for several years, but in June 1982, Parliament declared it officially so, and people the regime saw as opponents began to be harassed and intimidated. Many of them decided to go into exile abroad while others were pressured by the government to leave the country. Those deemed subversive were placed in detention. A number of them died in custody, where conditions were harsh and torture was common. Journalists were harassed when they reported such trials and arrests.

In August 1982, I was in Sweden attending a meeting when I learned that members of the Kenya Air Force had attempted a coup against President Moi. The coup failed, and after looting broke out in Nairobi, it is estimated that government security forces killed several hundred people, an action that they claimed was necessary to restore order. The president used the attempted coup as an opportunity to amass even more power and dismiss some elements in the government.

The University of Nairobi became a center of student resistance to the government's activities. Security forces clashed repeatedly with student demonstrators who called for more political freedom. In 1985, government forces killed at least twelve students, while two years later the government closed the university—as it was to do several times in coming years—and arrested student leaders. As a way to keep their opponents divided and insecure, elements in the government also played different ethnic communities off one another. This was to have devastating consequences in the early 1990s when tribal clashes broke out in different parts of the country.

In 1988, supporters of greater political openness in Kenya focused their energy and commitment on that year's national elections. The Green Belt Movement joined others in carrying out pro-democracy activities such as registering voters for the election and pressing for constitutional reforms and political space to ensure freedom of thought and expression. In this way, the Green Belt Movement was not only an environmental, women's, and human rights movement, but also part of the broader movement for democracy.

We hoped that these elections would provide the people of Kenya with a fairer and truer representation of their aspirations and beliefs. To our dismay and despair, however, the elections were the most disturbing and distorted in Kenya's history. The government introduced a highly controversial system of "queue" voting. Voters lined up behind their candidate and election officials counted each line and then told the people to go home. When election officials announced the winner, it was often the candidate with the shortest line of voters behind him! Since the voters were at home, there was nothing that could be done: The winner had been declared. The vote-rigging was so blatant that people who had lost their races were declared the winners in broad daylight with no embarrassment whatsoever on the part of the government.

After the elections, Parliament passed a bill to further limit the independence of the Kenyan judiciary. The press was harassed and intimidated, too. The *Daily Nation,* one of the country's most widely read newspapers, was banned from covering Parliament for four months. Many of us in the pro-democracy movement felt depressed and helpless. "This ruling party is going to be here forever," we said to one another. This was not helped by the fact that after the elections President Moi declared that KANU would rule for a hundred years.

I knew that we could not live with a political system that killed creativity, nurtured corruption, and produced people who were afraid of their own leaders. It would be only a matter of time before the government and I came into further conflict. The incident that brought me into direct confrontation with the authorities began, simply and essentially, with one person deciding that something had to be done to protect Uhuru Park.

9

Fighting for Freedom

In the autumn of 1989, I was working late in the office, as was
often the case, when a young law student knocked on my door.
Although I didn't know him, it was obvious he had some news for
me. He told me that he had learned from very reliable sources that
the government was planning to build a skyscraper in Uhuru Park.
The park, which is located west of Uhuru Highway in the very heart
of Nairobi, is the equivalent of Hyde Park in London and Central
Park in New York City or any central open space in any city of the
world—a large green swath amid the bustle of crowds and the concrete and steel of the metropolis. Its lawns, paths, boating lake, and
stands of trees provide millions of people in Nairobi with a natural
environment for recreation, gatherings, quiet walks, or simply a
breath of fresh air.

The young man had learned this information because he had
overheard his father and uncles, who were very close to powerful
people in the government, discussing the planned building project
and commenting on how terrible it was. He knew they wouldn't
make their concerns public and he didn't want to jeopardize their
positions, since at this time whoever openly questioned the government's actions was arrested and detained, and newspapers and jour-
nals were closed down. The young man, however, was aware of my
concern for the environment and knew that I was not afraid to speak
out on such matters.

"Don't let anybody know that I told you," he warned me. "But I
have heard that this tower is going to be a monstrosity and I was

wondering what could be done." I told the young man that I would not reveal his identity, a promise I have kept. "I've no clue about this tower," I replied, "but I will write a letter to the minister for environment and inquire." I had seen fencing in the park, but had assumed it had been put there temporarily for a major fun fair or religious gathering.

What this young man told me was shocking. Uhuru Park provided everyone, whether young or old, rich or poor, with some respite in a city that was growing rapidly, as sprawling housing estates and commercial buildings took over land that was previously grassland or forest. Nairobi was no longer the "Green City in the Sun" I had walked in over twenty years before. While there were other parks, they were not in the center of town and not as large. Even Uhuru Park itself was shrinking. Over the years, a hotel, a road, a members-only golf course, and a football stadium had all been built on land that had been part of the park.

In 1988, the government had further encroached on the park by building a monument near the intersection of Kenyatta Avenue and Uhuru Highway that celebrated ten years of President Moi's *nyayo* (or "step by step") political philosophy and twenty-five years of independence. It had cost almost a million U.S. dollars. It was a bitter irony that the park, named to celebrate our independence, was subjected, like so many of Kenya's public goods, to land-grabbers in the government.

By 1989, the park covered only thirty-four acres. Despite these past intrusions into the park, nothing would, literally, cast such a shadow over it as the proposed Times Media Trust Complex. Although the government disputed how much of the park would be consumed by the complex, what I discovered convinced me that it would be a sizable piece and that the construction would fundamentally alter Uhuru Park's character and role in the life of the city.

As envisioned, the complex would consist of a tower sixty stories high and would house, among other things, the headquarters for KANU, the *Kenya Times* newspaper (the organ of the ruling party), a trading center, offices, an auditorium, galleries, shopping malls, and parking space for two thousand cars. The tower would be the tallest building of its kind in Africa and the complex would cost in the region of four billion Kenyan shillings (then about $200 million) to construct. Most of the costs would be funded through a loan guarantee from the government to the private investors involved. The plan also called for a huge statue of President Moi.

As I learned the details, the plan for the complex seemed more and more absurd. Despite private investment in the project, the government could ill afford the huge loan it was offering. There were also many logistical questions: What about the enormous amount of car traffic that would be generated at an already congested intersection? The citizens of Nairobi didn't have adequate water pressure to keep a four-floor building functioning properly: How were they going to get enough water to flow around all sixty floors? What also annoyed me was that such grandiose and costly white elephants, which were more often monuments to ego than well-considered contributions to the public good, were being erected throughout Africa.

Soon after that young man visited me, I discussed the project with some members of the executive committee of the Green Belt Movement. We agreed that the way to go about it was initially to simply write letters to the relevant governmental and business offices inquiring about the project: whether it was true that there was such a project, who was responsible, and who could assist us with information.

On October 3, 1989, I wrote a letter on Green Belt Movement stationery to the managing director of the *Kenya Times* inquiring about the complex and urging him not to build it if the rumors about the plans were true. The park provided people with recreational facilities, I said, a break from life in the concrete jungle and a resting place where they could spend their free time. I reminded him that it was a space for public meetings and national celebrations, a playground for many city children, and that future generations were relying on us to keep the park in the form that it had been bequeathed to us. I sent copies of the letter to the office of the president, the Nairobi city commission, the provincial commissioner, the minister for environment and natural resources, and the executive directors of UNEP and the Environment Liaison Centre International. I also sent copies to the Kenyan press, and a small story about my appeal ran in the *Daily Nation* on October 4.

In the manner typical of the government of the day, instead of responding, the regime ignored me. When the office of the president did not reply, I started writing to other offices, and the more I wrote the more they knew that I knew, and the more the word spread.

Shortly after, I discovered that construction of the tower block would require the demolition of two historic buildings, so I wrote a letter to the director of the National Museums of Kenya, who had recommended that the buildings be preserved, asking for his support. In addition to the people I sent my first letter to, among those I copied this letter to were the executive director of the United Nations Educational, Scientific and Cultural Organization (UNESCO), the ministry of public works, the permanent secretary in the department of international security and administration, and the managing director of the *Kenya Times* (again). Nobody could say that they were unaware of our concern.

I also shared my letters with the press. Fortunately, many journalists were very interested and pleased I was raising this issue, and as they reported on my new campaign people around the country began to take notice. Kenya was still reeling from the blatantly rigged elections just a year earlier and many Kenyans, including the press, felt powerless against the government. They were, therefore, happy that someone was speaking out.

On October 26, three weeks after my initial letter, I wrote to Sir John Johnson, the British high commissioner in Nairobi, urging him to intervene with Robert Maxwell. Maxwell was, along with KANU, reported to be one of the major shareholders in the project and was then the proprietor of London's Mirror Group Newspapers. I requested that Sir John ask Mr. Maxwell to recognize that while many Africans might not know the full consequences of their environmental actions, people in Western Europe, Japan, and America had no such excuse. Surely the British and Americans wouldn't tolerate a tower block in the middle of Hyde Park or Central Park, I suggested to him, so why then should the people of Nairobi?

Still no direct response. A week later I wrote to the resident representative of the UN Development Programme (UNDP) about the complex. I complained that the owners of the *Kenya Times* and international investors were taking advantage of the Kenyan people, who were so busy trying to meet their basic needs that they "did not have time to complain, restrain, demonstrate and challenge the unadmirable locals who have collaborated [on the project] and the irresponsible financiers who have persuaded them to." I felt strongly that the issue extended beyond the preservation of the park to a matter of the government being responsible and accountable to its citizens.

There were millions of silent, despairing Kenyans, I explained to the UNDP representative, who wondered what had happened to their society, "to moral justice, to fair play and to responsibility and accountability of those who have been put in places of responsibility, those who are supposed to protect them, to guide them and to lead them to a brighter tomorrow."

I continued, "There are also the millions of Kenyans of tomorrow, our grandchildren and great-grandchildren, who will either curse us or feel deeply ashamed at the lack of foresight, at the magnitude of greed, and at the arrogance of those who are promoting destruction and want to call it development." I hoped he would "stand for the weak, for the poor, for the lonely, for the fearful, for the ignorant, and for the silent. We must not stand for the powerful only, or the rich only, or for the arrogant only. Justice does not demand that."

Although I had been writing all these letters, the authorities refused to reply to me directly. Instead, they spoke through the media. At a press conference in mid-October the minister for lands and housing told the *Daily Nation* that those who opposed the tower were "ill-informed" and said that the complex would be a "landmark." I replied with an open letter to the minister outlining my concerns, which I shared with the press.

In the November 7 edition of the *Standard*, a widely read daily newspaper whose shareholders at that time were mainly KANU officials or supporters, the minister for local government and physical planning denied that the *Times* complex would take more than a small portion of public park land. He lauded it as a "fine and magnificent work of architecture," and called those who opposed the project the "ignorant few." I wrote to him that same day and asked him to consider the environmental consequences of the decision to let the project go ahead. The logic behind the complex, I suggested, was the same as the attitude of development with destruction that had led to acid rain, poisoned rivers, deforestation, and climate change. I exhorted him to solicit the opinions of people whom I considered not the "ignorant few" but the "informed many" in Nairobi and to reconsider the plan.

I closed with an appeal: "We have tried to reach out and plead with all relevant authorities over the imposing *Times* complex at Uhuru Park. We appeal to Nairobi residents to raise their voices even higher, 'Do not be afraid of speaking out when you know that you are in the right. Fear has never been a source of security. Speak out and stand up while you can. If the ministers refuse to listen, the president will. If the ministers ignore us we will keep going until our faint voices reach the president at State House. He too claims to be an environmentalist and he cares for his people.' "

This last observation was true—to a degree. Earlier that year, President Moi had publicly burned millions of Kenyan shillings' worth of poached elephant ivory before the world's cameras and to the world's applause. It was perhaps a vain expectation, but I hoped that his newly burnished environmental image might influence his attitude toward the park as well.

At the heart of all my letters was a simple question: I was asking, "Is it true?" All the government had to do was answer yes or no. Fortunately, the press made it impossible for the government to ignore me entirely. Reporters went to the people I'd written to and asked them, "Have you told her whether it's true or not?" The officials would splutter and call me names and suggest that something was wrong with my head and the press would then faithfully come and tell me and the country what had been said about me. In turn, I would write to the officials and demand that they explain why they had told the press what they had. This went on until the building of the *Times* complex at Uhuru Park became a national discussion.

If the authorities had provided a convincing statement as to why the *Times* tower complex had to be built in Uhuru Park, I would have had to sit down and think of another reason to oppose it. As it turned out, the main justifications the project's proponents offered during the whole episode were that it would be a prestigious project, look magnificent, and that the tower would provide spectacular views of Nairobi and the surrounding area. This was not, of course, a serious answer to my question. Fortunately, those in power were so keen to appear good in the eyes of the international community that any exposure through the media forced them to respond. And respond they did.

The government was so arrogant at that time that in addition to not answering my letters directly and belittling my concerns via the press, it began to abuse me in public. On November 8, 1989, members of Parliament used a parliamentary procedure reserved for a national emergency to interrupt their ongoing debate to discuss . . . me. For forty-five minutes, MPs, including a minister and an assistant minister, lined up to express their outrage at what I had done. How dare I write to a foreign government over what they considered a sovereign issue! Had not Kenya achieved independence years ago? And yet there I was threatening to take them back to the colonial past! The complex would not affect the park at all, they said. Indeed, the government was looking at the possibility of building a public space even bigger and better than Uhuru Park. Furthermore, the president himself was internationally recognized for his commitment to the environment.

The Green Belt Movement was a "bogus organization," one MP claimed, that only erected billboards while I spent my time traveling the world collecting money for unknown purposes. Reflecting on my letter to the minister of local government, one MP claimed I had called for people to rise up against the government, a statement he considered "ugly and ominous" and that deserved to land me in court. After all, said another, I wasn't an MP, with the privileges of Parliament: What mandate did I have to speak for the people?

Then the abuse turned personal. To the cheers of a packed house, one MP said that because I had supposedly repudiated my husband in public, I could not be taken seriously and that my behavior had damaged his respect for all women. He accused me of incitement and warned Green Belt Movement members (my "clique of women" as he called them) to tread carefully. "I don't see the sense at all in a bunch of divorcées coming out to criticize such a complex," he concluded. Some MPs suggested that if I was so comfortable writing to Europeans, I should go and live in Europe. Members laughed while one parliamentarian even advocated calling down a curse, or *salala*, on me. All of this could have gone on much longer had not the Speaker stepped in and called an end to the farrago. But he had a final dig. "We hope Maathai has heard the sentiments of this House," he said.

Yes, I had, and I wasn't going to take those slanders lying down. As I read the newspaper headlines—"MPs Condemn Prof Maathai" and "Prof Maathai Under Fire in Parliament"—I knew that this was just what I needed to stake my ground. What had begun as my attempt to answer the call of a young law student had become a contest between me, asking the government to explain its actions, and the government behaving badly in response. As it turned out, the more the government misbehaved, the worse it seemed in the eyes of the public and, later, the international community.

The day after my vilification in Parliament, I wrote a letter to Philip Leakey, who was my constituency MP and an assistant minister for the environment, to respond to what, as I'd read in the papers, had been said in Parliament about me. I explained that the only reason I had written to the British High Commission was that one of the investors in the project was Robert Maxwell, whose whereabouts I did not know, and that it was absurd to call me anti-government because I had simply raised a question. I noted the president's interest in the environment, and said that it was precisely because of this concern, which I shared, that I had thought if I raised my voice about the *Times* complex he might hear me.

Far from acting against the spirit of the twenty-fifth anniversary of Kenya's independence from Britain, I continued, I was acting in the spirit of Uhuru, or freedom. "When I see Uhuru Park and contemplate its meaning," I wrote, "I feel compelled to fight for it so that my grandchildren may share that dream and that joy of freedom as they one day walk there." I reiterated that I was not against the complex per se, but its placement in the park. I also made clear that I had no intention of fleeing Kenya—for Europe or anywhere else. "This is home and this is where I will be. I hope that I will be buried right here in the heart of it."

At another time and in another forum, I told Mr. Leakey, I would discuss my marital status with the MPs, since they were so interested, but that I wanted to keep the focus on the issue at hand. "The debate is on the proposed *Times* complex at Uhuru Park," I wrote, and MPs should not be distracted by, as I put it, "the anatomy below the line (if they know what I mean)." In spite of what the MPs might think, I assured him, my being a woman was irrelevant. Instead, the debate over the complex required the use of "the anatomy of whatever lies above the neck!"

I'm sure the MPs were amazed that I was willing to tell them to concentrate on what was supposedly between their ears. That quote found its way into the press. Even though what had been said about me in Parliament was deeply unpleasant, it wasn't anything new, either for me or other critics of the government. I had been publicly humiliated during my divorce and denied reemployment at the University of Nairobi because I had dared to challenge the ruling party. Indeed, it was almost the price I had to pay to be free. I knew in this case I hadn't broken any law or done anything that warranted jail or mistreatment. I had asked a question, which I knew was a right guaranteed in the Kenyan constitution.

On November 16, I wrote to the president directly, urging him in an appeal of "last resort" to stop the construction of the complex. I suggested that saving Uhuru Park for Kenya's children, ordinary people, and future generations would be symbolic of his personal commitment to preservation of the world's environment. I felt, I wrote "like the Dutch boy at the dikes as the sea swelled," with the president as the last hope.

I never heard back.

As the public debate over the complex grew, some professional organizations, including the Architectural Association of Kenya, also raised objections to building in the park. More important, the people themselves spoke out. In fact, the more the government urged them to stay quiet, the more they raised their voices. I was thrilled when men and women dared to send letters to newspapers and weekly magazines in support of what I was doing. I was even more impressed that most felt courageous enough to use their own names and not to sign the letters "anonymous."

"This is where I escape from the crowded [housing] estates over the weekend or during the holidays," one letter-writer said about the park. "A green belt in the city creates a meaningful contrast to the concrete jungle," wrote another. Others recalled with pleasure their visits to the park after a day's work, or at lunchtime, or on the weekend. They complained that the skyline of the city would be obscured, the tower would block out the sun, and traffic would clog the entrances to the park, while trees and grass would be lost when the building went up. Children also wrote. "Uhuru Park is where my parents take me over the weekend," one said.

Many letter writers tied the fight for the park to the issue of democracy in Kenya and the government's reluctance to heed the people's wishes. "I have one suggestion to make," read one letter published in the *Weekly Review.* "The names of all MPs who vigorously bulldozed this project forward should be engraved prominently in the complex. This will allow future generations to know who robbed them of their favorite recreation facility, Uhuru Park." Another letter writer asked: "Our leaders, where is your sense of priority, your pride in the people you lead? When we write in protest we are called 'few,' 'ignorant,' and 'disgruntled.' . . . Democracy is of, by, and for the people." Yet another argued: "Kenyans should be allowed to debate matters freely without threats and abuse from our leaders. Their views and opinions should be listened to and respected because Kenya is acclaimed as democratic; this should not only be on paper but should be seen in practice." Although I knew from the press that the people were behind me, I never called for a street demonstration against the complex and I did not expect anyone to come to my rescue or protest in public when the government vilified me.

During the course of the struggle over the complex, I felt strongly that I was doing the right thing—popular opinion notwithstanding. So, I didn't experience fear on a daily basis. I don't tend to invite challenges, but I meet them. And once I do, I stick with it. I know the situation is not going to be resolved overnight, and I don't hurry to meet a second challenge until the first is concluded. That, perhaps, has been my strong point. I have seen time and again that if you stay with a challenge, if you are convinced that you are right to do so, and if you give it everything you have, it is amazing what can happen.

Nonetheless, it was hard at times to be the focus of so much negative attention and in the glare of the public spotlight. It was also very destructive for my children (Waweru and Wanjira were in the United States, and so had to follow the events from a distance), and for my family and friends.

Some days, as I walked from the Green Belt offices at the corner of University Way and Moi Avenue down the street toward the Khoja mosque, I could see people I knew crossing the road to avoid me. Or I would meet friends on the street and they wouldn't want to stand and talk because they were afraid to be associated with me. Some of them would ask me, "Why are you putting yourself in this situation? It's not your land. Why are you bothered?" And I would reply, "Because after they are done with what is owned by the public, they'll come for what is mine and yours."

This was the heart of the issue. Even though the immediate struggle was over the park and the right of everyone to enjoy green space, the effort was also about getting Kenyans to raise their voices. I was distressed at the audacity with which the government was violating people's rights, quashing dissent—often brutally—and forcing men and women from their jobs, especially in the university and the civil service. Ordinary people had become so fearful that they had been rendered nearly powerless. Now, they were beginning to reclaim their power.

Even though the debate had reached the floor of Parliament and the public arena, the fight was far from over. On November 15, at an official ceremony, ground was broken for the complex in Uhuru Park. At the end of the month, I sought an injunction in the Kenya High Court to halt construction, but the case was thrown out on December 11. By this time, the independence of the judiciary had been so compromised that the decision did not surprise me. I appealed to the acting attorney general, who was not sympathetic. While I lost the legal battles, these actions nonetheless helped generate publicity—I issued a press release about the court's decision—and we garnered more support from Kenyans. The controversy over the park, my court case, and the comments of President Moi and others regularly featured on the front pages of Kenya's newspapers and the international media were beginning to cover the story.

Still, the personal attacks continued. In early December, President Moi made his first public comments about the *Times* complex and the controversy. He gave the project his seal of approval and offered his opinion that those who opposed the complex had "insects in their heads." On December 12, *Jamhuri*, or Republic Day, when Kenyans celebrate independence from the British with a public holiday, the president gave a speech, in Uhuru Park no less. He condemned the Law Society of Kenya and the the National Council of Churches of Kenya for perceived criticisms of the government, and singled me out for opposing the complex. Moi also suggested that if I was to be a proper woman in "the African tradition"—I should respect men and be quiet.

Prompted by President Moi, who wondered in that speech why the women of Kenya had not spoken out against this "wayward" woman, the leadership of Maendeleo Ya Wanawake, our former National Council of Women colleagues and now a faithful branch of KANU, criticized me for "having belittled the president and the government." They held rallies and press conferences to denounce me. At one point they suggested that I had "gone astray and should seek guidance from [my] fellow women."

Not long after, the frustrated president declared that from then on all foreign assistance to Kenyan women's development had to be channeled through state organizations. This often made fund-raising for the Green Belt Movement difficult in subsequent years.

The furor increased when members of KANU asked for me to be expelled from the party and one claimed in a public speech that the Green Belt Movement had "done nothing that Kenyans could be proud of." This statement led to chants of "Remove her! Remove her!" from the crowd. MPs called for Green Belt to be banned because the sources of its finances weren't public (to his credit the attorney general dismissed their request). The movement and I were even barred by a local MP from his constituency, located around

Mount Elgon near the border with Uganda, because of my supposed disrespect for the president. In late November, I asked the Third World Network—a Malaysia-based association of groups and individuals engaged in development-related projects—to issue an international action alert to its members to urge the Kenyan government to stop harassing the Green Belt Movement and me. I was becoming an outlaw in my own country.

I knew that the government was using me as a mirror in which other women would look at themselves. They were being asked to decide if that image was who they would like to be. Because I couldn't go into the women's hearts and tell them, "It's all right. I haven't done anything wrong. It's them, not me." It was okay for me to be called crazy and told I had insects in my head: That is the way people using their own mirror saw me. But I offered women a different mirror—my own. What is important, indeed necessary, is to hold up your own mirror to see yourself as you really are.

Ten days before Christmas 1989, just when we thought things could not get more challenging, the government decided to evict the Green Belt Movement from the government offices it had been operating from under the auspices of the National Council of Women of Kenya. Jomo Kenyatta's administration had been very supportive of civil society in general and the NCWK in particular, and had given the NCWK office space many years previously. When President Kenyatta died and President Moi took over, we were moved from the house we were occupying and given an office next to the Central Police Station. This was a very old, wooden building, part of which was used as a book storage depot by the Ministry of Education. Our workspace consisted of subdivided offices and a meeting area in one long block. Although it was somewhat ramshackle and a little cramped, the situation was satisfactory.

Technically, however, the building was owned by the government, although it had forgotten we were there until I inadvertently drew attention to our address in a press interview. The government was outraged that it was housing this wayward woman and her organization. The day after the president's Republic Day speech in Uhuru Park, the police officer in charge ordered us to vacate the building—within twenty-four hours. I appealed the eviction order, but was told the decision was final. We weren't even allowed to take the dividers that separated our offices. When we looked for new space, our reputation, unfortunately, preceded us. Landlords either refused to give us office space because we were now blacklisted by the government or set the rent so high we couldn't possibly afford it. This left me with two choices: I either had to abandon the Green Belt Movement or move it to my house in South C.

The government seemed determined to do all it could to take an ax to the Green Belt Movement, and I was equally determined not to let it. Throughout the struggle over Uhuru Park, our work with communities around Kenya was still continuing, and millions of trees were still being planted. So, I used my own money and some Green Belt funds and converted my small bungalow and garden, where I had grown sweet potatoes and grazed two goats, into an office for our staff, which then numbered eighty. I had to add an underground water tank because we didn't have enough water for sanitation and I needed two extra toilets. The day we moved, police ransacked the old office, and threw papers and books out of the building.

As 1990 began, I decided to make a peace offering: I issued a statement thanking the president for abiding by the rule of law and allowing free speech to air the differences over the *Times* tower complex. My aim was not to be deliberately confrontational but to encourage movement on the issue. I also wanted to return the focus to our primary job, which was planting trees.

Just a few days later, however, the registrar general ordered the Green Belt Movement to provide its audited accounts for the past five consecutive years. I saw this as another attempt by the government to deregister the movement and make its activities illegal. But

I wanted to beat them at their own game. When I discussed the situation with Vertistine Mbaya, who as Green Belt's treasurer oversaw all the accounts, she said, "Let's send them *ten* years of accounts!" And we did. In the letter that accompanied the records, I asked the government to supply me with one year of its audited accounts of the ruling party, since I knew that KANU was not regularly audited. As you might expect, I never received a reply to that request.

If the office next to the police station was cramped, it was nothing compared to our accommodations at South C when all the staff moved in. While I kept my bedroom and Muta, my only child still living at home, kept his, the rest of the house became the general workspace. My office operated out of what used to be Waweru's bedroom and everyone else worked in the area we created outside, or in the living room, or in the two other bedrooms. None of these rooms is large! The receptionist sat at a table by the entrance to the living room and we made our meals and brewed tea in my kitchen.

I felt badly for Muta, who was a teenager at the time, an age when you want to bring friends home. I was sorry I couldn't provide more space for him than just his tiny bedroom. Muta understood the situation, although he'd have been happier not having to share his home with eighty Green Belt employees! In later years Muta worked for Green Belt and grew to be proud of his contribution and the part he played when the movement needed space.

We stayed this way for nearly seven years. It was crowded, but the situation worked, more or less. However, in 1991, we faced a disruption. Some months after the move to South C, a friend of mine who was a building contractor brought to the house a young man who had been involved in political activities in the university and was expelled. "He is wanted by the authorities," my friend said, "and so is undercover. He can't work in areas that are too exposed to the public. Construction work would be too visible." He asked me to help him. "He can knit sweaters and tablecloths, and that's how he makes a living at the moment. Perhaps you can help him earn something. He's desperate."

Like many young people in Kenya at that time, this youth had few skills, he'd been thrown out of the university because he had been involved in a strike, and he was considered a dissident. He was worried about being seen with anyone and operated under a pseudonym. I felt sorry for him, because he was *so* young. "I want you to sit next to my desk," I told him, "and help me with whatever I'm doing. We'll keep you away from the others at the moment, because we don't want them to alert the police." He was delighted with this plan. Unfortunately, in time he became so comfortable and got to know the staff sufficiently well that he tried to convince them that I wasn't paying them enough and that the working conditions were bad. "You should get out of there or she should get you a bigger office," he told them.

I had always been very straightforward with my staff. "If we can perform well," I informed them, "we will raise the money, and you will be paid. However, if I don't have it, I can't give it." They knew that no one had any pensions. "All I can give you is a monthly allowance," I said. "I'll try as much as possible to give you one month's notice if our money runs out and I can't raise it. But you need to give me one month's notice as well if you want to leave." I had put all this in a letter, and everyone had signed it.

The result of the young man's agitation was that one morning I woke up to find that forty-five members of the staff had walked out and some had formed a blockade outside my front gate. They were stopping everyone from coming in and telling them to go home because there was a strike on. What was worse was that Muta and I were prisoners in our own home: We couldn't go out and nobody could come in to see us. So I called the police, who came with officials from the Ministry of Labour to mediate the situation. The officials asked for the staff's contracts and demanded to know what I paid them. While I was talking to them, the policemen were looking around my house. They were astonished. "You mean you work here—with all these people?" they asked. "Where do you live?"

"I live in one bedroom," I replied, "and my son lives in the other one. The rest is the office." The policemen knew very well that the government had thrown us out of our offices and that we had had to relocate to my house, but the smallness of the space and my decision to keep the Green Belt Movement going impressed them. "Why would these people be so ungrateful?" they asked. "Look at the salaries they're being paid. They're even getting more than we are!"

After investigating, the officials found that there was nothing to warrant a strike and that the strikers were acting illegally in stopping Muta and me from entering and leaving our house. The strikers were amazed. They thought that my reputation as a troublemaker meant that the authorities would support them. Meanwhile, members of the press, whom the strikers had called, assuming they would take their side, were also unsympathetic to their claims against me. My biggest disappointment was that the organizer of the strike was the young man whom I had protected and sheltered. Naturally, I couldn't take him back after what he had done. I don't bear him any ill will: I think he was simply a mean-spirited person.

We worked at South C until 1996, when some friends visited and were astounded that the Green Belt Movement and I were squeezed into such a small space (by this time Muta was studying in the United States). While the Netherlands Organization for International Development Cooperation (NOVIB), a long-time supporter, wanted to help us purchase a permanent office, they did not have enough funds for this purpose. But they were quickly joined by other friends of the movement—the United Kingdom–based Tudor Trust and American philanthropists Steven and Barbara Rockefeller and Joshua Mailman. Together, they agreed to buy a house on Kilimani Lane near the Adams Arcade, not too far from the center of Nairobi, for the main Green Belt offices.

The other organization interested in helping us was CARE-Austria, but they were receiving their funds from the Austrian government, which did not want to purchase a building with a nongovernmental organization. As we looked for office space, we saw a house in Lang'ata that we decided could be a place to provide training, while we looked for another house to serve as our offices. The resources CARE-Austria had set aside were adequate to acquire the home in Lang'ata. The owners, a British couple, were pleased that Green Belt was to be the new owner because they knew we would not pave over any of the large garden or cut down the trees. In a demonstration of the Austrian government's confidence in us, it immediately had the building registered in the Green Belt Movement's name.

Naturally, I was very happy when everyone left my house—as were they, I'm sure. Afterward, that bungalow felt so huge I didn't know what to do with all the space! The day the staff moved into the house on Kilimani Lane, they basked in the sun, ate the guavas that were ripe on the trees, lay down on the green grass, and enjoyed Kilimani's roominess. This continues to be the Green Belt Movement's main office.

In spite of the difficulties we experienced with our office space, throughout the early 1990s we never wavered in our commitment to saving Uhuru Park and fighting for our freedom. By early 1990, despite the resistance of the authorities to any of my appeals, it was becoming clear that the government could no longer ignore the chorus of opposition both inside and outside Kenya to the *Times* complex. During the last months of 1989 I had written letters to many individuals abroad in Canada, the United States, the United Kingdom, and West Germany—politicians, media moguls, activists, and philanthropists—and asked them to put pressure on investors to ensure that the complex wasn't built in the park.

Once again, I appealed to them to recognize that while people in developing countries might not know about the kind of destructive development that the *Times* complex represented, or be able to stop it, there could be no such excuse for those in developed countries. I asked them to pressure their governments not to do business with dictators, whom they knew full well were oppressing their citizens and stealing their money, and not to hold poor people to account for the crimes of their rulers.

Journalists from some leading American and British newspapers, including the *New York Times*, the *Los Angeles Times*, and the United Kingdom's *Independent*, among others, reported on our struggle. This helped raise awareness among environmentalists and pro-democracy campaigners in Europe and North America. For the first time, many of them were hearing Africans raising their voices to protect their own environment and green spaces. Alerted by some of their citizens, foreign investors and donor governments now questioned the wisdom of spending such a vast sum of money on a building of dubious usefulness in a poor country that was already struggling with large domestic and international debts.

At last, our message was heard. On January 29, 1990, the government announced that its plans for the complex had changed. The sixty-story tower was considerably scaled back and the project's cost reduced to around $60 million (U.S.). The international media reported that, after a London meeting with the World Bank and other donors, Kenyan officials appeared no longer to be backing the project. For the next two years the project limped on as an idea, but nothing more was built on the site. The investment simply wasn't there and the costs all around were too high.

One day, late in February 1992, I woke up and learned that the fence surrounding the building site in Uhuru Park had been removed at about three o'clock that morning. That day, a group of women were meeting at the Kenyatta International Conference Centre in downtown Nairobi. When I got there, the women were eager to let me know that the *Times* complex was dead—as dead as a dodo. "Let's go to the park," I called to the women, "and dance, a dance of victory!" And so we did. On the way, I bought a wreath to hang at the site to declare the project dead and buried.

Looking back, I can see that there were two main reasons we

stopped the destruction of Uhuru Park. For one, the government's mismanagement of resources was exposed by the press. The press knew that what was being done was wrong and that the government was being arrogant and vindictive. The press was fantastic. I would never have gotten anywhere without them. What was also true was that, for the first time, many donor agencies and especially diplomats from wealthy countries that provided development aid to the government noticed that the Kenyan people were speaking out. Donor governments had seen the ruling party become increasingly dictatorial and oppressive, violating the rights of its citizens at every opportunity.

During the cold war, Kenya, like many other countries in the Western sphere of influence, was considered a bulwark against communism. Western governments had been content either to say nothing to the dictators who ruled many of these countries or preferred to whisper their concerns behind closed doors. With the collapse of the Berlin Wall at the end of 1989 and the rapid thawing of the cold war, the regimes that depended on Western governments' aid no longer had as free a rein to be as tyrannical as they had been.

Despite the changing circumstances in the world, Kenyans were so used to being silenced that most were still fearful of what might happen if someone challenged the government. That is why, when I started writing my letters, everyone was surprised. They were amazed not only that one relatively insignificant woman could stop a large project that those in power wanted to see completed, but astonished that it could be done only a year after we had watched in despair as losers of an election were declared the winners. I remember one man from the Central Region came over to congratulate me with the following words on his lips: "You are the only man left standing." We both laughed as we shook hands. People following the discussion were afraid that the government might harm me. But when the building was stopped and I was not harmed, people felt extremely empowered and they have never gone back.

Indeed, the slaying of the "park monster," as we called it, energized the Kenyan people. From that time on, we moved with more confidence, courage, and speed. To me, this was the beginning of the end of Kenya as a one-party state. Still, while we had won a victory, the struggle to restore our democracy would last another decade. During those challenging years, we would be led down further roads of violence and fear, and all of us—including me—would have to draw upon our deepest reserves of hope, conviction, and faith to keep going and never give up on freedom.

10

<hr/>

Freedom Turns a Corner

It is often difficult to describe to those who live in a free society what life is like in an authoritarian regime. You don't know who to trust. You worry that you, your family, or your friends will be arrested and jailed without due process. The fear of political violence or death, whether through direct assassinations or targeted "accidents," is constant. Such was the case in Kenya, especially during the 1990s.

After February 1990, when the *Times* tower complex was effectively dead, the government's attitude hardened toward the Green Belt Movement and me, and its actions against its opponents became even more hostile. The political climate was also becoming more oppressive. That same month, Kenya's popular foreign minister, Robert Ouko, who was considered a strong supporter of President Moi and was tipped as his possible successor, was murdered in mysterious circumstances on his farm in western Kenya. Several days of rioting followed, beginning in Ouko's home region of Kisumu and spreading to other areas.

I realized that I was now a political figure and that I had to take care, even as I knew I couldn't stay silent. Not long after Ouko's murder, I was in New York to talk about the Green Belt Movement's work. At one event, held at the Church Center of the United Nations, as I described my struggle to protect Uhuru Park and the political situation in Kenya, Peggy Snyder and other friends and supporters of Green Belt became increasingly concerned. They took me aside and convinced me I shouldn't return to Kenya just then. Instead, they secured a three-month consultancy for me at the

UNIFEM headquarters in New York, during which I stayed with Peggy, Marilyn Carr, who also worked at UNIFEM, and at the Vanderbilt YMCA, near the headquarters of the UN.

Meanwhile, far from suppressing the opposition, Ouko's death and the government's reaction only emboldened the pro-democracy movement. In May 1990, Kenneth Matiba, a former cabinet minister in the Moi government; Charles Rubia, the former mayor of Nairobi; and Raila Odinga, son of the veteran politician Oginga Odinga, all called for the reintroduction of a multiparty system. On July 7, a mass pro-democracy rally was held in Kamukunji Park, where we had planted the trees that marked the birth of the Green Belt Movement thirteen years earlier. Even though the government banned the gathering, hundreds of thousands of people walked, drove, or took the bus to attend the demonstration. However, the assembly descended into a riot when security forces attacked the crowd with live ammunition. Dozens of demonstrators were killed and hundreds more injured in the street battles that followed.

Still, Saba Saba (7/7 in Kiswahili, to mark the date of the rally) was a turning point in the history of the struggle for truly representative democracy in Kenya. It intensified the pressures inside and outside the country on the Moi government to be more open politically. It also showed me quite clearly that the struggle for freedom in our country had not ended in 1963.

I decided to honor those killed on Saba Saba by planting a small grove of trees in Uhuru Park. Over the next few years, elements suspected of being sympathetic to the government periodically tried to destroy the trees by slashing the trunks and branches or even burning them to the ground—this kind of vindictive vandalism was common among the regime's agents and supporters. Yet the trees, like us, survived. The rains would come and the sun would shine and before you knew it the trees would be throwing new leaves and shoots into the air. These trees, like Saba Saba, inspired me. They showed me that, no matter how much you try to destroy it, you can't stop the truth and justice from sprouting.

Since the late 1980s, foreign donors, international organizations, and diplomats—including the then-U.S. ambassador to Kenya, Smith Hempstone—had been expressing concern about political repression, corruption, and increasing instability in the country. Some governments suspended aid to Kenya, citing human rights abuses and economic mismanagement. In response to the pressure, the government had set up a review committee to look into issues of governmental reform.

In August 1991, Oginga Odinga and others founded the Forum for the Restoration of Democracy (FORD) as an opposition force to KANU, and invited many people active in the pro-democracy movement, including me, to join them. My work to protect Uhuru Park had raised my profile as an advocate not only for the environment but also for human rights. Although FORD was itself declared illegal, it scheduled a huge pro-democracy rally in Kamukunji Park in November 1991. The government naturally banned the event. Police officers cordoned off the park grounds, and when hundreds of demonstrators assembled despite the ban, they used tear gas and rubber bullets to disperse the crowd. At least two people died, and many opposition leaders and journalists were arrested.

The pressure, however, for multipartism was too great, and in December, President Moi was forced to accept its reintroduction and schedule national elections for the end of 1992. While the government gave up its claim as the sole party, though, it only tinkered with political and constitutional reform and retained laws giving the government disproportionate power to control political activity. We still faced the risk of being arrested on trumped-up charges and without guarantee of trial, and it remained difficult to discuss the need for real democracy without being harassed or detained.

It was in this political climate that, on January 10, 1992, a large group of us met in Nairobi's Ngong Hills Hotel, owned by Matu

Wamae, also a member of FORD, to strategize about how to propel our pro-democracy movement forward. During the meeting, one of us was called to the phone and given information that chilled me to the bone. "We have learned, reliably, that Moi wants to hand over power to the army," the caller said. Apparently, the president was scheduled to travel to Mombasa that day by train rather than plane, a change of transport that indicated a sense of uncertainty and insecurity within the government. The coup was scheduled to take place at any time, we were informed.

A government-sponsored coup would be the perfect way for President Moi to avoid having to face the electorate at the end of the year. It was possible that the rumor was started by the government itself to scare the opposition into silence and ensure that the authorities retained power. Nonetheless, I took what was said very seriously, not least because the person on the phone named me as one of a large number of people targeted for assassination. This was not an idle threat. Not long before this, Bishop Alexander Muge had voiced fears for his life after calling for civil rights in Kenya. He had died shortly afterward in a mysterious car "accident."

None of us felt we needed to apply to the authorities for permission to announce that our lives were in danger. We also hoped, Bishop Muge notwithstanding, that speaking out now would not only keep us alive but do the same for the many Kenyans who would likely be killed if the rumors proved true. We decided to alert the media. About ten of us went to the press center in Chester House office building in central Nairobi, where many of the foreign media outlets as well as local media have their offices. We issued a statement to the effect that, if the president felt there was a need for a change in the government, he should call a general election and not turn power over to the army. We also alerted the press to the existence of a list of potential targets for assassination.

The president denied rumors of the coup and attacked members of FORD for associating themselves with what he termed "loose talk." After we made our statement, we scattered. That afternoon, our phones started ringing with the news that all those who attended the press conference were being picked up by the police one by one and arrested. I decided to barricade myself in my home.

While the gate in the fence around the house was easy to climb over or force open, I had very secure doors and windows, which I had reinforced after a violent burglary six years earlier. That night I had come from a trip abroad and had, as usual, brought presents for the children. We had spent the evening of my return catching up with news and the children were excitedly opening the presents, long into the night. Eventually, we fell asleep exhausted—Wanjira and Muta in my bed and Waweru in his.

At about three o'clock in the morning, I heard a huge *bang* and then complete silence, and I began to drift back to sleep. Meanwhile, the robbers had gone to Waweru's room, shaken him awake, and asked where his mother was. By that time, other thieves had come in and woken us up. Everything was pitch-black, and we couldn't turn on the lights (we didn't realize that the robbers had cut the electricity). The next thing I knew there were flashlights all over the place and men in my bedroom. I screamed. "Don't make a noise," one of the robbers threatened, putting his hand over my mouth. "If you do, we'll kill you." In the darkness, I could see the glint of a machete, so I knew they were serious. We didn't make a sound after that.

Meanwhile, the other thieves were opening the closets and putting whatever they could find into a bag. My mother, who was visiting us at the time, had heard me scream and came into my room. "Grandma, you go back to sleep," one robber said to her. "Don't shout." My mother was scared and went back to the bedroom where she was sleeping, but couldn't hear anything from there so didn't know whether we were alive or dead. "Where does your mother keep the money?" another thief asked Wanjira. "Mommy doesn't keep money in the house," she replied. The robbers took all the clothes they could find, Waweru's tape deck and records, and the gifts I had brought. They also took the beaded necklace with nine strings I had worn on my wedding day.

The thieves had gotten into the house by throwing a heavy stone at the door and breaking it to the ground. I had never thought of getting an alarm system, since I didn't have much to steal. I did have a wonderful dog, who was partly a companion and a guardian, but they must have given her some meat because we didn't hear a peep out of her. The next day, when I saw her and asked her where she'd been the night before, she simply wagged her tail. I called the police, but they said our fingerprints had mixed with the thieves' and compromised the investigation. We hadn't much faith that the thieves would be caught in any case, since in those days the police themselves were often in league with the thieves.

Whenever I hear that someone has been robbed, my heart goes out to them, because I know how vulnerable you feel. After this experience, I decided that nothing should compromise the safety of my family and myself. So, even though it was very expensive, I made up my mind to secure my house—and that was the reason I felt I could safely barricade myself inside on that January day in 1992, when the police arrived to arrest me. Waweru and Wanjira were studying in the United States, and I had asked Muta to stay with his father so I could lock myself in. I thought nobody could get me.

Soon enough, the police arrived and knocked at the gate. I refused to let them in. They soon tired of knocking and about ten officers climbed over the fence into the compound and encircled the house. At that moment, I knew what a rabbit surrounded by dogs must feel like. "Open your door!" they called to me.

"I'm not opening it," I told them. "I know you want to arrest me." For several hours, a standoff ensued. They kept asking me to open the door and I refused. Eventually they left, but four armed officers remained to keep watch on the house throughout the night.

By the next day, news that I was under siege had spread and friends and the press had begun to gather in the street outside my gate, while people from the nearby slum peered over the fence behind the house to see what was going on. Among the friends was Reverend Timothy Njoya of the Presbyterian Church of East Africa. Reverend Njoya was himself a strong supporter of the pro-democracy movement and had himself been the victim of a violent assault in his home. He had brought me some bananas to eat, but the police officers said I'd have to open the door to get them, which obviously I couldn't do. "Dr. Njoya!" I shouted to him. "Please. I cannot open the door. If they won't allow you to pass on food to me, go back with it. I would rather be hungry than be arrested for no offense."

From inside the house, I talked to as many journalists as I could, Kenyan and international, who had gathered around the compound (some had jumped over the gate, too), as well as on the phone. I told them about the rumored coup and explained why we didn't want power handed to the army. I spoke about how the 1988 elections had been rigged and how the president was nervous about holding elections because he knew he would be defeated. I felt so safe behind those doors that I even did some work as the siege continued. After some time, though, the police cut my phone line, and then I was frightened. I was alone in the house, surrounded, my connection to the outside world gone. The rumors of the coup had set Kenyans on edge, including the security forces. I didn't know what would happen next.

The four policemen remained on guard, two at the front door and two at the door next to the kitchen, for the second night. It often gets cold in Nairobi in the evening, so I called out to one of the officers through the kitchen window. "I know you're here to do a job and that you have to arrest me. But I'm also doing my job, and I'm not opening this door. I know you're cold. I will make you a nice cup of tea," I continued, "but I don't have any milk. If I give you some money, would you go and get some?" The officer consulted his colleagues, which impressed me, and they agreed to the offer. One got milk from a nearby kiosk and I made tea, handing them the cups through the window. I had a cup myself, inside the house.

This was my way of creating a rapport with the officers and reducing the tension between them and me. I didn't think the officers really wanted to hurt me; they just hoped I'd give up and come out. While a number of police officers were strong supporters of the regime, others were sympathetic to the pro-democracy movement. They knew they were enforcing repressive laws and allowing corruption to go unchecked.

On the third day of the siege, however, the situation turned ugly. The locks on my doors and the steel bars on the windows must have annoyed the authorities greatly, since they acquired a pair of steel cutters from the army and went to work. When I heard the noise of them sawing through the window bars, I knew it was only a matter of time. Sure enough, I heard boots bashing in the doors, and suddenly three of the officers to whom I'd offered tea were in my living room. Taking me by the arms, they walked me through the broken doors and past a crowd of supporters at the gate, pushed me into a car, and drove me to the police station.

To my consternation, the officers left the house wide open. There were hundreds of people around and they could have helped themselves to everything inside. However, when Mwangi heard about the police coming to arrest me, he called a friend and asked him to send two security guards to look after the house. They protected everything that was there. Mwangi himself kindly came, closed and locked the gate to the house after I had gone, and made sure the guards stayed.

The charges against me were serious: spreading malicious rumors, sedition, and treason, the last of which carried the death penalty. Thankfully, by this time, I, as well as other targets of the regime, had a system whereby if I had been arrested or something had happened to me, people would spread the word to our supporters almost immediately. They would then inform the press and inquire about why I'd been arrested and what they could do to get me released.

Nevertheless, it was a dark time. I was in jail again, confined to a holding cell at Lang'ata police station. For a day and a night I tried to sleep without any covers on the floor of a cell that was wet, freezing cold, filled with water and filth. I wondered whether the floor had been flooded deliberately. Unlike the first time I was imprisoned, I did not have a blanket and I was alone in the cell. I was also fifty-two years old, arthritic in both knees, and suffering from back pain. In that cold, wet cell my joints ached so much that I thought I would die.

The guards left me alone, but I remember the near constant opening and closing of the cell door and the *boom, boom, boom* it made. The lights were kept on twenty-four hours a day, so it was impossible to sleep. I had no access to information or any idea about what was happening outside the bars of that cell. There was nothing I could do. I had to depend entirely on the guards assigned to contain me and the people outside trying to defend me. As I sat in those cells, denying me the ability to control what happened seemed to me to be the greatest punishment the regime could mete out to me.

By the time of my court hearing, my legs had completely seized up. Crying from the pain and weak from hunger, I had to be carried by four strong policewomen into the courtroom. It was strange for me to feel so helpless. People were shocked when they saw me unable even to stand to hear the charges read. "What have they given her?! They have killed her!" people shouted.

Some judges were sympathetic to the need for greater democracy but either had to act as the system demanded for their own personal safety or, less honorably, for their own personal comfort and privilege. In this case, the judge was fair, although he did require bail. He also demanded regular appearances in court that hampered my work and the work of my codefendants, who included the lawyers Paul Muite and James Orengo. Both of them, leaders in the pro-democracy movement, were also good friends. In those days, bail was often used as a way to curtail freedom and dissent, since it, or other deferred charges, made it impossible to travel and left you vulnerable to arrest at any time on numerous, vague accusations of wrongdoing.

While my codefendants and I knew we were innocent of what we had been accused, we had no guarantee that we would be publicly vindicated. As I was carried out of the courtroom to an ambulance to take me to Nairobi Hospital, I gained courage and strength from the women who wailed and wept around me. I was in physical agony, wondering whether the arthritis would ever let my legs carry me again. Then I saw a banner from the women's rights group Mothers in Action that warmed my heart and helped me realize that no matter what happened to me there were people who cared, who wished me well, and who understood what it meant to be a woman fighting for the future of her country: WANGARI, BRAVE DAUGHTER OF KENYA, the banner said. YOU WILL NEVER WALK ALONE AGAIN.

Such wonderful support came from many quarters. My son Muta, bless him, all of nineteen years old, talked to many members of the media about the case. Then there were my friends overseas, who, in these situations, would do what they could to ensure that I was safe. On this occasion, members of the Green Belt Movement sent out an alert that I was in danger. In the United States, Peggy Snyder, founding director of UNIFEM, Carol Coonrod of the Hunger Project, Caroline Pezzullo of GROOTS (Grassroots Organizations Operating Together in Sisterhood) International, which I had cofounded with others out of the Nairobi women's conference in 1985, and the late Bella Abzug and Mim Kelber, cofounders of the Women's Environment & Development Organization (WEDO) on whose board I served, called on members of the U.S. Senate Foreign Relations Committee to apply pressure to the Moi regime.

As a result, eight senators, including Al Gore and Edward M. Kennedy, sent a telegram urging the government to substantiate the charges against us. Senators Kennedy, Gore, and the late Paul Wellstone followed up with a letter cautioning the president that arresting pro-democracy figures could further damage relations between Kenya and the United States. The government must have listened to someone, because in November 1992 the state withdrew the charges against all of us. There was, and never had been, a case to be made. We were free again and ready to continue our advocacy work.

In Kenya in the early 1990s, outrages and abuses happened wherever you looked, and often simultaneously. Many young men landed in prison for political agitation. In January 1992, as I was still in the hospital recovering from my time in a police cell, Terry Kariuki, the widow of murdered politician J. M. Kariuki, acting as a friend of the mothers of these political prisoners brought the mother of one of the several dozen political prisoners then held by the regime to the hospital to visit me. The mother, Monica Wamwere, told me that she and a few relatives and friends had formed a group called Release Political Prisoners to appeal to the government to release their sons from detention. Some of the prisoners—such as her son, Koigi; Mirugi Kariuki; the brothers Rumba and Robert Kinuthia; Harun Wakaba; and Samuel Kang'ethe Mungai—were well known for their political activism, others were not; but all of them had been detained for advocating for greater democratic space.

The mothers hoped, they said, that I would join them and put pressure on the government to have these men released now that it was no longer a crime to advocate for multipartism. I had not been directly involved with the issue of political prisoners, but the case the mothers were presenting seemed very strong: Since it was no longer a crime for Kenyans to demand a plural political system, there was no reason for the sons to be in prison. I agreed to meet with them as soon as I was released from the hospital.

By late February, I had been out of the hospital for several weeks and had regained my ability to walk, although my knees would never quite recover. I was still out on bail so ran the risk of being rearrested, but I wanted to help the mothers and didn't want to allow a false charge to stop me from pursuing the truth. I suggested that we meet in my house. To my surprise, many of the relatives and friends were afraid, not merely to meet but even more so, to meet in my house: They were fearful of the system and knew that I myself was a target. I assured the women that my house served as an office, so if the police came we could always say we were members of the Green Belt Movement discussing tree planting and advocacy issues.

Indeed, some of the women were members of the Green Belt Movement, and I knew that the Release Political Prisoners campaign was an issue Green Belt was concerned about and was part of the movement's mandate to promote democracy and respect for human rights. So a few mothers and other relatives, most of whom were female, came regularly to my house and we discussed our strategy over cups of tea. As I listened to these women, I felt compassion for them. As a mother myself, I wondered what it would be like to have your child thrown into a cell with no sense of when he might be tried or released. I thought of my own sons and brothers: What wouldn't I do for them?

In the course of these meetings I suggested to the women that they meet the attorney general and petition him to free their sons and all the political prisoners. I agreed to accompany them to provide moral support and to serve as a translator. We agreed to meet at Uhuru Park and walk together to the office of the attorney general. "The government always responds to something that is done aloud and publicly," I said to the women. "If you go to the attorney general quietly and appeal to him, you'll be wasting your time. He'll say, 'Yes, yes, yes,' but he'll do nothing." I had another strategy. "When we see him, we'll tell him, 'We will wait in Uhuru Park for three days for all the sons to be released. During that time we'll go on a hunger strike and pray.' " I also recommended that we take our bedding with us to the meeting. Then the attorney general would know, I said, that the mothers wouldn't leave Nairobi for their villages without their sons and that we were prepared to sleep in Uhuru Park while they waited.

On Friday, February 28, 1992, about five mothers, their supporters, and I met in Uhuru Park and walked with our bedding to the office of the attorney general. He received us and I served as the translator as the women explained their case. When the meeting ended, we told him that we were going back to Uhuru Park to wait for the sons to be released. The attorney general was taken aback. "Don't go to the park," he said. "Go home. We've received your petition and we'll review the cases and we will take action." But we knew all about the government, how it never really listened or did what it promised. When we left the office, we walked back to the park and camped at the same intersection of Uhuru Highway and Kenyatta Avenue from which we had started. There we were joined by others, mostly men, who supported the initiative and wanted to make sure we would be safe spending the night at the park.

Evening arrived, and the sons had not come. We took fifty-two candles, one for each man we knew was in prison, put them in brown bags, and lit them. We almost caused a traffic jam at the corner, as people from all over the city slowed their cars to look at the flickering lights in the park. Pedestrians stopped, too, to listen to the women explain why they were on a hunger strike. By the time night fell, our camp had grown to include more than fifty women, many of whom were mothers and relatives of political prisoners. We built a fire to keep ourselves warm.

Kind gestures came from many ordinary people who supported our cause. One Indian man gave us a huge tent because he was worried that it might rain and several of the mothers, who were between sixty and eighty were frail. Some people donated money, while others brought water, juices, or glucose to keep the mothers healthy since they were not eating. Still others joined us as we sang freedom songs and hymns to keep our spirits up.

The mothers had many supporters whom I came to meet over the course of what became a long campaign. One of them was Dr. Ngorongo Makanga (also known by his Christian name, John), a member of the pro-democracy movement who ran a pharmacy at the Hilton Hotel in Nairobi. He and I later cofounded the Green Party in Kenya, of which he became secretary general. Dr. Makanga also joined me and the Green Belt Movement in many other struggles, including over the infamous tribal clashes in the Rift Valley.

The night came and went. Saturday dawned and a second night passed, and still the women had not been reunited with their sons. On Sunday, we decided to hold a church service, which Reverend Njoya and other clergy, dressed in their vestments and carrying Bibles, conducted for us in the park. As people left their own churches after Sunday services, many joined us and the gathering swelled. We decided to erect a sign, so I asked some friends to prepare a large board and write FREEDOM CORNER on it and bring it to us. We planted it where our encampment was, so the spirit of the corner matched the spirit in which the park had been named. That section of Uhuru Park has been called Freedom Corner ever since.

Over the three days, many people who had been victims of torture came to Freedom Corner and began to tell their stories. "What you do not know," they said, pointing to Nyayo House, a government building opposite the Nyayo Monument in Uhuru Park and immediately across the road from Freedom Corner, "is that underneath that house are torture chambers. Men have been maimed there. Some of them have died after what they have gone through."

As the victims related their horrific experiences, others, including grown men in their forties, embraced the freedom of that corner and found the courage to speak up. "Let me tell you my story," "I have never spoken about this before. I've been out of prison now for ten years, and this is the first time I have told anyone that I was tortured." Some related that they had been abused and beaten to the point where they would never be able to father children. While we listened to the men, we prayed and sang for comfort and courage.

Laypeople and the clergy bore living witness to what the government had been doing to its citizens behind closed doors. While some of us knew, or at least suspected, that such things were happening, it was nevertheless shocking to hear the details. However, some were hearing this information for the first time, and people could barely believe the horrific stories they were being told by fellow citizens.

Throughout Monday, there was still no sign of the sons. By this time, there were several hundred of us at Freedom Corner. Although we had told the attorney general we would wait in the park for three days, we knew we could not leave now. The next day, March 3, dawned mild and sunny. During the morning, we saw groups of paramilitary police, batons and guns at the ready, cordoning off the area to prevent anyone else from reaching us.

Around three o'clock that afternoon, the police ordered a member of the Release Political Prisoners campaign to tell us to disperse. There wasn't enough time to do anything before the police began firing tear gas into the camp and charging us from behind and in front, beating us with their batons. Chaos! People ran everywhere, including onto the streets surrounding the park. Some of the young men who had joined us fought back as the police chased them across the road to Nyayo House and down Kenyatta and Haile Selassie avenues as well as through the park.

As the battle continued throughout the afternoon, tear gas and the sound of gunshots filled the air. Police reinforcements stormed the tent where I was singing and praying with the mothers. When the police arrived in the tent, the fifty or so people inside were initially defiant, not believing the police would attack them. The protestors linked arms, which meant that when the police began their assault they could not easily take one without taking many. I saw people rise up in groups as police batons rained down.

In that immediate moment, I recall worrying that the paraffin lamps we lit at night would be disturbed and the tent would go up in flames. In the next instant, however, I was knocked unconscious. Even in the mêlée, good samaritans rescued me and rushed me to the hospital with two other women who were badly hurt.

The mothers in the tent refused to be intimidated and they did not run. Instead, they did something very brave: Several of them stripped, some of them completely naked, and showed the police

officers their breasts. (I myself did not strip.) One of the most powerful of African traditions concerns the relationship between a woman
and a man who could be her son. Every woman old enough to be
your mother is considered like your own mother and expects to
be treated with considerable respect. As they bared their breasts,
what the mothers were saying to the policemen in their anger and
frustration as they were being beaten was "By showing you my
nakedness, I curse you as I would my son for the way you are abus-
ing me."

By the time I arrived at the hospital I was dehydrated. Fortunately, my doctor, Dan Gikonyo, was on hand at the hospital and as
always attended to me promptly. It was important for those of us
in the pro-democracy movement to have doctors we could trust, and
Dr. Gikonyo was a man I trusted whenever I needed medical assistance. When I first came to, I had the strangest feeling, as though I
were hanging upside down. One of my friends and a Green Belt
board member, Lillian Njehu, was with me and I kept telling her I
felt like I was falling. Lillian stayed with me throughout my time in
the hospital, which was a big sacrifice for her, and made sure I was
protected day and night. Such was the spirit of sisterhood.

When I was sufficiently recovered, I called a press conference. I
was told that the police claimed I had incited them to beat me
unconscious and that I had asked to be given a black eye and a
baseball-sized lump on my head. I informed the press that although
after what had happened to me I would have to stay away from "dangerous ground," I wouldn't be silenced or deterred from telling the
truth and I wouldn't go away. "The mothers," I emphasized, "had a
right to seek the freedom of their sons."

The evening of March 3 the police forcibly removed all the
women who were still in the park and took them to their homes. As
they were being removed, the women cried, "We will only move
from this place when the government brings our sons here!" The
authorities ordered the women to end their hunger strike and told
them not to return to Nairobi. Freedom Corner was cordoned off

and we were unable to get to it again. By the time the police left, all our bedding and personal effects, including blankets, lamps, and the tent, had disappeared with the Nairobi City Council, never to be seen again.

When I think of what happened, I believe that it was the stories of torture that made the government decide that what we were doing was dangerous. Perhaps we had a false sense of security. We thought that even this government wouldn't hurt old women—mothers who simply wanted their sons to be released from prisons where they were being held for their political conscience(s). But the regime knew neither mercy nor justice and we were accused of threatening "the security of citizens and the nation." The government had decided that a revolt was brewing and that it could unleash as much venom and violence as it wanted to stop it.

The story of Freedom Corner did not end with my hospitalization or the dispersal of the mothers. We remained unbowed. The day after the police attack, many of the women, on their own, returned to Freedom Corner. Finding the area guarded by hundreds of armed soldiers, the women decided to seek help at nearby All Saints Cathedral in contacting the other mothers and their supporters. All Saints sits directly adjacent to Uhuru Park and is the seat of the Anglican archbishop. During the 1990s, the cathedral's clergy had begun to speak out against the government's oppression and provided space for prayers by and for pro-democracy groups.

The women met with the Reverend Peter Njenga, the cathedral's provost (and later the bishop of Mt. Kenya South Diocese), who agreed to give the women a temporary sanctuary so they could trace their colleagues. They learned that some of us were in the hospital, and indeed some of them came to the hospital to visit us while others remained at the cathedral. When night came, some of the women were still at the cathedral and had nowhere to go, so Reverend Njenga allowed them to stay in the cathedral's crypt. Reverend Njenga and the mothers expected the vigil to last for a night or two: It lasted for a whole year. During this time, the mothers rotated their hunger strike. As one woman became weak from lack of food, another would take over while the first one recovered.

When I was sufficiently healed and could walk properly again, I went straight to All Saints Cathedral to offer the mothers my help. Along with others, I organized supplies and support for the mothers during their yearlong vigil. Beside the mothers, there were male relatives who guarded the doors and acted as protection, because there were many visitors. Throughout their protest, most of the women remained strong despite intimidation and threats, both against them as individuals and their families, as well as police aggression.

I stayed with the women throughout. Unless I went out of the country, I made the cathedral my second home. I wrote and had printed up leaflets telling the stories of these women's sons, and had these leaflets distributed on the streets of Nairobi. I wanted people to know about these men: what they believed in; what had happened to them, their parents, and their families; how they had been declared enemies of the state or revolutionaries trying to overturn the government; and why they should be released.

The women also had their stories. One woman told me that the authorities had come to her home, claiming that her son had hidden guns there. "There are no guns," she told them. "We know your son has hidden guns here," they yelled back. "So dig." They pushed this mother to the ground and forced her to dig the earth with her bare hands until her fingers bled. They found no guns, because there were none! Such stories only made us more resolute.

One night, I was awakened and told that there were people saying they were policemen at the cathedral's door demanding that we open it and let them in. I looked out of the window and saw Nairobi's provincial commissioner and armed men in paramilitary attire, which was a relief since that meant it was the government and not hired thugs or hooligans outside. "Mothers, the president has heard your cry," the provincial commissioner called out to us.

"He sympathizes with you. Open the doors and go home, and your sons will follow you."

Some of the women wanted to open the doors. They still believed their president was honest and they were desperate to see their sons. But others knew that if the doors were opened, the police would rush in and arrest them and force them out. In the meantime, we realized there was a very large number of soldiers, perhaps five hundred in number, surrounding the church. We were fortunate that some of the soldiers were religious and refused to break down the church doors, even though they had been ordered to do so.

Eventually the provincial commissioner and others at the door gave up, but the soldiers remained on the compound. By morning, the news that the cathedral had been turned into a military barracks, with the soldiers surrounding the mothers, was everywhere. The government was forced to discuss the situation with the archbishop of the Anglican Church, Manasses Kuria. It was eventually agreed that the military should leave the compound but the mothers could stay in the crypt. As long as the soldiers remained, we never opened the doors.

Unfortunately, the continuous presence of the mothers in the crypt tended to divide the cathedral's congregation. All Saints, as the seat of the Anglican Church in Kenya, is expected to be proestablishment. It was the church of the state, especially during the colonial period. Because of this heritage, the clergy's giving support and shelter to the striking mothers of political prisoners shocked some in the congregation who expected their church to support the establishment. They questioned why the cathedral was getting involved in politics, and many failed to see the connection between their faith and the need for all people, including people of faith, to respect human rights. However, Reverend Njenga and the leadership of the Anglican Church upheld this pursuit of justice, good governance, and the rule of law. So the mothers continued their vigil in the crypt.

After the agreement between the archbishop and the government, we were able to leave the crypt and move out onto the church grounds during the day. The church became a center of pilgrimage. Many political figures in the pro-democracy movement, including Mwai Kibaki, Oginga Odinga and his son Raila, Michael Wamalwa, James Orengo, and Paul Muite, came and expressed solidarity with the mothers, while religious leaders from all denominations came and prayed with them. Soon the gathering at the cathedral turned into a national sit-in demonstration, a forum for everyone, including the press, to hear how people had suffered under the general misgovernance of the country.

The danger for the mothers was far from over, however. We were always afraid the government would apprehend us and abort the campaign. I suggested to the mothers that we keep ourselves chained together, so that if one of us was arrested, all of us would have to be dragged out together. The mothers trusted me. Not only could I speak English and translate for them, I was the leader who could articulate the connections and show how the struggle for the sons' freedom fit into the bigger picture of the pro-democracy struggle.

At that point, the government tried a different tactic. It attempted to break up the women's group by promising individual women that their sons would be released if they abandoned the vigil. About four women left the group and went to State House for tea with the president. They were told that I was misguiding them and that they should go home and their sons would be released. We knew it was all a ploy—and that the sons would not be set free under such arrangements. They were not, and one mother even came back to the church. The vigil continued.

Over the course of that year, the mothers' nonviolent protest became a focus, in Kenya and in other countries, for those wanting to end state-sponsored torture, random imprisonment, and the unjust suppression of the rights and voices of the people. Pressure on the government to release the sons intensified and came from many quarters. The vigil ended early in 1993 when suddenly all but one of the fifty-two sons were released en masse. (The fifty-second prisoner, we learned from informal sources, had been arrested on charges that were not politically motivated. Release Political Prisoners adopted his case and continued to fight for him, and he was eventually released in 1997.)

Upon the sons' release, we held a service of thanksgiving at All Saints. During the service, I gave each of the women a "certificate of endurance" that I hear still hangs in a special place on walls of their homes. After the ceremony the women proudly walked with their sons out through the cathedral's open doors and into the bright light of midday. They could sleep more easily now that their sons were free at last.

The Release Political Prisoners group decided not to disband but to continue pressing for the release of other prisoners and for the respectful treatment of all people in Kenya held behind bars. A good number of the sons, once they were freed, joined Release Political Prisoners and provided the leadership for greater freedom in Kenya and better conditions for people in jail, efforts that continue to this day.

When I left the cathedral, I returned to my home in South C, satisfied with what we had accomplished. I was also relieved to be back in my home and to sleep in my bed, instead of on a hard and very uncomfortable bench. I had been able to run home and take showers, and there was a shower for the women in the church, but the women and I slept in the same clothes we wore during the day and we lost all sense of privacy. Yet there was never any question in my mind of not seeing the vigil through. Having joined the women, I would not abandon their cause. We stuck together to the very end. In the months and years that followed, I sensed the bond we had formed with one another as mothers, and recognized the appreciation they had for what we had done for their sons.

Occasionally I would leave the women to travel. I felt it was prudent to maintain the international links I had established since, among other things, they offered a degree of security for myself and others from governmental attack at home. Sometimes I left to receive awards and honors in distant lands. For instance, in 1991, with five other people, I was awarded the Goldman Environmental Prize, which I traveled to San Francisco to accept, and that same year I also received the Hunger Project's Africa Prize for Leadership, presented in London. This visibility helped bring the issues of the environment and democracy, the work of the Green Belt Movement, and my personal profile to a wider audience, both nationally and internationally.

I spoke on how to protect and restore the earth, along with the need for democracy, human rights, and an end to rampant corruption. I knew that much of what I said would make its way back to Kenya and help expand democratic space there. The regime, however, often took what steps it could to silence or distort my voice. When CNN's report of the Goldman Prize winners was aired in Kenya, the three-minute segment on me and the Green Belt Movement was edited out. I later learned that journalists for the state-run broadcasting company were told not to air any interviews with me. When some staff of the state radio station did, they were promptly fired.

At times, particularly in the first few years of the 1990s, the government also made it difficult for me to travel. When this happened, I had to appeal to supporters abroad to ask the Kenyan authorities to guarantee my freedom of movement. In June 1992, for instance, I was due to address the UN Conference on Environment and Development (UNCED) in Rio de Janeiro, better known as the Earth Summit. But I was also due in court again because of my arrest for the coup rumors, so my lawyer had to appeal to Nairobi's chief magistrate for permission for me to miss a court date to attend the summit. This time, the magistrate agreed. So President Moi and I both went to Rio.

In Rio, I addressed the government delegates, spoke on several panels, and participated in a press conference with soon-to-be U.S. vice president Al Gore and His Holiness the Dalai Lama. I also conferred with environmentalists and friends from around the world, even as the media staff on Kenya's official delegation launched a campaign at the Earth Summit to discredit me and the Green Belt Movement. Preposterously, they accused me of inciting women in Kenya and encouraging them to strip at Freedom Corner. I was thus a bad influence on rural women, they said, and should not be allowed to speak at the summit. As it turned out, in spite of—or perhaps because of—the government's campaign, the international NGOs chose me to be their spokesperson at the summit. (It was during the two weeks I was in Rio that the government began its campaign to encourage the women to leave All Saints.)

The Earth Summit was the second time I had met with Al Gore. He had visited the Green Belt Movement in the autumn of 1990. We planted a podo tree together in Kanyariri in Kabete (it's still doing very well), and he had written about our work in his best-selling book *Earth in the Balance.* A few years after Rio, he invited me to accompany him to Haiti to look at the effects of deforestation there. We met with President Jean-Bertrand Aristide and other government officials. I then boarded a military helicopter and flew over the countryside. As I looked down, I realized I had never seen a country so devastated. People were cultivating crops on the tops of hills and nearly every tree had been cut down. It looked like someone had taken a razor blade to the land and shaved it bare. When the rains came, the soil just washed away.

In 2000, two Haitian women supported by GROOTS International came to Kenya to learn about the Green Belt Movement. When they returned to Haiti, however, they were unsuccessful in establishing an initiative. I tried to find funding to bring more people from Haiti to Kenya to train them in the Green Belt Movement approach, but I was unable to raise the resources. When, in September 2004, I heard the news that Hurricanes Ivan and Jeanne had together caused the deaths of more than three thousand people in Haiti through landslides and floods, I thought immediately of what I had seen a decade earlier. When people in Kenya call for forests to be opened for cultivation of crops, I think of the people of Haiti and vow that I will do all I can to prevent what happened there from occurring in Kenya.

We have continued to seek help and to reach out to the people of Haiti, but it has always been difficult because peace has been elusive in that country. Nevertheless, we hope one day to return and plant millions of trees and so realize Al Gore's dream of a green Haiti.

11

Aluta Continua: *The Struggle Continues*

The elections of 1992 provided a focal point for the democracy movement in Kenya. This was the first time since 1966 that more than one party would legally be able to contest elections, even though many restrictions remained. By the summer of 1992, after my return from the Earth Summit and even as the women's hunger strike in All Saints Cathedral continued, it had become clear to me and others in the opposition that we needed to present a united front in order to beat the incumbent president and KANU in the December elections.

As the largest party, and the party of government since independence, KANU had over a period of time changed the electoral system to make it harder for smaller or regional parties to form governments. The president also controlled the state-run television and radio and could draw on his and the state's large financial resources to support the ruling party. The government had disrupted independent media outlets and much of the political activity that had begun in the 1980s. Kenya's people hungered for change, but they needed the opposition to unite to satisfy their hopes.

Unfortunately, only a year after its founding, the Forum for the Restoration of Democracy, in which I'd been a keen participant, splintered. Kenneth Matiba and Oginga Odinga both ran for FORD's leadership, and the party divided. Odinga started FORD-Kenya, while Matiba led FORD-Asili. Mwai Kibaki, former vice president in the Moi administration, who left KANU in 1991, did not join FORD but formed the Democratic Party, further fracturing the opposition. This fragmentation would set back the cause of democratization for ten years.

As a result of this schism, some FORD members decided to form the Middle Ground Group, or MGG. I served as its chair. We hoped to create a "middle ground" on which the opposition parties could unite in time for the elections. We wanted to offer the public a space to learn about the opposition, give their opinions, ask questions, and engage with people of different views. To do this, we hit on the concept of "teach-ins." My colleagues liked the idea, but were not sure how to coordinate them. I drew on my American experience of the teach-ins of the 1960s. By this time I had also been holding seminars with Green Belt groups for years and I enjoyed leading group discussions. I therefore volunteered to conduct and organize them.

I led a number of teach-ins in a tent in downtown Nairobi to raise Kenyans' awareness about why it was so important for us to come together and reclaim our democracy at the ballot box. The tent was next to the Kenya Commercial Bank on Mama Ngina Street, in a central location that was also a transport hub for buses, so it was easy to gather a crowd. I would also inform the press of when I would be there, so that the word could spread. The teach-ins generally lasted all morning: I gave everyone an opportunity to speak and people to ask questions and debate. It worked very well. The MGG also organized several gatherings in All Saints Cathedral at which the public and sometimes opposition party officials came and prayed for unity.

The Green Belt Movement served as the secretariat for the MGG's public activities. Green Belt staff pitched the tent for the teach-ins, and if we needed them, made banners and signs. The tent was opposite Dr. Makanga's pharmacy at the Hilton, so he and his staff helped provide space to store our campaign materials. They also supplied first aid and medicines if we needed them.

The authorities never bothered us during the teach-ins, but not all of the MGG activities were free from police interference. Informers were busy keeping the police updated on the activities of people associated with the opposition. One evening, we were having an MGG strategy meeting at my house with about thirty activists, some of whom were lawyers. It was still not permitted for more than nine people to meet without first obtaining a permit—which, of course, no authority would give us. Suddenly, three armed policemen arrived at my door and I met them. "You're holding an illegal meeting. Where is the license?" they asked me.

"There are policemen outside! And they're armed!" I said loudly. I wanted to alert the people in my living room that police officers were at the door and vice versa. We wanted to show that we were not afraid of the government. In 1989, all of us would have been arrested and people would have fled from every conceivable exit when there was a knock on the door. While arresting all of us there that night was a legal option, by 1992 the security forces were somewhat constrained by the press, public opinion, a more powerful opposition, and, at times, the court. On that night, therefore, nobody moved. The police officers could see we were no longer intimidated enough to run for our lives, and that helped further the cause of democracy. That evening I used my wits and did something the police didn't expect: I decided to disarm them figuratively, even if I couldn't do it literally. I invited them into the house and led them to the living room where everyone was meeting.

The living room was not large. This evening, it was so packed that I couldn't even offer the officers seats. "This is my house," I told them, "and these are my friends. They came to visit me and we are talking about this country." I then introduced everyone by their first names, which to the police wasn't useful at all. Then I turned to the officers and said, "I guess you'd like to introduce yourselves now." Everybody, including the policemen, laughed, although they didn't give their names.

The officer who seemed to be in charge spoke up: "You're not supposed to have more than nine people in a meeting."

"Well," I replied, "this is my home and I can't tell people to get out because there are more than nine of them. They came to visit."

Then I turned to my guests and asked, "Why did all of you people come over together anyway?"

They laughed. "We're here discussing the future of this country," one of the guests, John Khaminwa, a very good lawyer, told the police. "Wangari is the secretary and whatever you want to know she can tell you, because she's been taking the minutes."

"Actually what I'd *really* like," I added, "is if the officers sat down and *they* took their own minutes."

Again, everybody laughed. With that, we started our pro-democracy "preaching." "We're trying to liberate you, too, because you're also being misused," we told the officers. "The law that says we can't meet if we're more than nine is a colonial law, an oppressive law. These are the laws we're trying to change so we can meet in our own houses, in our own country, without anybody telling us how many people can be here."

They listened for a few minutes and then prepared to leave. One of the officers said in as stern a voice as he could muster: "The only thing we would like to tell you is that it would be good to finish this meeting as soon as possible."

"We'll finish soon," I replied, "but we still have a few items on the agenda." Once the police left, we finished the meeting quickly, because they could have gone for reinforcements and come back to arrest us. There was only so far you could push. When the police came with guns, you didn't know whether they had live ammunition. If you tried to move too quickly you could easily be shot dead.

In tandem with MGG activities in the months before the December vote, Paul Muite, Ngorongo Makanga, Timothy Njoya, and I started the Movement for Free and Fair Elections, along with some others we knew from the Freedom Corner protest. We coordinated a series of seminars to educate people about the upcoming elections and translated materials about the elections and the opposition parties' platforms into local languages to make them more accessible to ordinary people. These efforts complemented the public education that the National Council of Churches of Kenya and the Catholic Secretariat's Justice and Peace Commission were doing in the lead-up to the general elections.

Between June and December 1992 we held many town hall–style meetings followed by open forums, where everyone could speak. We generally organized these seminars in church halls at the invitation of local communities, and each one attracted several hundred people. These open forums provided an alternative vision of Kenya's future from that of the government. At the seminars, local people were able to question leaders and politicians and organize themselves within their communities. In this way, we adapted the Green Belt Movement's approach to embedding decision-making at the local level and made sure the communities claimed ownership of their needs and aspirations.

Despite all of our efforts, the opposition failed to unite around a single candidate for president. All the opposition party leaders expressed a desire to come together to defeat the incumbent, but they all wanted to be the presidential candidate and expected the other party heads to come and talk to them first. The MGG invited the leaders to our forums: "You can talk to the people," we said, "and tell them why you feel you should, or cannot, unite." Most of the time, though, the heads of the parties didn't come, but rather sent a representative or had no presence at all. This turned into an education in its own right: We let the public know that these were their leaders and that they were not interested in forming a united opposition.

The year preceding the elections was bloody and difficult. It is estimated that as many as two thousand people were killed in early 1992 during the so-called tribal clashes stirred up by elements in the government. Throughout the campaign, opposition politicians were harassed and barred from holding rallies. For instance, an opposition rally in March that was due to be held in Uhuru Park had to move to All Saints Cathedral because heavily armed police squads barricaded the park. Even then, security officers pursued the demonstrators into the church and beat them in an unprecedented way: Never before had the police beaten people in church to the point where blood was spilled onto such holy ground.

During the nominating period, thugs hired by elements in the government barred fifty opposition candidates from handing in their candidacy papers. This meant that KANU was unopposed in nearly twenty constituencies, and it was reported that just before election day at least sixteen people—stoned, beaten, or assaulted in some other way—died. The Green Belt Movement was also publicly attacked for its role in the pro-democracy effort and one youth leader even called for the government to deregister the movement as an NGO. Fortunately, nothing came of that demand.

When it was held, the election was by no means free and fair. Reports were widespread of ballot boxes being stuffed and some voters intimidated. When the results came in, KANU had received only 36 percent of the vote. As those of us in the MGG feared, the opposition parties split the remainder among them, leaving KANU the largest party in Parliament and Moi still the president. After the elections, many people remembered what we had said: The opposition hadn't united and we were defeated despite the fact that, as seen in the voting pattern, a majority of Kenyans wanted change.

There was, however, some good news. A record nineteen women ran for Parliament and six of them were elected, the most ever. Five of the women MPs represented the opposition. Many more women won seats in local and town councils. I knew how tough they must have been to have survived parliamentary elections in a country where a good African woman was not supposed to be involved in politics.

Nineteen ninety-three did not start well for Kenya. When the newly elected Parliament met for the first time in January, the president suspended it, which he was free to do; and Parliament did not meet again until late March. Apparently, this gave KANU time to persuade some members of Parliament to rejoin the ruling party and to develop a strategy for dealing with opposition MPs. As the year continued, repression increased. People in the opposition were subject to verbal attacks and restrictions on their movement and the ability to do their jobs. As if to prove the president's contention that multiparty politics would degenerate into ethnic violence, the "tribal clashes" that had occurred in 1991 and 1992 flared up again at the beginning of 1993, around the time the mothers of Freedom Corner were ending their hunger strike. The conflict was most intense in the Rift Valley, where I had spent the early years of my childhood.

Ethnicity is one of the major strategies that politicians have used to divide Africans. In 1994, the world witnessed the horrendous genocide in Rwanda that killed nearly a million people, and interethnic violence in the Darfur region of Sudan has displaced and killed hundreds of thousands. I do not believe that people who have lived as neighbors for hundreds of years start attacking and killing one another with no provocation or support from those in power. What happens is that politicians stir people up and give them reasons to blame their own predicaments on people from other ethnic groups. This terrible tragedy has cost Africa many lives and many years that could have been used to promote development.

When ethnicity is linked to land, the result is often combustible. An example can be seen in the fate of the farm in Naivasha where the Green Belt Movement planted its second green belt in 1977. Then, much of the land on the farm was still largely virgin, full of acacia trees and giraffes, antelopes, and zebras. Since that time, however, a huge flood of settlers from the highlands has come into the area and begun cultivating crops. As a result, the wildlife has disappeared, our trees and the others that were there have been cut, streams regularly dry up, and the whole area is fast becoming a desert. This land, which was always fragile, really should have been kept as grazing ground and not converted into farmland. The soils cannot support the crops, especially from the highlands.

During the dry season, pastoralists (herders that move with their livestock to forage and find water) would bring their livestock to graze on this land. However, because of the destruction of the vegetation, the pastoralists were frustrated in their efforts to find grazing ground and streams. Now this area of Naivasha, on the edge of the Rift Valley, has seen repeated conflicts between the pastoralists, who come from one ethnic community, and the farmers, who belong to another. This is an all-too-common example of conflicts resulting from environmental devastation.

Moreover, since the arrival of the Europeans, the politics of land in Kenya has been fraught. When independence came and there was a program through which people could purchase land, Kikuyus like my father were in a position to buy some of the settlers' farms on which many had lived as squatters. In the latter years of Kenyatta's presidency, resentment had grown among non-Kikuyus about the power and land Kikuyus were perceived to have amassed during the Kenyatta years. The resentment is often highlighted and exploited by politicians.

When President Moi came to power, he gave the impression that he was correcting some of the problems of Kenyatta's administration when, in fact, his government was using ethnic politics to displace some communities and in the process appease others. Tribal clashes were witnessed in parts of the Rift Valley and on the coast. The communities most affected included the Kikuyus, Luhyas, Maasais, Sabaots, Kisiis, and Luos.

In Kenya, people depend on their land and primary natural resources, and are very attached to them. They can quickly make an enemy out of someone who has taken land that is seen as theirs. It was this history and attitude that made it easy in the early 1990s for agents in the government to stir up supporters in the Rift Valley to lash out against "other" tribes occupying "their" land.

The ethnic violence that erupted in early 1993 in the Rift Valley, Nyanza, and Western provinces was widely believed to have been kindled by senior members of the government and ruling party,

KANU. Because the government appointed the chiefs and subchiefs in towns and villages, it used them to maintain its control at local levels and to organize attacks on communities that the regime wanted "cleansed." It was partly for this reason that the pro-democracy movement recommended the dissolution of this provincial administrative structure. Unfortunately, when it came to power in 2002, the new, democratic government retained this system with vigor.

When I and others in the Kenyan opposition learned what was happening and detected the government's hand in it, we decided to bring the facts to light. We wanted people in Kenya and overseas to understand this was not just random tribal violence but rather cynical, political manipulation of the deadliest kind. As had happened with Uhuru Park and the protest by mothers of the political prisoners, people came and informed me about what was happening and asked for my help. Fortunately, I was in a position to take action.

In February 1993, I gathered several friends active in opposition politics, including Dr. Makanga, and visited the Rift Valley to verify what we had heard and read about. Local guides showed us houses burned and schools destroyed, leaving adults and their children with no place to go. Women had lost their husbands, men their wives, and many parents their sons and daughters. People had been displaced from their homes and were sleeping in churches. It was devastating—and it was all being done with the full knowledge of our government. "This is wrong," I thought. "The politicians must be stopped." We began to organize the victims of the violence. We held seminars, usually in local churches, where we would appeal to people not to engage in retaliatory attacks. I urged them to recognize that this was not an ethnic quarrel, but rather one that was politically instigated. "You can't beat them, so don't join in," I pleaded. "Things can only get worse." This was proved to me by what happened in Rwanda only a year later.

I also wrote, signed, and circulated leaflets to local communities with the same message. I warned of the dangers to Kenyan society if the clashes continued—escalating violence, further involvement of government security forces, anarchy, and the use of the army to restore order. This would result, I wrote, in soldiers turning their guns on citizens and on one another and the situation deteriorating into a chaotic showdown, "Somalia-style." I begged people to think about how their actions could ensure that this terrible future did not come to pass.

I also helped to establish the Tribal Clashes Resettlement Volunteer Service. We proposed activities that could quell the violence and reknit ties among the communities. We gave footballs to some adults and urged them to form youth football clubs. "The minute the ball is on the ground, the youth might forget their differences and come together to play," I said. We then encouraged the adults to discuss the violence with the young people and persuade them to be positive and peaceful in their interactions with children from other communities.

In some of the camps we discovered women who were practically going mad because they were used to cultivating their fields and were now sitting in camps day and night. We decided to lease land for them so they could do something with their minds and hands, for which they were very grateful. We also suggested to the communities that they establish tree nurseries. "When the seedlings are ready for planting," I told them, "invite the other communities and give them seedlings. Tell them, 'These are trees of peace. We are not interested in conflict. We want to foster peace.' "

At first, the other communities would not visit the nurseries. In time, however, they came and took the trees and planted them on their land. I'll never know whether they saw the trees as symbols of peace or took them because they were free. But communities on both sides of the conflict planted trees and, in many cases, I know they sustained the nurseries. On a few occasions, the two communities and I planted trees of peace together on land over which the two sides were fighting.

While the victims of violence were happy with what we were doing, the aggressors generally were not. As February wore on, it became increasingly dangerous to work within communities, since the government—not wanting people to see the truth on the ground—declared the clash sites "no go zones" and prevented people from entering. They accused those of us who visited the areas of inciting violence, even though we were there to do just the opposite.

I knew from my experiences the previous year that the government meant business: I could be hurt, jailed, or worse. So I took precautions. I tried as much as possible to stay within the law, because I knew the authorities were looking for any excuse to lock me away. This meant that whenever I was in trouble, my lawyers and supporters could say to the government, "She has not broken any law."

I also made sure I didn't deliberately expose myself to danger. As much as possible I traveled incognito and by night. I would leave Nairobi in the early hours of the morning, often with Dr. Makanga at the wheel, and arrive in the Rift Valley before dawn. Through a network of supporters, I could switch cars every twenty miles or so. This made it hard for the police to "mark" a car I was in. One time, I dressed like a nun (the nuns of Mathari and Loreto-Limuru finally got me into holy orders!). I removed the braids in my hair and wore a scarf, which made me virtually unrecognizable. Local people would inform us of what was happening around their area and help us avoid danger spots where security forces were operating.

I always made sure the press was with us, so they could record what was happening and take the news to Kenyans and the world. The people who were affected by the clashes were very happy because their only hope was that their stories got out. Otherwise, they were very isolated. Fortunately, the Kenyan press, while interested in selling newspapers, was also sympathetic to the need for political change, because journalists were also victims of the government's oppression. In this way, we did what we needed to do in the glare of the world.

· · ·

Immediate danger was never very far away during those first few
months of 1993. One night we drove from Nairobi to a town in the
Rift Valley called Burnt Forest, which lived up to its name since the
town was on fire. We left Nairobi in the middle of the night, because
we wanted to arrive early to learn what was happening before the
authorities knew we were there. We were in a convoy of two vehicles.
In the front car were Dr. Makanga and myself, along with Kenyan
journalists. In the second were a crew from the German television
station Deutsche Welle and more local reporters.

As we drove through the forest in the pitch-black night, we suddenly came upon a group of men dressed in traditional warlike costumes, including headgear and sheets across their chests, crossing
the road. They were carrying bows and arrows and machetes, and
while we did not see any, they may also have had guns. Even though
there was a sort of grace to their movements, as they hopped like
antelopes across the road, it was immediately obvious that these
men were ready to kill. While I couldn't quite make out what they
looked like, from the way they moved they appeared to be young. I
had never been so scared: Here in front of us was the killing machine
whose destructive actions we had come to witness.

We stopped to let them pass, keeping our headlights on at full
beam. I imagined that they were on their way to launch fatal attacks
in Molo! Those few minutes were terrifying. If we had switched the
lights off, the men could have easily attacked us. Fortunately, they
had no idea who was in the cars and kept moving. If they had looked
in our direction and discovered it was my friends and me, I am sure
they would have killed us on the spot. It was one thing to read about
the men who were carrying out the violence, but quite another to
see them on the move. Later, we discovered how dangerous our
encounter had been when we heard that the town of Molo, west of
Nakuru, had been attacked and that many were killed and injured.
Those young men had been heading for Molo.

We arrived in the morning in Burnt Forest, visited communities
affected by the clashes, and then attended a meeting between the
provincial administration and the elders of communities that had

been displaced. While the elders knew we were present, we deliberately did not draw attention to ourselves and so were not immediately recognized by the local government administrators. During the course of the meeting, both sides raised issues and after some time the district commissioner asked all those present to identify themselves. Soon it was my turn: "I'm Wangari Maathai," I said. The district commissioner could not believe his ears. How had we been allowed to attend this meeting? Why were we there? He was in a huff, and I knew that some heads would roll. With that the meeting was called to an immediate end and the police were ordered to remove us.

Both Deutsche Welle and the Kenyan press were there to witness this encounter. Earlier in the day, the German crew had taken some important footage of those who had suffered from the tribal clashes. Naturally, the police didn't want the international press filming our expulsion from the meeting, since they knew that that film, along with the other footage the crew had shot, would be shown outside the country. The police shouted at the camerawoman to get out and stop filming or they'd shoot. The woman shouted back, "Well, shoot then." I was thinking, "Why did she say that?" They could easily have shot her, and all of us.

They didn't, but instead forced us out with the barrels of their guns, very menacingly. It was fortunate that by then we had recorded what had been said at the meeting and shown the international and Kenyan journalists what was happening on the ground, so our mission was accomplished. But now the authorities would know we had been in Burnt Forest, so when we left the town late that afternoon, we took extra precautions. On the way back to Nairobi, we changed cars and drivers and arrived in the city only very late that night.

Through Deutsche Welle and other non-Kenyan media contacts, the news of the violence in the Rift Valley and other areas was spreading internationally. In addition, many human rights defenders, including Kerry Kennedy of the Robert F. Kennedy Memorial

Center for Human Rights and U.S. civil rights leader Jesse Jackson, traveled to Kenya and witnessed the atrocities being carried out through these tribal clashes. This was very important. We knew all too well that the Kenyan government could be completely untouched by the complaints of its people; but the minute the international community caught wind of what elements in the government were doing, it could move quickly, because it depended so much on foreign aid, military training funds, and goodwill overseas. Ironically, the Achilles' heel of so many oppressive governments is the positive international image they so desperately crave. It is perhaps just as sad that I had to turn so often to international supporters to protect me from my own government.

Initially, the government didn't complain about what the Green Belt Movement was doing in the Rift Valley. The first seminars held in early 1993 were not public, so the security forces may not have known they were taking place. Furthermore, how could the authorities complain about giving out footballs or planting trees? But as the clashes continued, the government lashed out, particularly after our visit to Burnt Forest.

In a speech the president gave toward the end of February 1993, which was reported on the front page of the *Standard*, he claimed that I had "masterminded" the distribution of leaflets in the Rift Valley that called for Kikuyus to attack Kalenjins and said that our visit to Burnt Forest had incited further clashes. He also asserted, rather ridiculously, that a "lucrative business" had been made by the victims of violence clearing household goods from their own homes and then setting them on fire, as well as by the National Council of Churches, which supported and funded camps to shelter the displaced people.

As usual, I wrote to the president to make my position clear and sent copies of my letter to the press. I had gone to Burnt Forest, I explained, because the victims' suffering had moved me and I wanted to listen to their concerns. I urged the president to use the machinery of government not to further the conflict but to end it. As usual, I did not receive a response. Instead, the attacks both on me and the Kikuyu community continued.

KANU's mouthpiece, the daily *Kenya Times*, claimed that I was "crusading for supremacy of the Kikuyu." A local councilor in Eldoret informed the public that I was out to topple the government and to turn Kikuyus against Kalenjins. He even claimed that the year before I had organized an infestation of aphids that had killed most of Kenya's cypress trees. Now that would have been quite an achievement! A KANU MP bluntly threatened to have me forcibly circumcised if I entered Rift Valley Province again: a chilling attempt to try to control and intimidate me as a woman. The National Council of Women of Kenya called the MP's statement "primitive and irresponsible" at a time when Kenya was working to end female genital mutilation (FGM). Indeed, President Moi himself had banned the practice five years earlier and many women's groups had been advocating for the eradication of FGM from Kenya.

Not all those leveling insults against me were men. Women from several Christian denominations in Nyandura District, northwest of Nairobi, called the government blameless and said that I was disrespectful to the president and out of step with African tradition. An African woman's most important duty, according to them, was "to obey."

Some of these accusations may have been ridiculous, but they were also frightening. During that time, it felt as though anything could happen, in an instant—and often did. On Saturday, February 25, hooded men abducted Dr. Makanga at gunpoint from his pharmacy. For three worrisome days no one, not even his wife, had any idea where he was. Dr. Makanga was a close ally in what we were doing and I was terrified to think what these men—whose identities were a complete mystery—could do to him, whether they were police or hired rogues. I felt terrible because I knew they had abducted him because he supported our work, and I worried about him being tortured in an effort to get information out of him.

After Dr. Makanga's arrest, I received several death threats and I began to fear for my life. I noticed unfamiliar vehicles following me in Nairobi and when I left the city. This was very unsettling, since I knew the recent history of "accidents" on the road. Never before had I felt as threatened as I did now. I decided that going public with my fears might protect me. I wrote an open letter to the attorney general.

At about the same time I organized a seminar at the church of Christ the King in Nakuru, the site of serious violence, and I asked the attorney general for assurances that the police would not harass me. This was not forthcoming. So, knowing the police would be looking for me on the road from Nairobi to Nakuru, I went to Nakuru two days early and hid near the church hall where the meeting was to take place. To the seminar, I had invited not only the affected communities but also the press and diplomats from countries that provided economic assistance to Kenya.

The attorney general replied in a manner of speaking: armed police prevented the seminar from taking place, as well as others we planned for later in March. I heard about the police activities from local guides on the ground and so did not go to the church hall that day. However, two days later, I learned that a delegation of diplomats and the press, guided by the Catholic Church and accompanied by the district and provincial commissioners and the police, had come to Nakuru to see the effects of the tribal clashes for themselves. I left the safe house in Nakuru where I had been staying and appeared at that meeting, knowing that the presence of diplomats made it unlikely I would be arrested. Together, we saw the burned houses, the charred ground, and the camps where displaced families were being sheltered. To ensure my safety, one of the ambassadors there that day gave me a ride back to Nairobi in his car and left me safely inside my home in South C.

Dr. Makanga's abduction and harassment gave me more than enough reason to preempt arrest. Therefore, on the suggestion of my lawyers, on March 4 I presented myself before a judge and told him I believed the police were intending to arrest me and that I wanted to plead to a charge and post bail (a process known in Kenya as bail before arrest or court arrest). This allowed me to preempt more serious charges. The next day, however, I decided that the danger to my life was very real, and did something I never thought I would have to do in my own country: I was forced to go into hiding. It wasn't simply being arrested that I was worried about. I could also have been beaten by the security forces or hired thugs. Friends believed I was targeted for assassination. I could only guess what might happen next.

Before I went underground, I issued a statement to friends around the world asking them to urge their governments not to resume the assistance that had been cut off prior to the reintroduction of the multiparty system unless the president ended the tribal clashes. "While the world is naturally focused on Liberia, Somalia, and the former Yugoslavia," I wrote, "there is ethnic cleansing going on in Kenya." Friends and colleagues in the United States and United Kingdom contacted their legislators, Human Rights Watch raised awareness of the situation, and Amnesty International sent out an urgent action alert about the dangers we faced. They and others called on their members to appeal to the president and his government to guarantee our safety and the freedom of the pro-democracy movement in Kenya.

One feature of living in an oppressive system is that you develop networks of information and protection. In a network, people sometimes know one another and sometimes don't. But when you need one another, a connection is made, often without your even knowing how. For instance, I would be home and someone would call or come by and say, "We must move you out of here." An informer might have heard that the government planned to pick people up for questioning or detention. Before the policeman had even put on his gear, that individual would know he or she was a target and head for a safe house. Only a few people would know where those who had gone underground were.

My network was quite broad. It included friends, members of the clergy, other pro-democracy advocates, and even foreign diplomats. During this time, I spent two weeks "underground" at a church guest house. This was a good safe place since it was an unlikely place to look for me. The archbishop agreed I could be hidden and gave me a room, where the church staff would bring food to me so I didn't have to come out and risk being seen by anyone. Nevertheless, it wasn't secure to stay in one place for too long. But going from safe house to safe house presented its own challenges. In the first half of 1993, I spent a lot of time crouched on the floor of friends' cars being transported around Nairobi under cover of darkness. I often wore a wig or scarf to disguise my appearance.

Even foreign diplomats from several countries helped me feel safer. Several of the Norwegian diplomatic staff were actively involved in efforts to protect me, and even assisted in moving me to safer ground. The Norwegians, in particular, were strong supporters of the pro-democracy movement in Kenya. When some Kenyan political prisoners were released and felt it was not safe to stay in the country, Norway gave them refuge. The Norwegian government's position on human rights so riled the president that he cut off diplomatic relations with Norway in the 1990s, and nearly all of Norway's diplomatic staff left the country. Unfortunately for the Green Belt Movement, this severing of relations meant that, like all other Kenyan organizations, Green Belt could no longer receive the support NORAD had been providing. After diplomatic relations were cut, one Norwegian diplomat, Arman Aardal, remained in Kenya; he was his country's representative to UNEP. Arman was very supportive and quite often during my time underground would help drive me from one safe place to another. He became a good friend and an ardent supporter of the disadvantaged children of the Mathare slum.

At the same time that I was moving from one safe house to another, I had been invited to a meeting in Tokyo by the Green Cross International, a global environmental organization set up that year by former Soviet leader Mikhail Gorbachev. I sent a message to the Green Cross meeting organizers to say I couldn't come because I did not have the necessary travel documents and was in hiding. To the surprise, I think, of the Kenyan authorities, President Gorbachev intervened, sending a message to President Moi asking his government to help me obtain the documents I needed to travel to Tokyo. The Kenyan president expressed shock. He claimed that he knew nothing about my inability to travel and sent a message through the press saying he could not understand why I thought I couldn't go to Tokyo.

My friends relayed this information to me in my safe house and suggested that I come out of hiding to get the travel documents. In their view, given what President Moi had said, it seemed likely that I would be safe. I was persuaded and presented myself to the immigration authorities, who gave me the necessary documents and never again questioned me at the airport in Nairobi about where I was going or why. Unfortunately, by the time I got the papers I needed, the Green Cross meeting was almost coming to an end and I would not have arrived in Tokyo in time.

I was, though, able to travel in late April 1993 to Scotland to receive the Edinburgh Medal from the Edinburgh District Council, as part of the Edinburgh International Science Festival. I'd written to the council and expressed my regret that fears for my safety and the fact that I couldn't get the necessary travel documents meant I could not attend. But thanks to President Gorbachev, I received my passport in time.

Working for justice and freedom is often a lonely and dispiriting business. Yet in my various struggles I have been fortunate to receive the encouragement and support of many individuals and institutions, both in Kenya and overseas, who have stood by me in difficult times. Often their phone calls, faxes, letters—or, later, e-mails—or simply their presence made the difference at a crucial moment. To all of them, I am eternally grateful, as I am to the powerful who were willing to use their positions to protect me.

It is no exaggeration to say that these friends, the awards I received, and the conferences I attended may have saved my life. As I told journalists in Edinburgh, "I don't want to die before finishing my work." After Scotland, in May 1993 I flew to Chicago to receive the Jane Addams International Women's Leadership Award and then in June I deliberately traveled to Vienna for the UN's World Conference on Human Rights. In addition to meeting with delegates and nongovernmental organizations, I organized an exhibition of photos of victims of the tribal clashes, and distributed copies of a Kenyan parliamentary report on the violence. Unfortunately, the photos and reports were stolen from the booth by members of the Kenyan delegation. Although I was angry and frustrated that they had wrecked my exhibit, their actions gave me an additional opportunity to expound at the conference, including to the media, on the tribal clashes and the violation of human rights in Kenya. I had turned my misfortune into an opportunity.

Gradually the clashes died down, although the effects of the violence linger to this day. Indeed, tribal conflicts tend to recur in different parts of the country whenever unscrupulous politicians incite their communities against other communities. They happened, for example, during the election campaigns of 1997, and even today they can be revived at the whim of politicans. Many people who were displaced by the violence of the early 1990s have still not returned to their homes and have been turned into internally displaced refugees. Unfortunately, the UN Commission on Refugees does not cater to internally displaced persons.

From the outset of the ethnic violence in 1991, I knew that the issues of land and governance had to be part of the civic and environmental education that Green Belt Movement members received. Too often, Kenyans were looking at one another as foreigners. It is the case that the various ethnic communities in Kenya are, for all intents and purposes, distinct nations, what I call micronations. We have our own languages, traditions, foods, and dances, and our own cultural and historical baggage.

However, in the late nineteenth century a large power with its own baggage brought us together and called us a nation. We cannot deny this fact of history, although being in one country does not mean we are identical peoples. We have to accept that our baggage can be divisive or destructive, and we should discard it. But this process has to be deliberate so that we focus on what brings us together, which will allow us to cooperate and respect one another. We need to honor the past but look to the future. In this way, we can consciously create a new idea of a nation, of Kenya and of what it means to be Kenyan. This concept of nationhood became a component of the Green Belt seminars after the tribal clashes.

From the outset of the ethnic violence, we held seminars in my house in the evenings, since during the day the house resembled a beehive, packed with Green Belt staff. People came over and sat in the living room and I'd teach, sometimes until one or two o'clock in the morning. Nearly all of those who attended were men, since it was easier for them to travel and many women were too scared to come or couldn't leave their children at night. At this time, we were still being constantly monitored by government informers. The informers got to know who came to my home and what kinds of activities were going on, as did the neighbors.

At first, people participating in the seminars would sleep over—forty or fifty of them at a time. As you'll remember, it's not a large house. I didn't have mattresses for them, but I kept a clean home so they could just lie down anywhere on the floor. After a couple of seminars, we decided it would be better if the men slept in hotels in town where there was more space and they were less likely to draw the attention of the police. I looked for funds to accomodate them.

Another feature of living under an oppressive regime is the element of absurdity that often accompanies moments that are potentially very dangerous and intimidating. I'll never forget one night when we'd had a seminar and the men had left shortly after midnight. Someone must have informed the police that I had held a large meeting at my house, because a few hours later, I heard my watchman calling me through the window. "Wake up," he said. "Some police officers are calling."

"Police?" I asked, sleepily. "It must be three o'clock in the morning!"

"Yes," he replied, "and they're already in the compound. They forced their way through the gate."

As soon as the watchman woke me up, he disappeared. He later told me he didn't want to be arrested and was watching from the other side of the back wall. So much for security!

"Open up," the officers called. "We know there are men here." They poked their batons through the open windows and tried to spread the curtains in the living room. "You know you're not supposed to have meetings," they continued. "We want to confirm that there are people in the house." To my relief, their tone wasn't threatening. "The people were in my house, but they've left. I'm alone here now," I replied with confidence, thinking about my security guard. But the police wouldn't believe me and became more insistent. So I went to the phone and did what anyone would do in the middle of the night when strange men demand to be let into your house: I dialed 999, the police emergency line.

"Hello," a policeman in the station answered.

"This is Wangari Maathai," I said. "I want to report that there are some thugs who've come into my compound and they're telling me that they are policemen."

The officer at the other end of the line didn't hesitate for a moment. "They're not thugs. They *are* policemen," he said.

"How do you know?" I asked him.

"We sent them there," he replied.

"Well, in that case," I retorted, "tell them to go home. There's nothing here."

But he remained unconvinced. "Open the door, so they can confirm there aren't any men in your house. There's nothing to fear."

I also was unconvinced. "Do you think I'm going to open my door to a group of policemen at this hour?" I asked him. "I'm not." And I put the phone down.

Now I had to deal with the policemen outside in my compound.

"Go away," I said through the window. "There's no one here." Then I heard a female voice. "Open up. I'm a woman!"

"What are you doing out there with those men at this hour?" I asked her, astonished.

"I'm a *policewoman!*" she replied.

"Then you can understand my apprehension," I insisted. "If you cannot believe me, I cannot believe you," I responded, and at that I started to pretend there *were* men inside, because even she wouldn't believe me. "OK. You men, you can sleep soundly, because there are policemen outside," I said loudly. This went on for some time, with them continuing to ask me to open up and me refusing. Eventually, I just sat down in my living room and stopped responding to them. The standoff continued until the officers got tired and became completely quiet, and I returned to bed. When I woke up the next morning, I saw that the police officers had gone and that my security guard had come back to tell his story of how he had seen everything that had happened—from a good, safe distance behind the fence.

In the fall of 1995, the UN held its fourth global conference on women in Beijing. That summer, I organized a "mini-Beijing" in Nairobi where Kenyan women could discuss and debate the issues the UN conference would address, including the environment, development, poverty, health, debt, and women's rights. That August I traveled to China for the first time and for two weeks participated in panels and workshops at the NGO Forum, held in the village of Huairou. At one of the panels, I presented a paper I had written called "Bottlenecks of Development in Africa," which described the obstacles to Africa's spiritual and economic renewal, including poverty, debt, corruption, destruction of the environment, and the fact that development was not focused on the people.

I also participated in the official government conference. On behalf of the Commission on Global Governance, of which I was a member, and which was then cochaired by the Swedish prime minister, Ingvar Carlsson, and Shridath Ramphal, former secretary-general of the British Commonwealth, I presented a statement to the government delegations. This was drawn from a report the commission produced titled "Our Global Neighborhood." I laid out some of the values that women around the world were trying to bring to our global neighborhood and that the commission had discussed. These were respect for basic human rights, justice, equality and equity, non-violence, caring, and integrity.

A neighborhood with such values, I said, "would seek liberty for all, would promote mutual respect and tolerance, and would demand that rights go hand in hand with responsibilities. Such a neighborhood would also require that the strong as well as the weak subscribe to a rule of law. It would combat the corrupted as well as the corrupting, and would encourage participatory and legitimate democratic governance within all relevant institutions."

During my time in Beijing, I also met old friends who for years had been working, like me, in the trenches for women's and environmental rights, including Bella Abzug and my fellow board members of the Women's Environment & Development Organization. I participated in several forums with Bella and shared my experiences in the Green Belt Movement. I also met with younger advocates. It was wonderful to see a new generation of women working for change and a joy to reconnect with friends and colleagues I'd known for decades. Given what I had experienced in Kenya in the first half of the 1990s, it was good to be with people whose support had sustained me during dark times. We were all a little older, and hopefully a little wiser, but we were as passionate in our beliefs as we'd ever been.

12

Opening the Gates of Politics

"A woman politician needs the skin of an elephant," I had told a reporter after the 1992 elections. In 1997, another round of national elections was scheduled for December. These held real promise for the opposition. Due to pressure from the pro-democracy movement and donor nations, the government had by this time given all political parties the official recognition they needed to field candidates. This expanded the scope of Kenya's emerging democracy, but it also made it a greater challenge to unite the opposition. In the months before the election, I again spoke publicly and appealed to the opposition parties to agree on one presidential candidate and to join together under a single umbrella coalition party. Otherwise, I warned, what had happened in 1992 would be repeated. . . . We would lose the elections.

In the runup to the 1992 elections, I had been asked by friends at home and abroad to run for president. Even though I had attempted to contest the by-election a decade previously, I hadn't thought seriously about a career in parliamentary politics since then. While I wanted to do what I could to ensure the opposition's victory, I still felt my primary role was to bring about societal change outside elective politics. Nevertheless, I recognized the limitations of what one could accomplish outside Parliament and active politics as a member of civil society.

In 1997, old friends, members of the pro-democracy movement who didn't want to suffer another electoral defeat, and men and, particularly, women from Nyeri began to talk to me seriously about entering Parliament. That September, nearly a thousand people in Eldoret and another thousand in Murang'a rallied to encourage me to run to be an MP and for the presidency. In Kenya, you need to be elected as an MP in order to also be the president, but you can run for both at the same time. I began to take these conversations, both public and private, more to heart, and wondered whether I had that elephant's skin.

The argument of those who wanted me to run was simple: Practice through mainstream politics what you have been preaching—and doing—through the Green Belt Movement for years. People would say, "If she can do so much and she's not in Parliament, guess what she could do if she was!" By then, I knew all too well the connection between bad governance and mismanagement of resources, environmental destruction, and the poverty of millions of Kenya's people. The Green Belt Movement had provided a laboratory of sorts to experiment with a holistic approach to development that dealt with problems on the ground but also examined and addressed their individual and systemic causes.

Even though internal and external pressure had since the early 1990s forced the government to reintroduce political parties and limit to some degree the reach of its power, government abuses (especially corruption) still continued. Poverty had deepened in Kenya, corruption was endemic, and most people felt powerless to change the direction in which the country was headed. Large areas of forest were still being logged legally and illegally, at a fast rate, or sold off to government cronies for development. These practices compounded the lack of water, fuelwood, healthy soil, and nutritious food in rural areas that so many Kenyans still experienced.

Running for the presidency intrigued me, especially as the election date of December 29 neared and the opposition showed no sign of uniting around a single candidate. Could I be the candidate that unified us? It wasn't outside the realm of possibility. My performance as coordinator of the Green Belt Movement was well known. People could judge me on what I had done.

I also wanted to challenge the perception among some people, including Kenyans, that good people don't go into politics, as if all politicians are tricksters and liars. Yet it was the politicians in Kenya who were making the policies that were repressing people and their aspirations and destroying the environment. It was their decisions that affected so much of our lives. To say that participating in politics is bad is to misunderstand the situation: Why leave your fate in the hands of liars or tricksters?

Before I could start a campaign in earnest, I needed a party to support me, since you couldn't be a candidate without a political party. By then it was customary in Kenya for people to register political parties and wait for candidates. To obtain the use of a party, the candidate would be expected to project that party's profile, carry its owners into the political process with them, or pay for the party and take it over. None of these parties had real ideologies or serious platforms. They were really organized more around personalities, and that is still the case in Kenya. In 1997, some people came and offered me the use of the Liberal Party, which was very small and unknown.

About five weeks before the election, on November 20, 1997, I announced my intention to run for a parliamentary seat in Tetu, a constituency that includes Ihithe, the village where I was born, and also join the race for president as the candidate of the Liberal Party. I was not alone: Twenty-seven parties fielded candidates in these elections, a huge increase from 1992, and fifteen people were running for president. Two of us were women, myself and Charity Ngilu, a sitting MP. One of the reasons I thought I could be useful to the opposition if I joined the race for president was that it would provide a way for me to engage my fellow candidates in dialogues and urge them to form a united front so that the opposition would not again lose the elections.

Once people become presidential candidates, it is nearly impossible to find a forum in which you can address them if you are not a candidate yourself. In addition, if you are not a candidate, it is much harder to reach the general public with your message; it is easy to become irrelevant.

In 1997, because I was among the presidential contenders, I used the campaign to try to talk with the others and have us work together to defeat the incumbent. As it turned out, what I was trying to do was completely misinterpreted. I began by trying to bring together the several presidential candidates that, like me, came from the central region of Kenya. After that, I thought, we could reach out to the candidates from other regions. But the minute I did this I was labeled, even by many in the Kikuyu community, a "tribalist."

It was not an easy campaign. I had begun late and had a lot of ground to make up. I also had very little money, although friends and supporters worked to raise funds to support my candidacy. Despite their efforts, I remained grossly underfunded. To my surprise, the press, which had written mainly favorable reports of my activities in the past, now questioned my interest in elective politics and suggested I could do more for the country if I kept focused on the Green Belt Movement. Unsurprisingly, those elements of the media friendly to, or controlled by, KANU, were particularly vocal in their skepticism about my motivations.

These attitudes, especially among the press, trivialized my candidacy and made it appear that I was not a serious candidate but rather a deliberate spoiler for Charity Ngilu, the other woman in the race. The reason I had wanted to join the race for president—to help unify the opposition so we did not make the same mistake we had in 1992—was lost. I felt bad, because I was being presented in a completely different light, far removed from my intentions. This presentation was unfair but it stuck, and whatever ideas I put forward didn't really matter.

I had hoped to introduce to people who had suffered so much from a single political party system a different understanding of the value of multiparty politics and what such a system offers voters: a greater freedom of choice of candidates, and an opportunity to be presented with different ideologies, philosophies, issues, and priorities from which to choose. What emerged from the experience, though, was something very different. It became clear during the course of the 1997 campaign that our society was still focused on ethnicity and personality cults. Communities rallied around one of their own, encouraging well-known personalities to compete with those from other communities, irrespective of philosophies or ideologies.

A favorite son or daughter of the community was the best candidate around which to build a "personality cult"; he or she would be most likely to bring goodies from the national treasury to each of their homes. The most important thing to the voters was that their candidate win and get into State House. There he or she would control national resources and the Treasury and ensure that his or her community got the biggest share. In this way the candidate became the ideology and the philosophy. There wasn't anything else. These personalities have enormous influence over their followers, who place all their hopes and aspirations on them. By doing so, the people re-emphasize their own disempowerment and powerlessness. In Kenya, communities talk of "our time to eat," if their own son or daughter wins!

Of course, each political party drew up a manifesto that articulated its objectives, philosophy, ideology, and values, but these were mostly for the purposes of registering the party and legitimizing candidates. Party manifestos, once written and presented to the registrar of parties, make good reading for students of political science. But as a people we had not matured politically to the point of using elective politics to debate philosophies, ideologies, and values, or of looking to the common good, rather than for narrow ethnic advantage. This even extended to members of the opposition, who, when they came to power too often resorted to the politics of ethnicity and personality cults (the "Big Man in Africa" syndrome). This culture permits easy corruption and misgovernance.

I was, therefore, a bit of a dreamer to expect voters in 1997 to elect the individuals they thought could do the best job and to avoid being influenced by ethnicity and personality cults. In the end, I didn't get the chance to see what kind of support I had won because, on the eve of the election, a rumor was circulated that I'd dropped out of both races and had told my supporters to vote for other candidates. I had made no such decision; it was a dirty lie from one of the local parties, whose candidate I was supposed to have endorsed. Nonetheless, the rumor spread quickly and was both in the print and electronic media on the day of vote casting! I received only a tiny percentage of the votes for president from those who either did not hear the rumor or did not believe it. I also lost the race for Parliament for the same reason. I was deeply disappointed, but I understood.

The reaction of the voters was not altogether surprising: Given the political culture in our land I was expected to support the local favorite son for president and seek a parliamentary seat through that presidential candidate's party and patronage. I could see that it was a waste of time for me to argue for a political ideology and philosophy or to run a campaign based on issues. That time was far into the future.

An international team of election observers reported vote-rigging and other irregularities, but concluded that the 1997 elections were an improvement over those held in 1992. While the fragmented opposition received the largest number of votes and increased its share of seats in Parliament, the incumbent ruling party was still the largest party and President Moi found himself elected to yet another term of five years. Again, the opposition, despite garnering about two-thirds of the votes had lost because it had failed to come together.

I was disappointed, of course, by the results; we had blown it again! There was so much work to do to overcome the political culture and give merit a chance. After the campaign, I returned to my office at the Green Belt Movement and consoled myself with the fact that if I had been elected to Parliament, I would have been limited in what I could have achieved as a member of the opposition. KANU still exerted a lot of control and refused to distribute national resources to constituencies represented by the opposition. If I had been elected an MP I probably wouldn't have been reelected in 2002, since I wouldn't have been able to do much for my constituents, who expected much from their member of Parliament.

In the hope that I could still contribute to changing the political culture, my supporters and I eventually founded and registered the Mazingira Green Party to allow candidates to run on a platform of green values, like those embodied in the Green Belt Movement, and to make these values more mainstream in Kenyan politics and society. "Mazingira" means "environment" in Kiswahili. We joined the Federation of Green Parties of Africa as well as the Global Greens, an international network of green parties in nearly seventy-five countries.

In Kenya, the Green Party is still young and while there are people who care about the environment even in many of the other political parties, the idea of "green politics" in the way it is understood in Germany, for instance, is not in evidence in Kenya—yet. Indeed, this is true of Green Parties in many African countries. There is still a lot of work to be done to create a "Society of Greens" and build support for green values not only within the other political parties but also in the country at large. Only then would candidates with such values be voted in on that platform.

After the disappointing experience of the elections of 1997, I resumed my position as the head of the Green Belt Movement, which was more than enough on my plate. This was partly because KANU continued to mismanage the country's natural resources, especially forests. Our efforts to protect these resources, especially Karura Forest in Nairobi, placed the Green Belt Movement in direct confrontation with the government yet again.

. . .

One of the areas where green values have been challenged most in Kenya is in the way the government uses public land. During its years in power, the past regime had regularly given thousands of acres of forest or parkland to politically connected people for private use in return for political support. While the government was no longer able to parcel out land as spectacularly as it had tried to do with the *Times* tower complex in Uhuru Park, the practice of "land-grabbing," as it is known in Kenya, was still widespread.

The Green Belt Movement helped stop some of the most outrageous examples, including the selling off of Jivanjee Gardens, a botanical park given to the city of Nairobi by a prominent Indian family. Whenever a piece of public land was threatened with privatization, the Green Belt Movement erected a billboard painted in the colors of the Kenyan flag to alert the public of the threat so that members could protect the land from being "grabbed."

Still, we lost some battles and many of the deals were made by the government in extreme secrecy. People wouldn't know that public land had passed into private hands until they saw a building being erected. In Nairobi today you can see many office blocks, shopping centers, and even places of worship built on what was once state land.

I felt very strongly about land-grabbing, since the destruction of the forest mirrored the government's looting of the nation's treasures, whether it was money from the treasury or natural resources from the environment. I knew that all of the Green Belt Movement's work would be in vain if the government continued to sell off or exploit natural forests. If we didn't do something about it, the Sahara Desert would continue to spread south and life for millions of people would only get harder as land suitable for agriculture and habitats for wildlife got scarcer.

In 1997, I had written to the minister of environment and natural resources to protest the deforestation of Ngong and South Western

Mau forests, as well as of Karura Forest. Then, in the summer of 1998, I learned of an example of land-grabbing so blatant and extensive that I knew this would be a fight we could not afford to lose. The government was taking public land in Karura Forest to the north of Nairobi and giving it to its political allies for executive offices and private houses. For the government to earmark forest for a research institute, tree nursery, or even a school was one thing. It was quite another to give a forest to friends. I soon learned that as far back as 1996, a vast swath of the Karura Forest that had previously been protected, or gazetted, had been allotted to private developers.

I was outraged. For generations, Karura Forest had acted as a break between the winds off the savanna to the south and those descending from the highlands to the west and north. Its 2,500 acres of natural forest serve as a catchment area for four major rivers, while its dense undergrowth and canopy are home to many rare species of flora and fauna, including *mīhūgū* trees, Sykes monkeys, bush pigs, antelopes, and hundreds of species of birds. Situated on the edge of Nairobi, Karura Forest serves as the lung of the congested metropolis.

By this time the Green Belt Movement had developed its own unofficial network of informers. In Karura, these included men and women from a nearby village who herded their goats in the forest and others who rode horses or hiked there. They passed on information to us about what was happening. When, in September 1998, I went to Karura to see the situation for myself, I discovered that a road had already been dug and workers were laying down what looked like a drainage system. Even though work had not yet begun on the houses, several structures to house the construction workers had been erected.

I wrote to the attorney general on September 28 requesting a halt to any further construction in or clearing of the forest. As usual, the government's immediate response was to ignore us. However, we also alerted the press, and the *Daily Nation* newspaper hired a helicopter to fly over the forest and published the photographs on its front pages. The aerial shots brought home how much of the forest had been cleared and destroyed.

We began our campaign to reclaim what had already been destroyed and to stop any more land being cleared in much of Karura Forest in the same way the Green Belt Movement began other campaigns: We would inform government officials of our concern and, if they didn't respond after some time, we would hold a press conference to let the media and the public know that the government was not responding. Eventually we would move in and try to reclaim the land by planting trees.

In the days after my letter to the attorney general, we visited Karura Forest on several occasions to raise awareness of the land grabbing and the destruction under way, always informing the government of when we planned to be in the forest. On the very first day that we arrived at what was now a building site in Karura Forest, we saw a large tractor, housing for the workers, and a group of young men hanging around. We had our suspicions, but went into the forest anyway. What we did not know was that the young men intended to attack us. As we were planting trees, they descended on us with machetes. The young men uprooted all the trees we planted and we were saved from being hurt only by the arrival of the construction workers, who had been given instructions to stop us from planting trees. They had followed us and now calmed the young men down, telling them not to beat the women but only to force us out of the forest. That day we got out without any confrontation.

But we returned several more times and even established a tree nursery inside the forest. These visits became like teach-ins or the seminars we held with Green Belt groups. We would talk to the workers and explain the role the forest played in Nairobi's environment and inform them that Karura was being cut down so that wealthy people could live there and that they and their families wouldn't benefit at all. Sometimes our arguments were persuasive because the workers would agree that we could plant our trees. We also invited the press so that our message got out to the public.

But on October 7 the campaign took on a new dimension. That morning, when we arrived at the forest, we went straight to the camp where the building site was, accompanied by twelve opposition MPs who shared our unhappiness with the government's mismanagement of environmental issues. The press joined us. We again asked the workers, who were each armed with a *panga,* or a short machete, to stop destroying the forest and let us plant trees, but this time, they wouldn't listen to our appeals. It appeared they were ready for battle. In no time all hell broke loose.

I had walked farther into the forest with the other women to plant our seedlings. Suddenly, there was a commotion. People were running in all directions. Suddenly there was smoke. The reporters with me asked what I thought was burning. "I hope it's not the forest!" I replied anxiously. I hurried back toward the smoke to see what had caused the fire. We saw trucks, tractors, and the buildings that the contractors had brought into the forest all aflame.

Luckily, no one was hurt. While I regretted the destruction of property, I couldn't help but wonder what vehicles and buildings were doing in the forest in the first place, since they weren't part of any biodiversity I knew. The contractor was unable to take anyone to court because the workers had run away, and he didn't know who to charge. It is also true that public opinion in Kenya was by now against anyone who was perceived to be destroying our forests, wherever they were.

By the time we announced that we were going again to Karura on October 17 to plant trees and stop further construction, the section of the forest slated for development had been blocked off by a fence and a huge gate, plastered with a big sign that said, PRIVATE PROPERTY. We informed the chief forester of Karura, the chief conservator of forests, and the police of our planned visit. But two days before, the police denied us permission to enter the forest, citing "security reasons." We refused to be intimidated: After all, this was a *public* forest. We came as we had promised but were prevented from entering. That day our party included members of Green Belt groups, the public, and a few students. Since we could not enter the forest, we planted two trees at the gate and left. When we returned the next day, we found that those trees had been uprooted.

We still needed to get into the forest, because the seedlings in the tree nursery we had established needed constant tending. We also needed to maintain our surveillance activities because once the fence was erected we didn't know how far construction had proceeded. Of course, we also wanted to ensure that the building did not go any further. So we informed the authorities that we would be in the forest again and asked them not to interfere with our activities. Their response was to send a large battalion of armed policemen into the forest to guard every possible entrance and keep us out of the forest.

Fortunately for us, the authorities did not think about the possibility of our entering the forest through the strip of marshlands about three hundred yards across the border on the north side of Karura. Having been denied entry through the main gates, and knowing there were guards at the other entry points to the forest, we decided that going through the marshes was our only option. Once more our unofficial network of informers helped by providing us with a guide who knew his way through the swampy area. A group of about twenty—the women hitching up their dresses, the men rolling up their trousers, and all of us removing our shoes—stepped into the wet ground, using the footprints of our guide in front of us. I was armed with my watering can, and the press was with us, too.

As we made our way across the marshes, at one point we had to walk along a log partly submerged by the fast-flowing river. You had to balance carefully to make sure you didn't fall into the water. Alas, some of those with us did tumble in, but fortunately the water was not that deep. It was only after many of us had crossed the river and were inside the forest that the police realized we were there. They were astonished to see me watering the seedlings in the nursery. The police thought they had the forest completely covered, and yet we had crept in. We beat them to it!

Everybody but me was cleared from the nursery by the police, but they allowed me to go to the river, dip my can in, come back, and water the young trees again and again for over an hour. One officer stood guard and watched me work to make sure he could tell his superiors that he had caught up with me and that all I was doing was watering trees. I was all business with him. "If you aren't going to water these trees for me," I said, "then you shouldn't bother me. All I'm doing is watering them. I don't want them to die." He let me finish, which was nice. By the end of that hour, my dress was soaked and I was tired.

The trees watered, the police officer offered me a ride in his car and escorted me out of the forest through the main gate, which was now wide open. Our supporters who had walked through the marshes and the press were there to meet me, barefoot and with my shoes hanging from my neck. The next day, the Kenyan newspapers carried an interview with me, which was greeted with astonishment by many. They didn't expect to see me emerging from the forest, but rather stuck on the outside trying to get in past the big gate. They were very supportive.

After the fires of October 7 and the standoff of October 17, the struggle for Karura Forest became an international affair, as the media and global organizations began to take notice. On October 27, Klaus Toepfer, executive director of the United Nations Environment Programme, the headquarters of which had been carved out of Karura Forest some twenty-five years previously, issued a statement that Karura Forest was "a precious natural resource that the city cannot afford to lose."

Many UNEP staff members were appalled that Karura Forest was being privatized and came incognito to our rallies in support. UNEP officials told us, either directly or through their staff, that they had contacted senior members of the Kenyan government and expressed the hope that the forest would be saved. This encouraged us, because not only did we feel that we weren't alone but we had an important agency working with us.

On December 5, I invited one hundred delegates—Africans, Europeans, and North and South Americans—then attending the Euro-African Green Conference in Nairobi to visit our tree nursery in Karura and to plant symbolic trees there. We informed the police that we were coming to the forest and were able to get in through one of the entrances that was not guarded that day. We warned the delegates that there might be a confrontation with the police, who, when we arrived, were there in full force and armed to the teeth. But they didn't bother the delegates, whom I thanked for being there and for participating in saving the forest. It was great, I added, that the police were also in our company. And with that, we all planted trees in the forest.

After this, rather than do what was right, the government decided to ratchet up the tension and the level of violence. In December it told those who'd been given plots in the forest that it was up to them to protect their property. That meant hired security. It was easy to pick up unemployed men in downtown Nairobi and pay them enough to make sure that Wangari and her team would not only get nowhere near the forest but be hurt if they did. The presence of armed thugs posed a much greater threat than we'd experienced before. These men were scattered throughout the forest, away from the cameras and anyone who might be able to stop an "accident" from happening. We decided, therefore, that when we visited again on January 8, 1999, we would not try to enter Karura Forest. Instead, we would plant a tree at the gate to make our statement that the government should return the land to the public.

I knew it was important to have people of standing with us who might protect us from violence. That day we were accompanied by six members of Parliament, journalists, a few international observers, Green Belt group members, and supporters from affiliated groups, such as Friends of Forests and the Kenya Human Rights Commission, an organization independent of the government that had been established to monitor human rights abuses in the country. When we arrived early on the morning of January 8, we were confronted by two hundred guards armed with machetes, clubs, whips, *pangas,* and bows and arrows. Some even had swords.

They walked toward us and surrounded our group. "You can't get into the forest," they said.

"We're not trying to get into the forest," I replied, trying to keep calm. "We just want to plant a tree here."

"You can't do that," responded the men, shaking their heads. Some of them also shook their *pangas.*

"I can't leave this place today until I plant a tree," I said.

"This is private property," they snapped back.

That was not true. "This is public land, and we're entitled to plant a tree on public land." This conversation, if it could be called that, went on for some time before I had had enough. "It is time for me to plant a tree," I declared, and set out to dig a hole with my hoe.

No sooner had I started digging than the men got aggressive and began hurling abuse and obscenities at us. "Who do you think you are, woman?" they shouted. This was hurtful, because these men were young enough to be my children. It was also frightening. These young men seemed unstable and could easily have been on drugs or drunk on alcohol.

It is hard to know precisely when violence starts, but in a heated atmosphere, it can take an instant, like a coal bursting into flame. In this case, we suddenly found ourselves under assault from whips and clubs, and stones began flying through the air around us. When the blow came, I felt not so much pain as surprise, even though from the beginning the thugs clearly wanted to hurt or even kill us. I put my hands to my head and found it was bleeding. Strangely, my mind was very clear and calm. "Now, why would he do something like that?" I asked myself. "Why would he hit me?"

We always encouraged people to run when they were attacked. It was one thing to shout, "Leave the forest alone"; it was another to nurse a wound in the hospital. Some of those who joined our campaign for Karura and who were with us that day were also young, and we didn't want them to be so afraid that they wouldn't protest again. In all our campaigns it was our persistence that won the day more than our bravery.

Even as I saw people running, I remained still, almost transfixed. I found it difficult to move until Dr. Makanga and Lillian Muchungi caught hold of me. They were longtime Green Belt staff members and friends, and the three of us ran. As we all scattered, the thugs began howling and hurling even more stones at us and smashing the cars that some of us had arrived in. I was very worried, because people were falling on top of one another as they fled. Four of the MPs, some of the journalists, and two German environmentalists were hurt, and there would be many broken legs and arms. Thankfully, the thugs didn't follow us as we made our way to the main road, climbing over fences to reach it, and then to the nearest police station. It was two miles away and it took us about forty minutes to get there.

By then, I realized I had a deep gash on the top of my head and blood was streaming down my neck. I was furious, not so much with the thugs as with the police. My head still warm with the blood, I reported the assault and told the officers that we knew who the attackers were. We offered to take them back to the scene of the violence so they could arrest our assailants. If you can believe it, the police didn't move at all. Instead, they asked me to sign a formal complaint testifying to my assault. So, sign it I did: I took my finger and dipped it into the blood pouring from my head and wrote a red "X" on that paper—so they would know how I felt about what had happened and also be unable to avoid the evidence in front of them. After that, I went to Nairobi Hospital, where my doctor told me I was very lucky. If I'd been hit again, he said, I might well not have lived.

Why the police did nothing did not remain a mystery for long. That evening, KTN ran a story with footage showing that a cameraman who had arrived before us had a shot of an officer conversing with the thugs at the gate. It showed us, and all Kenya, that the attack was organized and approved by the police. That report, and the coverage in both local and international papers over the next few days, led to universal condemnation of the attack; the U.S. ambassador, members of the Kenyan clergy, opposition MPs, and the press all spoke out. In an unusually frank statement, the UN secretary general, Kofi Annan, on whose Advisory Board on Disarmament I served, condemned the beating and the violence that accompanied it.

Subsequently, I learned that many embassies, international organizations, and individuals raised their voices, asking the president why it was necessary to destroy the forest, why we had to be beaten when we demonstrated, and why it was a crime to demonstrate in the first place. After the violence of January 8, the clergy got fully involved and brought the weight of their authority not only to the selling off of a public forest but also the violent assault on members of the public and MPs.

The president offered his opinion: He couldn't understand why people would be opposed to the luxury development in Karura Forest. After all, he said, much of Nairobi had been built out of forest land, and this was just another example of the city striding forward into the future. Others begged to differ, and what had happened on January 8 only further inflamed already existing tensions in the country. University students, completely independently from the Green Belt Movement, organized their own protest.

At the end of January, a number of students commandeered a tractor from the University of Nairobi, along with public buses and other vehicles, and rammed the gate that denied access to Karura Forest. When the tractor hit the gate, it stalled and the police pounced. The students scattered everywhere, many running into UNEP's compound with the police in riot control trucks hot on their heels.

UNEP's governing council was meeting that day and the students thought they would be safe on UNEP's grounds, since nobody was supposed to be followed onto UN property. The students had other reasons to feel secure. Under its executive directors Mustafa Tolba and then Dr. Toepfer, UNEP had supported the Green Belt Movement and other organizations financially and had tried to ensure that we weren't threatened by the government in our efforts to protect the environment. UNEP officials often spoke out against governmental mismanagement of the environment and its harassment of the Green Belt Movement, diplomatic protocol notwithstanding. This was a serious matter of environmental and other human rights.

The students were, however, wrong in assuming that the police would respect this understanding. Once on the UNEP compound, the police beat them savagely. At least two students were admitted to the hospital with serious injuries. Klaus Toepfer himself broke all protocol and lodged a formal complaint with the government. The next day riots broke out throughout the city. The students were on fire—angry about the destruction of the forest and angry about the government's repression and its abuse of citizens. For six hours they battled with the police. Tear gas and bullets flew, causing the universities in Nairobi to be closed and the president to realize that something had to be done to stop Karura Forest from becoming a tinderbox that set the whole country on fire.

Thankfully, as 1999 progressed, tempers on both sides cooled. Green Belt Movement members visited Karura a few more times to plant trees. Then one day we learned from an old man who was one of our informers that the developers had left the forest. On August 16, 1999, the president announced that he was banning, with immediate effect, all allocation of public land. Soon all construction in the forest ceased and, according to our informers, even the hired thugs were moved out.

Illegal logging of trees in Karura Forest continued, however. Despite our complaints to the conservator of forests and the fact that forest guards were posted inside Karura, it appeared that the people who had been given the plots by the government were determined to clear the forest of its trees. This logging continued with the full knowledge of the forest department until the 2002 elections, when a new government was voted into office. After the 2002 elections, the Green Belt Movement and the government developed a new relationship and formed a partnership for the restoration of Karura Forest, an initiative that continues to this day.

Many people assume that I must have been inordinately brave to face down the thugs and police during the campaign for Karura Forest. The truth is that I simply did not understand why anyone would want to violate the rights of others or to ruin the environment. Why would someone destroy the only forest left in the city and give it to friends and political supporters to build expensive houses and golf courses?

For me, the destruction of Karura Forest, like the malnourished women in the 1970s, the *Times* complex in Uhuru Park, and the political prisoners detained without trial, were problems that needed to be solved, and the authorities were stopping me from finding a solution. What people see as fearlessness is really persistence. Because I am focused on the solution, I don't see danger. Because I don't see danger, I don't allow my mind to imagine what might happen to me, which is my definition of fear. If you don't foresee the danger and see only the solution, then you can defy anyone and appear strong and fearless.

This is not to say we were reckless. We found ways to protect ourselves. When we were confronted with a tense situation, we would sing about the need to protect the forest, and dance. This was a way to disarm the armed men in front of us—and it worked. We could see their frowns and scowls vanish and their faces soften. We were only women singing and dancing, after all, and those things didn't pose a threat. As far as they were concerned, we could sing and dance all day! What they didn't know is that the singing and dancing made us feel strong. It also ensured that nobody got hurt.

In the end, what was important was that we showed we were not intimidated. We were in the right and had stood up for what we believed in. We were making a statement that this was a public forest and no houses should be built there. To put a gate and fence and guards around public land to stop us entering was to interfere with our right of access. And how did we register our protest? Well, you can talk all day about how something is wrong, but how do you tell a government in this situation that it is violating your rights? Our answer was to plant trees. Today, that beautiful forest is still there, helping Nairobi breathe, and more trees are being planted to reseed what was lost and restore its biodiversity and beauty.

As the Green Belt Movement matured so also did its vision for how to meet the challenges that continued to unfold. We had already achieved great success with individual farmers planting trees on their own land and meeting the needs that they had envisaged more than twenty years previously for firewood, fencing material, fodder, and food. Even as we continued supporting Green Belt groups to plant trees on their individual plots, the experience of Karura and other forests clearly demonstrated the importance of including public lands within our scope of activities. These need to be retained for the people, protected from privatization and encroachment, and their biodiversity preserved, especially when they are catchment areas. From the year 2000, this has continued to be the main focus of the Green Belt Movement.

Women's groups are producing seedlings and planting them in designated degraded parts of many of Kenya's forests in an effort to rehabilitate and restore them to their natural state. In another major shift, this is being done as a partnership between the Kenyan government's department of forests and Green Belt Movement communities living near the forests. This work provides the greatest hope for the conservation and restoration of the five water "towers" in Kenya—Mount Kenya, the Aberdares, the Mau complex, the Cherangani hills, and Mount Elgon—that control the country's water systems. This includes the flow of rivers, rainfall patterns, and groundwater, all of which are necessary for agriculture, hydropower, people's daily needs, and the wildlife that are at the heart of Kenya's tourism industry.

This initiative of the Green Belt Movement has also inspired greater awareness of the need to protect other forest ecosystems in Africa that are under threat, especially the Congo Basin Forest. The Congo and Amazon forest ecosystems are two of the most important "lungs" of planet Earth.

In 2000, I suffered the greatest personal loss I have had so far: My mother died on March 8, International Women's Day, aged ninety-four. I found it poignant that she died on the day women around the world celebrate their solidarity. My mother had come to live with me in the late 1990s, when she became ill. I took great joy in looking after her. Throughout the years she had always supported everything I did. I'm not sure she always understood why I wanted to put my life on the line and she probably worried about me, but I am glad she lived to see what I managed to achieve.

My mother continued to work well into her eighties. Her life in the country became a little easier. While her house never received electricity, running water arrived during the 1960s and this meant she no longer had to go to the river to fetch it. While my mother was happy to come to live with me in Nairobi at my house in South C, she always wanted to go home to Ihithe, to her farm and the tree nursery she managed for the Green Belt Movement. I did take her home once, but she became unwell the next day, so I had to bring her back to the city. Later, we would drive to her homestead to have a look. What I find amazing was that she never thought she was dying. She believed she was going to get well and go home again to tend to her tree seedlings and food crops.

She fought to the end. Even in her last years in Nairobi, she mixed herbs and bark from Ihithe in traditional preparations that seemed to give her energy. She walked, even when it was nearly impossible, and would sit in the wheelchair I bought for her only when she became very tired. She was operated on in her late eighties, but her digestive system was weak and she wasn't getting enough energy. Eventually her muscles, and then her body, gave out. I had taken her to the hospital because she was dehydrated, and she came down with pneumonia. I felt terrible, because one part of me was saying, "Take her back home," while the other said, "But you're not a doctor." I have always regretted that she slipped away in the hospital while I was away from her deathbed.

My sister Beatrice Wachatha and I accompanied my mother's body in the car to Nyeri and passed by her house, which she had built in the 1960s. My hand rested on her coffin the whole journey. "This is it," I kept thinking. "I will never see her again." We buried her in the homestead. I couldn't bear to see the coffin disappearing into the ground, and walked away. The next day, the whole family gathered at the grave and we planted flowers and a tree. My sister Monica died a couple of years later and was buried next to our mother. I haven't yet gone back to the grave site. It is still too painful. But I hear the tree has grown tall and reminds visitors that there lies a loving mother of mine.

By the time of my mother's death, I had already lost my father (in 1978, aged seventy-five), my brother, and some friends. But when she passed away, I was more upset than I have ever been in my life. Afterward, I wasn't able to look at her picture or enter her room for a long time. It is a consolation that she died knowing my children were doing well. They phoned her often when they were in America and Muta was able to spend time with her when he returned to Kenya before resuming his graduate studies in the United States. I will never forget the many wonderful evenings my mother and I shared, sitting in her room and talking. My mother is a forever friend.

My mother was certainly not an environmentalist in the way we would understand the concept today, but she knew the beauty of nature when she saw it and how it made her feel. My mother told me a story of when she was a young woman. She used to walk through the forests from Nyeri to Naivasha on the western side of the Aberdare range. As she walked, she crossed numerous tributaries of the Gura River, which I could hear from our house in Ihithe when I was a child. The Gura and all the other tributaries, known collectively as Magura, flowed down the Aberdares, and my mother told me they were teeming with trout. Kikuyus didn't eat fish at that time, so there was no fishing. But she and her friends would rest by the streams, watch the trout, and marvel at how beautiful they were.

My mother is gone, as are many of those rivers, and with them the trout and a way of life that knew and honored the abundance of the natural world. Now, because of the devastation of the hillsides, instead of rivers there are only little streams and the Gura River no longer roars. Its waters don't run over the stones so much as seep into the riverbed, and even when I stand next to it, the river says nothing . . . its roar has slowly been silenced.

As my people would traditionally say: *Arokoma kuuraga,* "May she sleep where it rains." For me, that place is wet with morning dew and is therefore green. Well, perhaps heaven is green.

13

Rise Up and Walk

By 2000, I had been working to address the consequences of poverty in Kenya through a holistic approach to development for twenty-five years. Poverty was not only the result of bad governance and environmental mismanagement, but also an outcome of the global economic system, one of the key realities of which, for poor countries, was crippling debts. As the new millennium approached, a small group of advocates consolidated the campaign for debt cancellation and tied it to the year 2000 being a "Jubilee" year, like all years that end in "50" or "00." The tradition of the Jubilee year comes from the Bible, which says that every fifty years people should let their fields lie fallow, pray, celebrate God's bounty, forgive any outstanding debts, and let the slaves go free.

The call for rich countries to cancel the debts owed to them by poor countries became a global campaign. Many of these loans had been advanced to leaders of developing countries who were often known by the lenders of private banks and the World Bank to be corrupt. Not surprisingly, many of these leaders and their cronies in government had not spent the money to benefit their people through health care, education, employment creation, or environmental restoration. Instead, much of the money had been sent out of the country back to bank accounts in the industrialized nations. I had seen the effects of such corruption and poor governance all too often in Kenya, especially through deepening poverty and increasing insecurity. It was estimated that in 1999, Kenya spent $2 billion (U.S.) simply on servicing its debt to the rich countries.

In 1998, I became cochair of the Jubilee 2000 Africa campaign. Through a network of individuals and groups across the continent, we worked to gather one million signatures on petitions calling on the world's richest countries to cancel Third World debts in 2000. To me, the campaign's greatest opportunity lay in educating ordinary Africans about how the debts were incurred and what their relationship was to good or bad governance. The Green Belt Movement cofounded the Kenyan Debt Relief Network (KENDREN) as an umbrella organization for groups concerned about the effects of our international debts. Besides the Green Belt Movement its members included the Kenya Human Rights Commission, other civil society organizations, and church bodies such as the Catholic Church's Peace and Justice Department. As in many countries, members of the clergy in Kenya were very active in the Jubilee campaign.

Despite the fact that we were advocating for the dropping of the debt to benefit all Kenyans, our government didn't value our efforts. In fact, the police violently broke up one of the marches we held in Nairobi in April 2000. Several hundred of us were walking to the office of the World Bank to deliver a letter to its representative in Kenya calling for the debt to be canceled. Just before we arrived at the bank's office, the police rushed into the crowd with clubs and tear gas and pushed nearly sixty of the marchers into waiting police vans. They then arrested them for participating in an "illegal assembly," and locked them in police holding cells.

While I was part of the protest that day, I had stopped to talk with some colleagues and by the time I began walking again, the rest of the marchers were out of sight. I rushed to catch up, but my knees wouldn't let me run very fast. When I arrived, the march had been broken up and the vans were on their way to the police station. It broke my heart to hear from some marchers still left at the scene, as they wiped tear gas from their eyes, that thirteen nuns and two priests had been arrested along with members of the Green Belt Movement, students, and others.

I hurried to Nairobi's central police station and was furious to see members of the clergy, many of them elderly, locked in those filthy, cold cells. It was the first time any of us could remember that the government had gone so far as to jail nuns and priests. We alerted the international Jubilee 2000 network, which called on its supporters to fax letters of protest to the Kenyan government. Ann Pettifor, then head of the Jubilee 2000 campaign, sent a letter to Kenya's attorney general expressing her deep concern about the arrests. Even the World Bank representative called for the marchers to be released.

The Catholic archbishop of Nairobi, Ndingi Mwana N'zeki, could not believe what had happened. Unfortunately, none of us was able to secure the marchers' release until the following day and only after everyone, including the nuns and priests, had been taken to court and charged. Only a group of underage schoolchildren who had been part of the march was allowed to leave without spending a night in jail.

Those who had been arrested at the march were held overnight in a twelve-by-twenty-four-foot police holding cell that was already crowded with drunkards and petty thieves. After our failure to secure their release, a priest from the Catholic Church's Peace and Justice Department and I decided to keep vigil outside the cell in solidarity with the marchers. I wanted to join them inside, but this time the police refused to incarcerate me. They argued that I had not been arrested. The sisters told me not to worry and encouraged me to go home and sleep, but I couldn't. How could I leave? These were sisters like the nuns who had taught and mentored me for years. They were like my mother and sisters. I couldn't leave them in a police cell and go home and find sleep on a bed.

Throughout that long night, we sang and prayed and kept our spirits up. But I was irate at this latest example of the government's harassment of peaceful, nonviolent protestors—people who weren't even protesting against the regime. Indeed, they were trying to help the regime by seeking the cancellation of the government's debt! It was not until late the next afternoon that most of the marchers were released on bail and ordered to appear in court at the end of May.

Some couldn't be released until evening, when sufficient bail money had been gathered. I told the press how outraged I was by what had happened and assured them, and the government, that the members of the clergy involved were even more committed now to our campaign to cancel the debts.

In May, we organized a service at All Saints Cathedral to pray for the marchers and educate the public further about the Jubilee 2000 campaign. While all of the nuns and priests were brave, some never recovered from the shock of being in that crowded police cell with no personal privacy, where buckets served as toilets. I wondered, having experienced being in such cells myself, how the nuns could handle these indignities. To this day, they still nurse injuries— physical and psychological. That, too, breaks my heart. For the government to treat the religious this way was, to me, the lowest level to which the system had sunk.

Although the Jubilee 2000 campaign was extremely successful at mobilizing millions of people in wealthy and poor countries alike, debt is still a crucial issue for Africa.

Between 1970 and 2002, African countries obtained about $540 billion (U.S.) in loans and paid back $550 billion. However, because of interest on that debt, by the end of 2002 the debtor countries still owed the lending agencies nearly $300 billion. Good governance and democratic space are essential to Africa's development. But even together, they cannot overcome this crushing debt burden. The debt still must be lifted if we seriously want to make poverty history. Recent efforts by musicians like Bono and Bob Geldof and other celebrities have given the campaign to cancel poor countries' debts, including through the Make Poverty History initiative, renewed energy and a greater response from the world.

As the new century began, many of us who had been working for years to expand democratic space and protect the environment had more hope—and conviction—that we could peacefully restore democracy in Kenya. Elections were to be held in 2002, and there were strong indications that President Moi would finally step down. The international community had grown weary of the corruption and misrule in Africa, where strong men drove their nations deeper into poverty and despair. Foreign capitals were quietly and not so quietly encouraging such men to retire.

Despite this, Kenyans still had to contend with the realities of a government hell-bent on its own enrichment and power. The century had changed, but the government's attitudes and behavior had not. It was still absolutely opposed to the Green Belt Movement and our work. In March 2001, I felt this reality all too clearly. The previous year, the government, sensing that its end might be near, announced plans for a huge land-grab. Nearly 170,000 acres of virgin forest were to be degazetted and given to members of the government and its political supporters. Kenya's forested area had been gradually reduced to less than 2 percent of the land. This is dangerously below the UNEP recommended minimum of 10 percent required to protect watersheds and ensure regular rainfall and good harvests.

Only a third of land in Kenya is arable. The rest is arid, semi-arid, or desert, and Kenya's forests are found only in the one third that is arable. Even there, the forests are largely confined to the mountains, so the loss of any forestland was and is very serious. In 2001, Kenya was also in the grip of a two-year drought, with thousands of people depending on food aid to survive.

Notwithstanding these realities, the government's excision plan was massive. It covered nearly 10 percent of Kenya's remaining woodlands, including forested land on Mount Elgon, in the Mau and Nakuru forest reserves in the Rift Valley, and on my beloved Mount Kenya. The environment minister defended the plan, assuring the public that poor, landless Kenyans would get the land. He argued that since 1933 successive Kenyan governments had excised forests when they needed to and turned them into plantations of timber trees and farmlands for human settlements.

It was common for those in power to dish out forested land to their friends and supporters. One particularly extreme example included in this grab was the allocation of a thousand acres of the Kaptagat Forest, near Eldoret, to a powerful government minister so he could build a monument to his late mother. He denied this, claiming that the forest was excised legally, amounted to less than two hundred hectares, and would be donated to an educational trust. Unlike in the past, however, any destruction of the forest did not go unnoticed.

On March 7, 2001, I traveled to Wang'uru, a village two hours from Nairobi and not far from Mount Kenya, to join Green Belt members who had been working to raise awareness of the government's latest attempts to grab more of Kenya's forests. We planned to collect signatures and petition the government to change its plans for excising the forests. We also erected a billboard warning that a village plot was in danger of being grabbed.

After planting a few trees in the village, we moved to a nearby shopping center. While I spoke about the land-grabbing through a bullhorn from the backseat of the office Land Rover, Green Belt members attempted to collect signatures from the people shopping. Suddenly, the police arrived. Even though the Land Rover was still moving, one officer opened the driver's door, pushed my driver out of the car, and got behind the steering wheel. I had been carjacked! While other policemen chased away the women who tried to follow us, the officer drove me to Wang'uru police station. We didn't say a word to each other as he drove wildly to the police post. When we arrived, he pushed me into a cell and locked me up. Later, I was transferred to a police station where I was thrown into a crowded and filthy cell.

Jail, again. Another night in a dirty, cramped police holding cell. Only two days before, President Moi, opening a women's seminar in Nairobi, had told the women assembled that "because of your little minds, you cannot get what you are expected to get." People were appalled and many Kenyans protested. But I knew this attitude all too well. March 8 was International Women's Day. I could almost smile at the irony.

The government's heavy-handed tactics against me backfired. The Green Belt Movement and friends in the U.S. faxed and e-mailed news of my latest arrest to friends and supporters throughout the world. The Kenyan authorities were so bombarded with complaints about the illegal arrest that by the next afternoon they had to charge or release me. I was taken to court three times in the morning as the police tried to come up with a charge that would withstand the scrutiny of the presiding judge. They could not and the doors of the jail were thrown open for me to walk through to freedom. I was released without charge.

Spitefully, the police had stolen the Green Belt Movement billboard we had erected at the side of the highway the day before, but at least I had a few hours in which to celebrate International Women's Day. Unfortunately, I also learned upon my release that the government minister for lands had announced plans to degazette a further ten thousand acres of forestland. It appeared that both victory and suffering were my constant companions.

Given the changes we knew were coming to Kenya, I had thought I wouldn't be harassed or arrested again in 2001. But I was wrong. That July 7, a rally was held in Nairobi to commemorate ten years of the multiparty system and the eleventh anniversary of the Saba Saba demonstration. The government didn't want any such commemoration, which it considered a political statement. I decided not to go to the rally. Instead, I invited members and friends of the Green Belt Movement to come to Freedom Corner in Uhuru Park to plant new trees for Saba Saba and honor the heroes of Saba Saba, like Kenneth Matiba. We had just finished our planting when we heard the news that the Honorable James Orengo had been arrested at the Saba Saba commemorative rally. Suspecting that the police might come for us next, we dispersed.

It was a nice sunny morning in Nairobi, so three of us who had been at the tree planting—Vestistine Mbaya, Marion Kamau, and I—

walked to the nearby offices of the department of forests, sat down on a bench inside the compound, and began to chat. Suddenly, the gates were thrown open menacingly by burly policemen in civilian clothes. They held walkie-talkies in their hand and appeared to be in a hurry. "She's here!" I heard them shout as they approached us. They came up to the bench where we were sitting and announced that I was under arrest. "Why are you arresting me?" I inquired.

"Because you have been holding an illegal meeting," they replied.

"But you found me seated here, just talking to my friends!" I answered calmly. But they weren't listening. They just threw me into a police car and drove me to Gigiri police station near the UNEP headquarters. "When will they leave me alone?" I wondered to myself.

When I got to the police station, I was questioned and explained what I'd been doing: planting trees at Freedom Corner to mark the anniversary of Saba Saba. "Lock her up alone," thundered the offi-cer in charge. My friends spent the whole afternoon trying to find out where I had been taken. At about four o'clock in the afternoon, some members of the opposition, including Dr. Makanga, Honor-able James Orengo, and Honorable Beth Mugo, discovered me in the police station. They brought me tea and I was allowed to visit with them outside the cell. At about six o'clock that evening, I was released without charge and went home. All they wanted was to humiliate and intimidate me. They achieved the former, but never the latter.

That was the last time I was held in jail or a police holding cell in Kenya. I can only hope that those days are over. Even though the country truly changed after the 2002 elections, to this day I cannot say for sure that I will never be arrested again or spend another night in police custody. You can never tell. Things can change overnight.

Meanwhile, a wonderful opportunity opened for me to return to the classroom I had left twenty years previously. In New York in late

2001, I met with James Gustave (Gus) Speth, the former head of the UNDP, at the office of my longtime friend Mary Davidson, then a banker in New York who also introduced Green Belt to the Marion Institute, of which she is a cofounder. Gus was also a friend from the time he served as the principal White House adviser on environmental issues to President Jimmy Carter. He invited me to be the Dorothy McCluskey Visiting Fellow for Conservation at Yale University's School of Forestry and Environmental Studies, where he was the dean. I would be there from January to June 2002. It was a great opportunity to reconnect with Gus and a privilege to be invited to teach at such a prestigious institution.

I enjoyed my time at Yale immensely. I cotaught a course on sustainable development that focused on the work of the Green Belt Movement, and spoke on many panels on the environment, Africa, and women. I discussed students' research and interests with them, and had some time to think and write. As part of the coursework at Yale, I was able to bring some of the students to Kenya, where they participated in a Green Belt Safari. This is an experiential learning ecotour that exposes visitors to all aspects of the Green Belt Movement's work, from the realities of environmental degradation in Kenya to the theory behind what we do, to spending several days in rural homes of Green Belt group members, to planting trees. Participants also go on a traditional wildlife safari and learn about how this type of tourism is not always sensitive to its environmental impacts and often leaves behind destructive footprints.

This experience made a great impression on the students from the School of Forestry and Environmental Studies and I hoped that it could be a regular arrangement. An opportunity came in 2004, when a Yale graduate, James Leitner, sponsored another group of students to come to Kenya on a Green Belt Safari. We hope this continues in future years. In 2004, Yale awarded me an honorary doctorate in humane letters. I received this wonderful honor at the commencement ceremony in May along with Willie Mays, the legendary American baseball player; medical researchers David Baltimore and

Bernard Fisher; writer Tom Wolfe; educator Nannerl Keohane; Egyptologist Jan Assmann; and photographer Lee Friedlander.

Throughout my life, I have never stopped to strategize about my next steps. I often just keep walking along, through whichever door opens. I have been on a journey and this journey has never stopped. When the journey is acknowledged and sustained by those I work with, they are a source of inspiration, energy, and encouragement. They are the reasons I kept walking, and will keep walking, as long as my knees hold out.

In 2002, another opportunity arose for me and my country to fulfill a long-held dream—realizing a truly representative democracy. Once again, the question of whether I should run for Parliament in the elections scheduled for that December came up. Even though I had run in 1997, it was still a big decision for me to join elective politics. I told my supporters that I had to finish at Yale and would then return to Kenya. Once the semester at Yale was over, in June 2002, I returned home to begin a new adventure.

Once I got back, I decided to contest the parliamentary seat in Tetu again. In preparation for these elections, the opposition that had been frustrated at the polls for a decade finally agreed to unite, coming together under one umbrella, the National Rainbow Coalition, or NARC. All the major communities—the Luhyas, Luos, Kikuyus, Kambas—united, too. With that, momentum built. It looked as if, finally, the opposition could win the elections.

I knew I wouldn't be elected unless I was part of NARC. I was causing consternation among my supporters, because they wanted me to run as a candidate of the Democratic Party, which was dominant locally, and not as a Green. NARC had agreed, however, to field one candidate for each seat. Whichever individual won the first round of voting in November 2002 would become the NARC candidate, so it wouldn't matter, after all, which party candidates came from. When the primary vote for the Tetu constituency was held, I polled higher than the other candidates and was chosen to represent the Tetu constituency as the NARC candidate.

My slogan was "Rise Up and Walk," which was inspired by the story from the Bible (Acts 3:1–10) when the disciples Peter and John come across a beggar, who has all the characteristics of a disempowered person: He is poor, self-effacing, dejected, and has no sense of pride in himself. On seeing him in such a dehumanized and humiliated state, Peter says to him, "Silver and gold we do not have, but what we have we give to you." And, taking him by the right hand, Peter helps the lame man stand up. "In the name of Jesus Christ of Nazareth, rise up and walk!" Peter says.

What I wanted the voters to understand was that I could not give them alms or even miracles, but together we could lift ourselves up and address the conditions of our poverty and disempowerment and regain our sense of self-respect. Together, we could establish governance that was responsible and accountable to the people. The slogan was the essence of what the Green Belt Movement had been trying to do all those years: "Rise up and walk!"

It took people some time to understand that we had formed a coalition and came from different parties. Once they understood it, however, campaigning was easier. The Green Belt Movement was not directly involved in the campaign, but everywhere I went Green Belt members came out in support. I spent quite a lot of time campaigning for NARC and its presidential candidate around the country—so much, indeed, that my own constituency organizers became worried that I wasn't spending enough time campaigning in Tetu! I knew, however, that I had a good chance of winning the seat, because the opposition was working together and I was finally in a position to present my candidacy as I was. Unlike in previous years, the campaign was not marred by wholesale violence or intimidation, and people knew that this time the elections would be free and fair. Democracy, they felt, had finally arrived.

Election day itself was marked by huge numbers of people across the country and from all the communities exercising their democratic rights and responsibilities peacefully—even euphorically. While I had been prepared to win the parliamentary seat, I had not expected the large turnout. When the ballots of the first free and fair election in Kenya in nearly a quarter century were counted, I was astonished and gratified to discover that the voters had elected me to Parliament with 98 percent of the votes cast—a truly humbling experience. The people of the region that nurtured me had put their hopes and trust in me, as I had in them. I was determined that we would rise up and walk along the new path that we would create together.

It was a wonderful time in Kenya. After twenty-four years of struggle and difficulty and setbacks, of jailings and beatings and insults, and of determination and perseverance and hope, we had finally come together and could proudly proclaim that December day: "We made a change in Kenya. We brought back democracy!" And we had done it without bloodshed, and the people knew that their government would now be accountable to them, and that if we did not govern them well, we could be dismissed from power, democratically.

There was an electric atmosphere as the country anticipated the end of repression and looked forward to the beginning of a new era. This spirit was captured at Uhuru Park—the scene of so many of my struggles—where tens of thousands of citizens celebrated, sang, and danced in jubilation as KANU fell. On December 30, people climbed trees, leaned out of office buildings, and packed the park to watch President Moi handing over the instruments of power to the newly elected President Kibaki. It was a moment for which people had been waiting for decades, and no words can describe how wonderful it felt. It was a moment of great pride for all Kenyans, leaders and citizens alike.

I stood on the platform only a few yards from the presidents. President Kibaki had been seriously injured in a car crash only a few weeks before, and I could see how his physical pain mixed with joy as he fulfilled his lifelong dream to be president. I was overwhelmed. The day we had fought for over many years had finally arrived. It was as if we had finally crossed the deep and seemingly endless valley and were approaching the summit of the ridge.

Even as I savored the peaceful exchange of power, in the back of my mind lingered the knowledge of the many challenges that awaited Kenya. The years of misrule, corruption, violence, environmental mismanagement, and oppression had devastated our country. The economy was in ruins and many institutions needed rebuilding. But on that day, the future looked bright—not only for me, but for the whole country. A few weeks later, in January 2003, I was appointed assistant minister in the Ministry for Environment and Natural Resources.

Democracy does not solve problems. It does not automatically combat poverty or stop deforestation. However, without it, the ability for people to solve problems or become less poor or respect their environment is, I believe, impossible. Government itself is about compromise and consensus and I know that, since those heady days of December 2002, the sometimes slow pace of change has frustrated people. They look at me and see someone who now has a degree of power and they do not understand that that power is bound by the constraints of governance. However, I do feel that it is better to try to bring about some change from the inside than hammer in vain on the doors from the outside. It is a start; only a beginning.

What I have learned over the years is that we must be patient, persistent, and committed. When we are planting trees sometimes people will say to me, "I don't want to plant this tree, because it will not grow fast enough." I have to keep reminding them that the trees they are cutting today were not planted by them, but by those who came before. So they must plant the trees that will benefit communities in the future. I remind them that like a seedling, with sun, good soil, and abundant rain, the roots of our future will bury themselves in the ground and a canopy of hope will reach into the sky.

I am one of the lucky ones who lived to see a new beginning for my country. Others were not so fortunate. But I have always believed that, no matter how dark the cloud, there is always a thin, silver lining, and that is what we must look for. The silver lining will come, if not to us then to the next generation or the generation after that. And maybe with that generation the lining will no longer be thin.

Canopy of Hope

On the morning of October 8, 2004, I was on my way from Nairobi to my parliamentary constituency, Tetu, for a meeting when my cell phone rang. I moved closer to the window of the van I was traveling in so I could hear better amid the static and the bumps on the road. It was the Norwegian ambassador, asking me to keep the line clear for a phone call from Oslo. After some time, it came. It was Ole Danbolt Mjos, chair of the Norwegian Nobel Committee. His gentle voice came through clearly, "Is this Wangari Maathai?" he inquired.

While I receive calls from all over the world, I may not catch the name of the caller or recognize their voice until the reason for the call has been explained. So I paid attention to the caller for the message. "Yes," I said drawing the phone closer to my ear. He gave me the news. It left me speechless.

I was not prepared to learn that I had been awarded the Nobel Peace Prize; I wonder whether anybody ever is. The news hit me like a thunderbolt. How was I supposed to handle it? How did this happen? How did they find such a person as me? I could hardly believe it.

It was clear now why the Norwegian ambassador had called. "I am being informed that I have won the Nobel Peace Prize," I announced to myself and those around me in the car with a smile as I pulled the cell phone away from my ear and reconnected with my fellow passengers. They knew it was not a joke because happiness was written all over my face. But at the same time, tears streamed from my eyes and onto my cheeks as I turned to them. They, too, were by now smiling broadly, some cheering loudly and hugging me as if to both comfort and congratulate me, letting my tears fall on their warm shoulders and hiding my face from some of my staff, whom they felt shouldn't see me cry. But these were tears of great joy at an extraordinary moment!

I thought of the long journey to this time and place. My mind went back and forth over all the difficult years and great effort when I often felt I was involved in a lonely, futile struggle. I didn't know that so many people were listening and that such a moment would come. Meanwhile, the car rambled on to Nyeri's Outspan Hotel, where I often take a break before continuing to my rural Tetu constituency.

The news spread so fast that some journalists were already at the hotel waiting to record my arrival and hold interviews. They too were ecstatic and eager to hear my reaction. As I tried to answer their questions, I received what seemed like an endless series of calls from other journalists on my cell phone from all over the world. So numerous were the telephone calls that it became necessary to use every mobile phone at hand to respond to them. There was an instant media frenzy and I was right in the middle of it. I was completely unprepared for such media attention!

The news spread quickly throughout the hotel and among the guests. The manager and his senior staff were quick to come out to congratulate me. Then the enterprising manager responded to a request to provide a tree seedling and a shovel so that I could celebrate the best way I know how: by planting a tree.

A member of the hotel staff quickly dug a hole as a small crowd of onlookers and journalists gathered to witness and record the planting of a Nandi flame tree. Surrounded by the local and international press, the hotel guests, and workers, I prepared to plant this hardy tree seedling along the edge of the green yard, overlooking the imposing Mt. Kenya to the distant north. I kneeled down, put my hands in the red soil, warm from the sun, settled the tree seedling in the ground. They handed me a bucket of clean water and I watered the tree.

I faced Mt. Kenya, the source of inspiration for me throughout my life, as well as for generations of people before me. I reflected on how appropriate it was that I should be at this place at this time and celebrating the historic news facing this mountain. The mountain is known to be rather shy, the summit often cloaked by a veil of clouds. It was hidden that day. Although around me the sun was bright and strong, the mountain was hiding. As I searched for her with my eyes and heart, I recalled the many times I have worried whether she will survive the harm we are doing to her. As I continued to search for her, I believed that the mountain was celebrating with me: The Nobel Committee had also heard the voice of nature, and in a very special way. As I gazed at her, I felt that the mountain too was probably weeping with joy, and hiding her tears behind a veil of white clouds. At that moment I felt I stood on sacred ground.

Trees have been an essential part of my life and have provided me with many lessons. Trees are living symbols of peace and hope. A tree has roots in the soil yet reaches to the sky. It tells us that in order to aspire we need to be grounded, and that no matter how high we go it is from our roots that we draw sustenance. It is a reminder to all of us who have had success that we cannot forget where we came from. It signifies that no matter how powerful we become in government or how many awards we receive, our power and strength and our ability to reach our goals depend on the people, those whose work remains unseen, who are the soil out of which we grow, the shoulders on which we stand.

The Nobel Peace Prize has presented me with extraordinary opportunities. As I travel, both at home and abroad, the biggest challenge continues to be the capacity to respond to countless requests to visit and see, celebrate, encourage, and empower the huge constituency that felt honored by the prize: the environmental movement, those who work on women's and gender issues, human rights advocates, those advocating for good governance, and peace movements. There continues to be lot of interest among government leaders, academic institutions, development agencies, the corporate sector, and the media.

This interest was partly due to the connection the Norwegian

Nobel Committee made between peace, sustainable management of resources, and good governance. This was the first time such a linkage had been forged by the Nobel Committee and it was the first time that the committee had decided to recognize its importance by awarding the Nobel Peace Prize to somebody who had worked in these areas for over three decades. As we had said for many years, humanity needs to rethink peace and security and work toward cultures of peace by governing itself more democratically, respecting the rule of law and human rights, deliberately and consciously promoting justice and equity, and managing resources more responsibly and accountably—not only for the present but also for the future generations.

In trying to explain this linkage, I was inspired by a traditional African stool that has three legs and a basin to sit on. To me, the three legs represent three critical pillars of just and stable societies. The first leg stands for democratic space, where rights are respected, whether they are human rights, women's rights, children's rights, or environmental rights. The second represents sustainable and equitable management of resources. And the third stands for cultures of peace that are deliberately cultivated within communities and nations. The basin, or seat, represents society and its prospects for development. Unless all three legs are in place, supporting the seat, no society can thrive. Neither can its citizens develop their skills and creativity. When one leg is missing, the seat is unstable; when two legs are missing, it is impossible to keep any state alive; and when no legs are available, the state is as good as a failed state. No development can take place in such a state either. Instead, conflict ensues.

These issues of good governance, respect for human rights, equity, and peace are of particular concern in Africa—a continent that is so rich in resources and yet has been so ravaged by war. The big question is, Who will access the resources? Who will be excluded? Can the minority have a say, even if the majority have their way?

Fortunately, new leadership is emerging in Africa and, with it, new opportunities and commitments. Such leadership should be encouraged and challenged to stay on course. This is why I agreed to become a goodwill ambassador for an initiative aimed at protecting the world's second "lung," the Congo Basin Forest Ecosystem. Thankfully, the nations of central Africa came together to see how we can ensure the survival of this vital resource. I am also the presiding officer of the African Union's Economic, Social and Cultural Council (ECOSOCC), which is working to bring the energy and ideas of civil society organizations throughout the continent to Africa's leaders in a common forum. This would give civil society and the voice of the African people an opportunity to be listened to and advise the African leadership. It is a great vision by the African Union and demonstrates the importance of respecting the voices of the people in whose name leaders govern and chart the future of Africa.

As women and men continue this work of clothing this naked Earth, we are in the company of many others throughout the world who care deeply for this blue planet. We have nowhere else to go. Those of us who witness the degraded state of the environment and the suffering that comes with it cannot afford to be complacent. We continue to be restless. If we really carry the burden, we are driven to action. We cannot tire or give up. We owe it to the present and future generations of all species to rise up and walk!

One day a group of young men and women went to a dance. (At that time it was very common for young men and women to dance both separately and together.) The men danced and the women watched. There was one man who was extremely handsome and a beautiful dancer, and four young women at the dance thought him very attractive. One of the women, who was very romantic at heart, fell in love at first sight.

As the evening passed, three of the women noticed that the young man behaved very strangely. At one point as he danced he broke one of his fingernails, took the nail, and popped it into another mouth hidden at the back of his neck. As the mouth opened a swarm of flies came out, buzzing noisily. "Did you see that?" the first girl asked the second, shocked and amazed.

"Yes I did," answered the second.

"Wow!" said the third. "I think this young man is not what he seems. I think he's a dragon."

Now the third girl was right, but the fourth girl, who had fallen in love, was very naive and love blind. She saw only good in people, no matter how manifestly evil that person was. "What are you talking about?" she huffed. "I didn't see anything. He is a lovely man!"

"Well, we all saw what he did, and it was disgusting," responded the three other young women. "No human being has two mouths."

At this, the love-struck young woman became even more indignant. "Well, you girls never see anything good in anyone; and if you do you're always ready to tear them apart." And they began a furious conversation, full of mutual recriminations.

Meanwhile, the mysterious young man continued dancing until, looking around, he caught sight of the four young women and stared at them. They stared back and three of them saw that his eyes could open very wide and close just like the eyes of a chameleon. "Did you see that?" shouted the three young women to the lovesick fourth. "What human being has eyes like that?"

"Those eyes are the most beautiful eyes you could ever see," murmured the fourth woman. "You girls have never seen anything you didn't want to criticize."

The girls continued bickering until the dance ended and the handsome young man walked over and invited them to come to his compound. (This was typical practice in Kikuyu culture. It was quite acceptable for girls to go with boys and sleep in the same room together. No sexual intercourse was allowed, but the boys and girls would sleep together in a common area. Girls at that time had what might be termed chastity belts they wore before they went to sleep. This was only a precautionary measure, since young women and men always socialized in groups. This was a deterrent among unmarried young men and women.

On the way to the compound, the young man once again lost a nail and threw it behind him, where it was consumed by his second mouth even as a swarm of noisy flies emerged. Once again the three girls asked the fourth whether she'd seen it, but once again love had made her blind. This was too much for one of the three, who was too scared and returned to her home. The remaining three, including the love-struck maiden, were too intrigued to depart. They didn't want to leave one another alone with this fascinating young man.

It was nearing six o'clock and dusk was drawing in when the young man turned to them. "If you look straight on, over this ridge to the ridge beyond, you will see some white dots. Can you see them?"

The young women strained their eyes and, sure enough, there were the dots. "Yes, we can see them," they replied.

"Those are my sheep," said the young man. "At the rate we're walking it will be too dark for the sheep to be outside. I'll go ahead and put them inside the house and you can come at your own pace."

The women agreed to this plan and set off at their own speed. It turns out that the white dots on the ridge were not sheep, but the blanched bones of the people the dragon-man had eaten, and he wanted to go on ahead to remove them.

By the time the young women arrived at his compound, the dragon-man had cleaned the bones and lit the fire in the two huts of his compound—one for him and one for the girls. He had slaughtered a goat and the meat was boiling on a big fire in the young women's house. After adjusting themselves to their surroundings, one young woman became curious and decided to finally confirm her suspicions about the young man. Full of trepidation, she crept up to the entrance of his hut and peeked her head through the door. There he was, eating not the leg of a goat but the leg of a human being.

"Young woman," the dragon-man said sternly. "What did you find me eating?"

"Nothing," stuttered the girl in a fright. "I didn't find you eating anything. I just found you happy and enjoying the fire."

She ran back to the hut to the other girls. "This is no ordinary man!" she cried. "This is a dragon. Guess what he was eating?!" And she told them.

Yet again, the infatuated girl would not listen. So the second young woman decided to see what he was doing. This time she found the dragon-man eating a head, not of a goat but of a human being.

"Young woman," said the dragon. "What did you find me eating?"

"I didn't find you eating anything," stammered the second girl in fear. "I just found you nice and happy."

But when the second girl returned to the hut, the lovelorn young woman still didn't believe her. That was it for the two other women; they had to get out of there. However, they were fearful that if they left the compound through the normal entrance the dragon-man would catch them and put them in the boiling pot, so they decided to dig a tunnel. Unfortunately, they didn't have any tools. Therefore, as nonchalantly as they could, the two girls went to the dragon's house and asked him for an ax.

"What do you need an ax for?"

"Oh, we need to add more wood to keep the fire under the cooking pot going."

"Shall I come and help you cut some wood?"

"No, no, no," replied the young women hurriedly. "We'll do it ourselves."

The dragon gave them an ax, and shortly afterward heard the chopping. After several hours of chopping, however, he became curious to know why they needed so much wood.

"What are you so busy cutting out there?" he yelled.

"We're trying to get the meat from the pot and it's proving to be very difficult."

"Shall I come and help you?" he asked.

"No, no, no, no," replied the two young women. "It's almost done." And so it was—the tunnel, that is. The two women crawled through it and ran home, leaving their love-struck friend behind.

The love-struck girl became the dragon's wife. In the course of time, she produced a baby boy, which looked like his father (dragons could procreate with human beings but their offspring was always a dragon) and was called Konyeki. Because her son and husband were dragons, the woman lived completely separate from them. Every day the father and son went out hunting for human beings or whatever they could find and brought back the bodies for her to cook. As you can imagine, the woman was miserable, but she was stuck with her dragon-husband.

Now it turned out that the woman's sister had been baffled about why her sister had not come home after the dance. (In the stories, you didn't go home when you married the dragon.) So, even though she was heavily pregnant, she set out to visit her sister. Finally she found her at the dragon's compound. Amazingly, the woman was deaf to her sister's pleas to go away with her. Instead, she became alarmed and urged her to leave. "The dragon and his son will kill you and eat you," she said. "You must leave now. It looks like it's going to rain. As you go home, no matter how much it rains, don't take shelter at the fig tree near the river. That tree is where Konyeki and his father rest on their way home. Go anywhere else, but don't go there."

"Okay," agreed the sister, and she left in a hurry.

Sure enough, before the sister had gotten too far it began to rain cats and dogs and she ran to the nearest fig tree—the very fig tree she had been warned about. Even though she realized she'd made a mistake, she decided to climb to the top of the tree. "They won't see me up here," she thought. "I'll wait for them to pass by." In the way these stories usually work, Konyeki and his father came and rested under the tree. But Konyeki was a curious child. He looked up into the tree and saw a little black dot like a bird's nest at the top.

"Father," said Konyeki. "Isn't that a bird's nest at the top of the tree?"

His father looked up. "I think it's always been there," he said.

"No," responded Konyeki. "I've looked at this tree quite a lot and I've never seen anything like this. Let me check it out." (At this point in the story, we'd be holding our breath. They're going to find her!) Up he went, higher and higher, the spot getting bigger and bigger, until Konyeki arrived at the top and discovered the woman.

"Be still. Don't say a thing," said Konyeki. "If you give me one of your fingers, I won't say I found you." The woman hesitated. "Just one," Konyeki said persuasively.

"Okay," said the terrified woman. "You can have one finger."

So Konyeki took one finger and gobbled it up. "Give me just one more finger," said Konyeki, "and I'll never say I saw you."

The woman agreed, so Konyeki took another finger. This went on until Konyeki had eaten all the fingers on one hand. "Now you must give me a toe," said Konyeki, smacking his lips. "Just one toe and I'll never say I ever saw you." The woman, who did not know what to do in her situation, gave him a toe and he ate it. "Give me another toe," Konyeki said. "If you don't give me another toe, I'll say something. My father's down there, but if you give me the toe, I'll keep quiet." This went on until her feet had no toes. Then Konyeki, still unsatisfied, decided to work on the woman's breasts.

Now the woman had only one hand to hold on to the tree. Once Konyeki had eaten all the fingers of the other hand he called down to his father. "It's coming down, Father," and he pushed the woman off the tree. When she hit the ground, her womb burst open and out came baby twins, both boys. The two dragons were very happy with their extra food source: They both ate the woman but Konyeki took the babies back to the compound.

Once they arrived home, Konyeki turned to his mother. "Could you cook these two little moles for me?" The woman recognized them as her sister's children. She put the babies in a basket she used to ripen bananas and trapped two moles and put them in the cooking pot. When the son came for his meal, the mother gave him the two moles. "These moles are too small and they have fur. My moles didn't have fur," grumbled Konyeki.

"These are your moles," insisted the woman. "You eat them." So Konyeki ate them.

Over the next few years, the woman nurtured the boys alone during the day as Konyeki and his father went out hunting. The boys would play outside during the day, and every night she would hide them. Konyeki, however, was shrewd. He went to his father. "Father," he said, "if you watch around the homestead there are too many footprints. I wonder whose footprints these are? They are small. They are not like my mother's."

The father told him to ask his mother, who didn't bat an eyelid. "How many times do you think I go in and out of the house?" she asked Konyeki. "The whole day! Those are my footprints!" Konyeki was still suspicious and kept asking her about the footprints, and every time the mother had the same response.

Eventually, the boys became young men and the woman wanted them to escape. In order to escape, however, they needed weapons. The mother went to Konyeki and his father. "You know, you go from my compound every day and leave me alone. If there were an ambush I would never be able to protect myself."

"What do you need?" Konyeki asked.

"I need a spear for both hands."

So Konyeki gave her two spears. Another day, the woman raised the issue of security again, and Konyeki asked her what she wanted. "I need a shield for both hands." And Konyeki gave her what she wanted. The next day she wanted a sword, and she got one for each hand. Each day she would arm the young men and during the day they would duel and exercise. Eventually, they became very strong and she felt the young men were ready.

One thing remained. She needed to know just how strong Konyeki and his father were. She tied some grass, sweet potatoes, and grain together and went to the two dragons. "I really want to know how strong you are," she said. "If we were ambushed, I need to know whether you are strong enough to protect me. Try to lift these loads." Because the dragons were stronger than any human they could lift the loads easily. The woman continued to increase the weight of the loads, adding heavy stones from the river and putting them inside the bales. Every so often she would tell the dragons to try their strength and they would lift the loads.

One day, however, the load became so heavy that even they could not lift them. They pulled and heaved and tried to help each other: They were desperate to prove they could do it. Just as they were struggling to lift the bales, the woman opened the door and out came her two nephews, who butchered the dragons on the spot. The sons and the woman escaped and the woman went back to her people, perhaps a little wiser.

"And that is the end of the story," my aunt Nyakweya would say. "Now you tell me a story, or you will be eaten by a mole!"

By then the food would be ready and would be served whether we had another story to tell or not. After the meal, we would all fall asleep, and storytelling would be put aside until the following evening, when the family would gather again around an open fire.

INDEX

PHOTO CREDITS

AP/WIDE WORLD PHOTOS: Wangari Maathai plants a tree with Gordon Brown.

GREEN BELT MOVEMENT ARCHIVES: Canadian ambassador hands key to Wangari Maathai; planting a tree in Kibwezi; march to protest logging in Karura Forest; Wangari Maathai before gates to Karura Forest.

WANGARI MAATHAI ARCHIVES: Wangari Maathai with her mother and aunt outside mother's home in Ihithe; Consolata Missionary Sisters; Wangari Maathai yearbook photo; Wangari Maathai at the University of Munich; Wangari Maathai's wedding reception; Wangari Maathai on honeymoon; Wangari Maathai and husband in scholarly robes; Muta, Wanjira, and Waweru Maathai as children; Wangari Maathai in Uhuru Park; Wangari Maathai, her mother, and Vertistine Mbaya in Ihithe.

MIA MACDONALD: Ihithe Primary School; the path Wangari Maathai walked to school; reinforced door of Wangari Maathai's home; Wangari Maathai on the telephone with the Norwegian ambassador.

MARTIN ROWE: valley near Ihithe; Freedom Corner in Uhuru Park.

FLORENCE CONRAD SALISBURY: four young women at Mount St. Scholastica.

STANDARD GROUP (KENYA): Wangari Maathai leaving the office of the Deputy Supervisor of Elections; dismantled fence in Uhuru Park; Reverend Timothy Njoya speaking to journalists; Wangari Maathai in Nairobi after winning the Nobel Peace Prize.

the
green belt
movement
international

As this book reflects, my life's work evolved into much more than planting trees. Two organizations that I founded, the Green Belt Movement and its sister group, the Green Belt Movement International, demonstrate that evolution. By planting trees, my colleagues in this grassroots movement and I planted ideas. The ideas, like the trees, grew. By providing education, access to water, and equity, GBM empowers people—most of them poor and most of them women—to take action, directly improving the lives of individuals and families.

Our experience of thirty years has also shown that simple acts can lead to great change and to respect for the environment, good governance, and cultures of peace. Such change is not limited to Kenya or Africa. The challenges facing Africa, particularly the degradation of the environment, are facing the entire world. This is why the Green Belt Movement International was founded. Only by working together can we hope to solve some of the problems of this precious planet.

It's my fervent hope that you will seek to learn more about the work of the Green Belt Movement and the Green Belt Movement International by visiting our Web site, www.greenbeltmovement.org. Please share in our message of hope.

Wangari Maathai

A NOTE ON THE TYPE

The text of this book was composed in Trump Mediæval. Designed by Professor Georg Trump (1896–1985) in the mid-1950s, Trump Mediæval was cut and cast by the C. E. Weber Type Foundry of Stuttgart, Germany. The roman letter forms are based on classical prototypes, but Professor Trump has imbued them with his own unmistakable style. The italic letter forms, unlike those of so many other typefaces, are closely related to their roman counterparts. The result is a truly contemporary type, notable for both its legibility and its versatility.

Composed by Creative Graphics, Inc.,
Allentown, Pennsylvania

Printed and bound by Berryville Graphics,
Berryville, Virginia

Designed by M. Kristen Bearse